WITHDRAWN

W9-BLG-124

Lean
FOR
DUMMIES®
2ND EDITION

by Natalie Sayer and Bruce Williams

WILEY

John Wiley & Sons, Inc.

Lean For Dummies®, 2nd Edition

Published by
John Wiley & Sons, Inc.
111 River St.
Hoboken, NJ 07030-5774
www.wiley.com

Copyright © 2012 by John Wiley & Sons, Inc., Hoboken, New Jersey

Published by John Wiley & Sons, Inc., Hoboken, New Jersey

Published simultaneously in Canada

No part of this publication may be reproduced, stored in a retrieval system or transmitted in any form or by any means, electronic, mechanical, photocopying, recording, scanning or otherwise, except as permitted under Sections 107 or 108 of the 1976 United States Copyright Act, without either the prior written permission of the Publisher, or authorization through payment of the appropriate per-copy fee to the Copyright Clearance Center, 222 Rosewood Drive, Danvers, MA 01923, (978) 750-8400, fax (978) 646-8600. Requests to the Publisher for permission should be addressed to the Permissions Department, John Wiley & Sons, Inc., 111 River Street, Hoboken, NJ 07030, (201) 748-6011, fax (201) 748-6008, or online at http://www.wiley.com/go/permissions.

Trademarks: Wiley, the Wiley logo, For Dummies, the Dummies Man logo, A Reference for the Rest of Us!, The Dummies Way, Dummies Daily, The Fun and Easy Way, Dummies.com, Making Everything Easier, and related trade dress are trademarks or registered trademarks of John Wiley & Sons, Inc. and/or its affiliates in the United States and other countries, and may not be used without written permission. All other trademarks are the property of their respective owners. John Wiley & Sons, Inc., is not associated with any product or vendor mentioned in this book.

LIMIT OF LIABILITY/DISCLAIMER OF WARRANTY: THE PUBLISHER AND THE AUTHOR MAKE NO REPRESENTATIONS OR WARRANTIES WITH RESPECT TO THE ACCURACY OR COMPLETENESS OF THE CONTENTS OF THIS WORK AND SPECIFICALLY DISCLAIM ALL WARRANTIES, INCLUDING WITHOUT LIMITATION WARRANTIES OF FITNESS FOR A PARTICULAR PURPOSE. NO WARRANTY MAY BE CREATED OR EXTENDED BY SALES OR PROMOTIONAL MATERIALS. THE ADVICE AND STRATEGIES CONTAINED HEREIN MAY NOT BE SUITABLE FOR EVERY SITUATION. THIS WORK IS SOLD WITH THE UNDERSTANDING THAT THE PUBLISHER IS NOT ENGAGED IN RENDERING LEGAL, ACCOUNTING, OR OTHER PROFESSIONAL SERVICES. IF PROFESSIONAL ASSISTANCE IS REQUIRED, THE SERVICES OF A COMPETENT PROFESSIONAL PERSON SHOULD BE SOUGHT. NEITHER THE PUBLISHER NOR THE AUTHOR SHALL BE LIABLE FOR DAMAGES ARISING HEREFROM. THE FACT THAT AN ORGANIZATION OR WEBSITE IS REFERRED TO IN THIS WORK AS A CITATION AND/OR A POTENTIAL SOURCE OF FURTHER INFORMATION DOES NOT MEAN THAT THE AUTHOR OR THE PUBLISHER ENDORSES THE INFORMATION THE ORGANIZATION OR WEBSITE MAY PROVIDE OR RECOMMENDATIONS IT MAY MAKE. FURTHER, READERS SHOULD BE AWARE THAT INTERNET WEBSITES LISTED IN THIS WORK MAY HAVE CHANGED OR DISAPPEARED BETWEEN WHEN THIS WORK WAS WRITTEN AND WHEN IT IS READ.

For general information on our other products and services, please contact our Customer Care Department within the U.S. at 877-762-2974, outside the U.S. at 317-572-3993, or fax 317-572-4002.

For technical support, please visit www.wiley.com/techsupport.

Wiley also publishes its books in a variety of electronic formats and by print-on-demand. Some content that appears in standard print versions of this book may not be available in other formats. For more information about Wiley products, visit us at www.wiley.com.

Library of Congress Control Number is available from the Publisher upon request.

ISBN 978-1-118-11756-9 (pbk); ISBN 978-1-118-22446-5 (ebk); ISBN 978-1-118-23772-4 (ebk); ISBN 978-1-118-26258-0 (ebk)

Manufactured in the United States of America

10 9 8 7 6 5 4 3

WILEY

About the Authors

Natalie J. Sayer is the owner of I-Emerge, an Arizona-based global consultancy, and co-author of *Lean For Dummies*, 1st Edition. She has traveled the world extensively, working with leaders in English and Spanish to improve their daily lives, businesses, and results. Natalie began studying and applying Lean in the automotive industry in the United States and Mexico before it was formally known as *Lean*. She has trained, coached, mentored, and rolled up her sleeves to implement Lean in organizations ranging from Fortune 130 companies to micro-businesses.

She brings a unique blend of people, process, and cultural skills to every project. Natalie has a Bachelor of Mechanical Engineering, a Masters of Manufacturing Systems Engineering, is a graduate from Coachu, a professional speaker, a Six Sigma Black Belt, a Global Leadership Executive Coach, and an actress. She is a passionate people person who lives her life with the convictions that "there is always a better way," "change won't happen without the people," "adjust yourself accordingly," and "learn from every life experience and move on."

"To strive, to seek, to find and not to yield" —Alfred, Lord Tennyson

Bruce Williams strives for perfection and added value as a scientist, educator, consultant, entrepreneur, and executive. Leveraging the Lean principle of standardized work, this is now his seventh *For Dummies* work, dating from 2005, on topics including Six Sigma, Lean, Business Process Management, and Process Intelligence.

His undergraduate degrees in physics and astrophysics from the University of Colorado testify to his early passion to uncover the ultimate nature of root cause. He then was a sculler in the value stream of aerospace systems, where he shot the rapids in the tumultuous whitewater of the Hubble Telescope program. With graduate degrees in technical management and computer engineering from Johns Hopkins and the University of Colorado, Bruce then elevated his value stream role to tugboat captain, leading and managing technical teams and projects.

Decades of *kaizen* inspired his continuous journey through high technology, software, process improvement, and strategic management. A *kaikaku* moment once unleashed his entrepreneurial self in 1999; he is now charting the deeper value-stream waters as an executive with Software AG.

He lives with his standard family in the rural desert foothills of northern Scottsdale, Arizona, flowing just-in-time value in response to their continuous demand pull. He regularly suffers the *muri* of 5S'ing around the house and occasionally pursues the unattainable ideal state of par golf.

Dedication

To all Lean leaders who "get it," who know that Lean happens through the people, is sustained by the culture and is a long-term journey of excellence in enterprise. To my inner circle: you enrich my life by supporting, guiding, cheering, and challenging me at every turn. To my family who is always there no matter what. Thank you all.

— Natalie J. Sayer

To my children: my daughter, Hannah, who has always been keenly able to help net-out just what is and what isn't "value-add," and my son, Evan — the greatest personification of 5S I'll ever know. You both just seem to practice *kaizen* naturally, and inspire me to do the same. I dedicate this work to you.

— Bruce Williams

Authors' Acknowledgments

The authors acknowledge many people who have directly and indirectly contributed to this second edition of *Lean For Dummies*. We are especially thankful to Christine Dicken for her voice of the customer feedback, relentless pursuit of excellence and those trés cool ARIS value-stream maps.

As members of the Lean community, we have the highest regard for the outstanding service and contributions to industry excellence delivered by the team at the Shingo Prize, and recognize Bob Miller for his vision and leadership. And thank you, Bob, for your august and inspirational foreword.

For their contributions of connections, experiences or case studies, Linda LaGanga of Mental Health Center of Denver, Erica Gibbons, Elissa Torres, Frank Cooney, Todd McCann, Jon Miller, Tim Briones, Scott Kurish, Eleanor Clements, Pamela Oakes, and from Healthcare Performance Partners, Inc., Charles Hagood, and Jason Baldwin.

Thanks to Tim Mullett for contributing his years of wisdom as our technical editor. His practical experience has been an invaluable resource to this project. We appreciate his time, efforts and suggestions.

Thank you to Patricia Hatem and Mary Miller for obtaining permission to use the excellent wall chart from Diversey Inc., part of Sealed Air.

All people interested in Lean owe their ongoing gratitude to Mark Graban and his contributors, who through the Lean Blog (www.leanblog.org) translate Lean to the world around us.

As authors and researchers, we humbly bow to the continuing miracle that is Google, and also to the ubiquitous multi-sensory stimulative and collaborative experience that is Starbucks, whom we recognize both as consumers and for their Lean initiative.

As consumers, and on behalf of consumers everywhere, we acknowledge the contributions of the brilliant pioneers who have contributed to the evolution and dissemination of what we now know as Lean: W. Edwards Deming, Taiichi Ohno, Shigeo Shingo, Norm Bodek, James Womack, and Jeffrey Liker.

But most of all, we acknowledge the many thousands of leaders and Lean practitioners globally, who regularly confront established structures, functional silos, challenging business environments, arcane accounting practices, and entrenched procedures to cut waste and find the real customer value. You make Lean thrive. You are our heroes.

Publisher's Acknowledgments

We're proud of this book; please send us your comments at http://dummies.custhelp.com. For other comments, please contact our Customer Care Department within the U.S. at 877-762-2974, outside the U.S. at 317-572-3993, or fax 317-572-4002.

Some of the people who helped bring this book to market include the following:

Acquisitions, Editorial, and Media Development

Project Editor: Susan Hobbs

Acquisitions Editor: Michael Lewis

Copy Editor: Susan Hobbs

Assistant Editor: David Lutton

Editorial Program Coordinator: Joe Niesen

Technical Editor: Tim Mullett

Editorial Manager: Carmen Krikorian

Editorial Assistant: Rachelle Amick

Art Coordinator: Alicia B. South

Cover Photos: © iStockphoto.com / José Carlos Pires Pereira

Cartoons:
Rich Tennant (www.the5thwave.com)

Composition Services

Senior Project Coordinator: Kristie Rees

Layout and Graphics: Claudia Bell, Corrie Niehaus, Mark Pinto, Christin Swinford

Proofreader:
BIM Indexing & Proofreading Services

Indexer: Sherry Massey

Publishing and Editorial for Consumer Dummies

    Kathleen Nebenhaus, Vice President and Executive Publisher

    Kristin Ferguson-Wagstaffe, Product Development Director

    Ensley Eikenburg, Associate Publisher, Travel

    Kelly Regan, Editorial Director, Travel

Publishing for Technology Dummies

    Andy Cummings, Vice President and Publisher

Composition Services

    Debbie Stailey, Director of Composition Services

Contents at a Glance

Table of Contents

Foreword

. . . .

Something deep inside of almost every person tells us that it is good to improve. It is better to move forward than it is to move backward. It is better to move faster than slower. Personal contribution to a relentless pursuit of perfection is perhaps the most exhilarating thing that can happen to an individual, followed closely by being recognized for that contribution.

I love being a part of an organization that has its roots in recognition. Recently, we substantially raised the bar for what is required to receive a Shingo Prize to include an evaluation of the culture. Many very experienced Lean leaders, when first exposed to this much higher standard, strongly advised against what we were attempting to do. They said, "The standard is too high; no one will be able to meet it. Your expectations are far greater than almost any organization is capable of performing." This was exactly what we wanted to hear.

We knew that something had to shake business out of the wasteful cycles of program- and tool-oriented improvement initiatives that have become commonplace. In my role as executive director of The Shingo Prize for Operational Excellence (named for Japanese industrial engineer Shigeo Shingo who distinguished himself as one of the world's thought leaders in building operational excellence), I have observed firsthand the many failed improvement programs that have come and mostly gone in most organizations all over the world. "flavor of the month" is the universal descriptor for these initiatives.

Everyone seems to recognize this wasteful practice, but few know how to stop it. Each new flavor seems so attractive, so logical! Doing nothing is never an attractive option, so in we jump, hoping against hope for a different outcome. Lean has the potential to become one such flavor.

This new edition of *Lean For Dummies* goes a long way toward exposing the necessities of a successful Lean deployment. The authors not only teach the tools and methodologies associated with Lean, but more importantly help to make the connections between the tools and techniques and the principles and concepts behind them. Shigeo Shingo said, "It is not enough to teach people how to do something; they need to know why." Correct principles are "the why."

When people understand "the why" behind "the how," they become empowered to act independently and to take initiative. Creating a culture of Lean requires every single individual in an organization become fully engaged in continuous improvement. When people understand the principles behind the tools, they become capable of innovating the application of the tools to their unique problems. One successful improvement followed by another, slightly different, and then another, different yet, unleashes a continuous flow on innovation, enthusiasm, and commitment to a never-ending journey.

No one that has tasted the fruit of continuous improvement can ever again be satisfied in an environment of mediocrity and stagnation. Associates who learn the principles and tools associated with Lean become change agents, leaders, inspirational and powerful. This happens from the very top of an organization to the very bottom. I have observed over and over that a powerful leader at the bottom of the organization is no less impactful than one at the top.

This second edition of *Lean For Dummies* rightfully acknowledges that organizations cannot afford to implement Lean the same way they implemented JIT, TQM, and a plethora of similar programs. By emphasizing Lean principles and insisting on cultural transformation, Sayer and Williams empower the reader to break the cycle of failed programs and create a lasting culture of continuous improvement.

Robert D. Miller
Executive Director, The Shingo Prize for Operational Excellence

Introduction

● ●

*L*ean is recognized globally as a one of the most powerful and effective ways known to build, improve, and sustain businesses and institutions. Following a Lean path, any business in any industry of any size or type can improve itself continuously — both in the short term and over the long term. Led by advancements first pioneered at the Toyota Motor Corporation over 50 years ago and since translated and refined by experts and practitioners world wide, the principles, methods, and practices of Lean constitute a successful approach to organizing and operating any enterprise.

If you're in certain manufacturing industries, healthcare facilities, or public institutions, you've probably heard about Lean. You may even have been through a *kaizen* event or been part of implementing standardized work. If so, you've already experienced some of the power of Lean tools. But if you're like many people, while the term *Lean* itself may be familiar to you, its principles and practices are not.

The Toyota Production System (TPS) was the incubator where the methods, techniques, and tools of Lean were pioneered and refined. But for decades, the whole system of Lean principles and practices was known only to specialized manufacturers, certain academic researchers, and quality gurus. Its full potential was a mystery to most organizations and professionals.

All that changed in the late 1980s, as the term *Lean* was coined to describe the fundamentals of TPS to the rest of the world. As the understanding of Lean spread across continents, industries, and organizations, it became less of a mystery and much easier to understand and implement.

Simply stated, Lean is a proven long-term approach to aligning everything in a business or institution to deliver increasing customer value. It's about engaging people and aligning systems into processes that deliver a continuous stream of value to customers while continuously eliminating waste and deficiencies in the process. But Lean techniques are not just for specialists; Lean is an everyday practice, performed by everyone, at all levels, to consistently improve performance.

About This Book

This book makes Lean accessible to you. We wrote it because Lean is applicable everywhere — it's applicable in large and complex corporations, but also in small businesses and industries, as well as public-sector institutions — and it applies at all levels.

We wrote this book for you, the individual. You may be a small-business owner, an ambitious career person, a hospital administrator, or a manager who wants to know what Lean is and how to apply it. Your company may be adopting and applying Lean. You may be a college student or job applicant who wants to have an edge in upcoming job interviews. No matter who you are, if you want to know more about Lean, this is the book for you.

Lean For Dummies is not just an overview or survey of Lean. It's a comprehensive description of the principles of Lean, as well as the methods and tools to put Lean into practice.

This book is

- A reference book that's organized into parts, chapters, and sections, so that you can flip right to what you need, when you need it
- A comprehensive text that addresses both the common tools of Lean and the improvement principles and practices
- A guide for leading a Lean initiative, helping you identify and manage Lean projects and using Lean tools
- A guide to engaging people successfully in a Lean organization
- Step-by-step instructions for value-stream mapping and the methodology of Lean projects
- Instructions on where you can go for additional help, because the field of Lean is much too large to fit in just a few hundred pages

Lean *is* different, and it contains Japanese terms and ideas that may be foreign to you. But we've taken this difficult subject and made it understandable through examples, simple explanations, and visual aids.

Conventions Used in This Book

When a specialized word first appears in our book, we italicize it, and provide a definition. We also italicize any foreign-language words, including the many Japanese terms that make up the lingo of Lean.

For terms and phrases that industry practitioners use as acronyms, we define the term first and then use it in its abbreviated form going forward.

We put any web addresses and e-mail addresses in `monofont` to set it apart from the rest of the text. When this book was printed, some web addresses may have needed to break across two lines of text. If that happened, rest assured that we haven't put in any extra characters (such as hyphens) to indicate the break. So, when using one of these web addresses, just type in exactly what you see in this book, pretending as though the line break doesn't exist.

We use some business-management and statistical concepts and language in the course of the book. To get extra smart on the statistical and problem-solving aspects, check out *Six Sigma For Dummies,* by Craig Gygi, Neil DeCarlo, and Bruce Williams; *Six Sigma Workbook for Dummies* by Craig Gygi, Bruce Williams, and Terry Gustafson. Also check out *Managing For Dummies,* 2nd Edition, by Bob Nelson, PhD, and Peter Economy; *Statistics For Dummies,* by Deborah Rumsey, PhD; and *Coaching & Mentoring For Dummies* and *Managing Teams For Dummies,* both by Marty Brounstein (all published by John Wiley & Sons).

Foolish Assumptions

We assume you've heard something about Lean and are intrigued and compelled to find out more, for one or more of the following reasons:

- ✔ You're contemplating using Lean in your business or organization, and you need to understand what you might be in for.

- ✔ Your business or organization is implementing Lean, and you need to get up to speed. Perhaps you've even been tapped to participate in a *kaizen* event or a value-stream-mapping exercise.

- ✔ You believe Lean is the pathway to better performance in your job and can help you advance your career.

- ✔ You're considering a job or career change, and your new opportunities require you to understand Lean practices.

- ✔ You're a student in business, international business, operations, or industrial engineering and you realize that Lean is part of your future.

We assume you realize Lean demands a rigorous approach to analyzing the value stream of business processes. We also assume you believe that change only happens through engaged people working together, intelligently to solve problems and improve processes and designs. And we assume you accept that Lean practice calls for capturing data and applying analytical tools to discover the true nature of value creation and the causes of waste in your environment. In addition, we assume you might be from any industry, including manufacturing, service, transactional, healthcare, or even government. For these reasons, we have devoted several chapters of this book to describing and defining the Lean toolset.

How This Book Is Organized

We break this book into six separate parts. Each chapter is written as an independent standalone section, which means you can move around the book and delve into a given topic without necessarily having to read all the preceding material first. Anywhere we expound upon or extend other material, we cross-reference the chapter or part of origin, so you can tie it together.

Part I: Lean Basics

Part I is an overview of Lean, including the principles and language of Lean. Chapter 1 is a comprehensive overview of Lean. Chapter 2 addresses the key principles as well as the language and lexicon of Lean.

Part II: The Lean Culture

Part II focuses on the often overlooked Respect for People aspect of Lean. Chapter 3 looks at Lean in the organization, including principles, behaviors, and change. Chapter 4 shows Lean and change at an individual level. Chapter 5 covers the organizational strategy and evolution of Lean.

Part III: Understanding Flow and the Value Stream

Part III gets into the essence of Lean: understanding the way value is created and flowed to the customer. In four chapters, we thoroughly describe the flow of value. Chapter 6 defines value precisely, in terms of the customer and the end consumer. Chapter 7 introduces and explains the process of value-stream mapping, one of the key tools of Lean. Chapter 8 explains how to use a value-stream map to define where you want to go and how you'll approach getting there. Chapter 9 explains the principles and practices of *kaizen* — the basis for continuous improvement.

Part IV: The Lean Toolbox

In this part, we present a comprehensive listing and overview of the many customer, value stream, flow, pull, perfection, and management tools of Lean in four chapters. Collectively, Part III and Part IV cover the tools that form the Lean toolkit.

Chapter 10 describes the many tools used to understand customer needs/ wants and to deliver customer value. Chapter 11 describes the flow and pull tools. Chapter 12 covers the perfection tools used within Lean to reduce variation, create standardized work, enable management-by-eye, and improve every day. Chapter 13 addresses the management tools of *hoshin, gemba*, and management information tools.

Part V: The Lean Enterprise

Part V contains three chapters and describes how Lean becomes part of the enterprise. Chapter 14 explains how Lean works in the different functions and organization of an enterprise. Chapter 15 addresses Lean in different industries. Chapter 16 shows five real-life case studies in different organizations.

Part VI: The Part of Tens

This part, in the *For Dummies* tradition, is a compilation of key points of reference. Chapter 17 discusses ten practices for success. Chapter 18 addresses ten pitfalls to avoid. And in Chapter 19, we tell you about ten additional places you can go for help.

Icons Used in This Book

Throughout the book, you'll see small symbols called *icons* in the margins, and these highlight special types of information. We use these to help you better understand and apply the material. When you see any of the following icons, this is what they mean:

These are key points to remember that can help you implement Lean successfully.

When you see this icon, we're cautioning you to beware of a particular risk or pitfall that could cause you trouble.

This icon flags a detailed technical issue or reference.

We use this icon to summarize information into short, memorable thoughts.

Where to Go from Here

The beauty of a *For Dummies* book is that you don't have to start at the beginning and slowly work your way through. Instead, each chapter is self-contained, which means you can start with whichever chapters interest you the most. You can use *Lean For Dummies* as a reference book, which means you can jump in and out of certain parts, chapters, and sections as you want.

Here are some suggestions on where to start:

- ✔ If you're brand-new to Lean, start at the beginning, with Chapter 1.
- ✔ Interested in the organizational and people elements of Lean? Go to Chapters 3 and 4.
- ✔ Want to know about the basics of value-stream mapping? Check out Chapter 7.
- ✔ If you want to know other Lean tools, jump in at Chapter 10.
- ✔ If you are interested in real world examples, go to Chapter 16.
- ✔ If you want to understand all the Lean lingo and terminology, flip to the glossary in the back of the book or check out the online version at www.dummies.com/go/leanfd2e.

Lean is a journey. Like any journey, it is exciting and exhilarating, stretching and life altering, challenging and unexpected. But it *is* worth it. We wish you well on this journey. With this book by your side, you have what it takes to live Lean and thrive!

Part I
Lean Basics

The 5th Wave   By Rich Tennant

"I'm writing the corporate bylaws. How do you spell 'guillotine?'"

In this part . . .

Think of Lean as a fitness program for your business. Like a diet and exercise regime for your body, Lean is a way to get your business fit for life, through a focus on your customer, the implementation of new business practices, and the ongoing commitment to continuous improvement. In this part we fill you in on the foundations, philosophies, and basics of Lean.

Chapter 1

Defining Lean

. . . .

. . . .

*W*hen you first hear the word *lean,* it conjures up an image. Most likely, you're seeing a mental picture of thin people — like long-distance runners, or those aerobics junkies who somehow don't seem to have an ounce of extra fat on them. Maybe you're thinking about lean food — the foods that are lower in fat and, of course, much better for you. The term *lean* also implies a sense of speed and agility, with a sort of edge or underlying aggressiveness that recalls the rhyme "lean and mean."

That's because the word *lean* suggests not only a physical condition, but also a certain discipline — a mental toughness. The notion of lean carries with it a commitment to a set of principles and practices that not only *get* you fit, but *keep* you fit. People, who are lean, seem to be that way not just temporarily, but continuously. Lean people are committed to being lean; they act a certain way in their habits and routines. Lean isn't a fad or diet — it's a way of life.

Now take this concept and apply it to a business or organization. What does *lean* mean, business-wise? Back in 1988, a group of researchers working at the Massachusetts Institute of Technology (MIT), led by Dr. James P. Womack, were examining the international automotive industry, and observed unique behaviors at the Toyota Motor Company. Researcher John Krafcik and the others struggled with a term to describe what they were seeing. They looked at all the performance attributes of a Toyota-style system, compared to traditional mass production. What they saw was a company that:

- Needed less effort to design, make, and service their products
- Required less investment to achieve a given level of production capacity
- Produced products with fewer defects
- Used fewer suppliers
- Performed its key processes — including concept-to-launch, order-to-delivery, and problem-to-repair — in less time and with less effort
- Needed less inventory at every step
- Had fewer employee injuries

They concluded that a company like this, a company that uses less of everything, is a "lean" company. Table 1-1 shows a contrast between a traditional mass production organization and a Lean enterprise.

And just like that, the term *lean* became associated with a certain business capability — the ability to "do more with less." Lean organizations use less human effort to perform their work, less material to create their products and services, less time to develop them, and less energy and space to produce them. Lean organizations are also better oriented toward customer demand, and develop a higher quality of products and services in the most effective and economical manner possible.

The practice of *Lean* — from here on capitalized because, in this context, it's a proper noun — is therefore a commitment to the set of principles and behaviors that not only gets your organization fit, but keeps it that way.

Table 1-1	The Lean Enterprise versus Traditional Mass Production	
	Mass Production	*Lean Enterprise*
Primary business strategy	Focus is on exploiting economies of scale of stable product designs and non-unique technologies. A product-centric strategy.	A customer-focused strategy. Focus is on identifying and exploiting shifts in competitive advantage.

	Mass Production	*Lean Enterprise*
Organizational structure	Hierarchical structures along functional lines. Encourages functional alignments and following orders. Inhibits the flow of vital information that highlights defects, operator errors, equipment abnormalities, and organizational deficiencies.	Flat, flexible structures along lines of value creation. Encourages individual initiative and the flow of information highlighting defects, operator errors, equipment abnormalities, and organizational deficiencies.
Operational framework	Application of tools along divisions of labor. Following of orders, and few problem-solving skills.	Application of tools that assume standardized work. Strength in problem identification, hypothesis generation, and experimentation.

In this book, we fill you in on the origins, applications, and continuing evolution of Lean, which is now an established science and a mature global practice. Although Lean has a toolset, it is much more than a set of tools. Lean is a philosophy, an approach to your life and work. Lean is a journey, without a predefined path or end state. It's a way to go forward that guarantees continuous improvement. Lean isn't a diet or a fad; it's a disciplined way of life.

What Is Lean?

Lean is a broad catchphrase that describes a holistic and sustainable approach to using less of everything to give you more. Lean concepts aren't new; companies large and small around the globe have practiced the techniques in various forms for decades. The term *Lean* can be described by the following ideas:

- ✔ Maintaining an unrelenting focus on providing customer value
- ✔ Respecting people most of all
- ✔ Adopting a philosophy of continuous learning and everyday improvement

- ✔ Using techniques for reducing variation and eliminating waste

- ✔ Taking the long-term view

- ✔ Improving value not just locally, but globally — across the whole "value stream"

- ✔ Providing exactly what's needed at the right time, based on customer demand

- ✔ Leading by focusing not just on results, but *how* results are achieved, where customer value is created, and by building capability in employees

- ✔ Building long-term relationships with all its stakeholders, including employees, managers, owners, suppliers, distributors, customers, the community, society, and the environment

- ✔ Keeping things moving — flowing — in a value-added, effective manner

Lean means less of many things — less waste, shorter cycle times, fewer suppliers, less bureaucracy. But Lean also means more — more employee knowledge and empowerment, more organizational agility and capability, more productivity, more satisfied customers, and more long-term success.

Although the term *Lean* was originally associated with manufacturing and production processes, Lean covers the total enterprise, embracing all aspects of operations, including internal functions, supplier networks, and customer value chains. A broad range of industries — including automotive, aerospace, banking, manufacturing, retail, construction, energy, healthcare, and government — have applied Lean.

The Shingo Prize, called "the Nobel Prize of Manufacturing" by *Business Week,* was developed to promote Lean practices, and has been awarded in North America each year since 1988. Honoring the renowned engineering genius Shigeo Shingo, its purpose is to "promote awareness of Lean manufacturing concepts."

These broad definitions and history are all interesting enough, but what really matters is that the world's customers are the better for it — much better, in fact. It's been invisible to many people, but Lean has brought to everyone vastly improved products and services, and it's brought them faster, cheaper, and more reliably. Its successes have saved billions of dollars. Its competitiveness has forced traditional functional organizations to retool themselves and focus on customer value. And it has equipped struggling companies and industries with methods and techniques to improve performance.

The logic of Lean

In Lean, you pursue the ideal state of perfect processes and performance. You seek to understand the sources and root out the causes of waste (more on this in Chapter 2). The practice of Lean as the root-cause eliminator of wastefulness is based on a core set of fundamental assumptions. Follow this logic:

- ✔ **You provide products and/or services to your customers.** The customer has the need and defines the purpose. It all begins and ends with what your customer requires. Everything else is fluff.

- ✔ **The customer is the one true arbiter of value.** Your customer is willing to exchange their capital for your product or service only when they believe it's a fair exchange of value. It has to be the right combination of the right quality of products and services, in the right place, at the right time and at the right price.

- ✔ **Value-creation is a process.** You create value for your customer through a combination of steps — such as marketing, design, production, processing, delivery and support — rightly performed, that result in the products and/or services that the customer will properly value.

- ✔ **Waste diminishes the process of value creation.** Things that creep in and prevent the steps in your processes from flowing quickly and effectively will inhibit your ability to create customer value.

- ✔ **A perfect process has no waste.** If every step in the process is fully capable, acts only when necessary, flows perfectly, and adapts to perform exactly as needed, the process will develop and deliver products and services perfectly — without waste. This is the ideal state.

- ✔ **Pursing perfect processes maximize customer value.** The closer to perfection your processes become, the more effective the creation of value, the more satisfied the customers and the more successful the endeavor.

 People create value. They implement the processes and utilize technology and equipment. Rooting out waste through Lean depends on creating the right culture and environment, where people are engaged, innovative, and perform meaningful work.

 Some organizations believe in "being practical" and don't strive for the "perfect process." Lean warns you to not set your sights too low. Perfection through Lean is a journey, not a destination. Although your next practical implementation may be far from the ideal, you must always have a vision for what the ideal could be.

Where is Lean?

You can apply Lean wherever there is waste, and anywhere there is opportunity for improvement. In other words, Lean applies everywhere. It's not confined to any particular part of the organization or within any particular function. Lean practices apply across the board.

It's in the enterprise

Lean is a business-improvement initiative, best applied enterprise-wide and ingrained in the organizational culture. A common misconception holds Lean is a sort of manufacturing quality program. Not so! The philosophy, principles and practices of Lean are applicable anywhere, and they are most effective when applied across the entire organization (see Chapter 14).

Think of Lean in the enterprise not as a group of functional or departmental practices, but as a set of multidisciplinary practices that cross functional lines. This is because Lean focuses on the processes that create customer value, which by their nature are cross-functional. Examples include the:

- Supplier-assembler process
- Assembler-distributor-customer process
- Marketing-design-development process
- Patient care-administration-insurance process
- Employee acquisition-on-boarding-training-evaluation process
- Order-to-cash process
- Procure-to-pay process
- Company-government-regulatory process

In each of these cases, work is not aligned by classic Western-style functional departments. Instead, multidisciplinary teams facilitate the process.

It's in the people

Lean calls for everyone to adapt a certain mindset and to utilize a particular set of facilitating tools and techniques to eliminate waste and maximize customer value (covered in Parts III and IV). Although the Lean tools are important, Lean is first about the people, then the tools. This is a critical point — companies that have failed to recognize this have met with disastrous consequences.

Organizations on a successful Lean journey value and respect their people. They put the primary emphasis on the people in the organization. The journey must engage everyone, continually educate and train them, challenge and empower them. Employees must be safe and feel secure in their work environment and job situations. They must be stimulated and incentivized, celebrated and properly compensated.

A Lean organization views people as their most valuable assets. They are more important than tools and fixtures, equipment, material, or capital. Some Lean organizations have promised work for life, in return for individual commitment and dedication to pursuing perfection.

It's in the culture

In a Lean organization, the tenets and philosophy of Lean are fundamentally part of its fiber — embedded in the organization's culture. Everyone practices Lean techniques habitually. When you observe an organization practicing Lean, you will see that:

- Leaders have a long term vision of the business and understand that you must continue to improve it.

- People always see activities as processes; they strive to standardize these work processes, eliminate non-value-added activities (see Chapter 6) in them and work to the standard they've created.

- People routinely communicate through value-stream maps, team meetings in the work area, process flow diagrams, communication centers, graphical analyses, control charts, and other explicit instruments.

- Leaders frequent where the organization creates value. They are in touch with their customers and their organization.

- Visual signs and cues are everywhere. People are in deliberate and decisive motion, performing standardized work. Meetings are short and crisp.

- People naturally and regularly use *kaizen* to eliminate wasteful non-value-added work and follow the Plan-Do-Check-Act (PDCA) methodology. (See Chapter 9 for more about *kaizen*.)

- Everyone makes improvement suggestions — continually.

- People regularly take on new roles and tasks in order to be more complete team contributors. They embrace learning, share knowledge, and are open to changes and new ways of doing things.

- The business builds long-lasting relationships with employees, suppliers, providers, and customers.

What Lean is not

Lean is a lot of things — it's a philosophy; a set of principles; a language (complete with its own jargon and acronyms); a management strategy; a methodology; a set of techniques, behaviors, tools, and even includes some specialty software — all of which support you in reducing waste and delivering long-term customer value. Lean is often associated with other process improvement programs and initiatives, and in particular it's frequently paired with Six Sigma (more on this later in this chapter). And Lean, as a way of thinking and behaving, can be part of many initiatives.

So Lean is a lot of things. But there are a number of things that it isn't:

- ✔ **Lean isn't consulting foo-foo dust.** It's not just a bunch of manager-speak, arcane mapping sessions, or feel-good teaming exercises sprinkled with hoity-sounding Japanese terms. Lean is a well-grounded, mature, and very real framework for developing and sustaining performance excellence. Although some Lean concepts might sound counterintuitive at first — and are very much counter to how many organizations are run — the tools and techniques of Lean have been around for decades and are fully complementary to long-standing proven methods.

- ✔ **Lean isn't onerous.** Unlike most other process improvement initiatives, Lean does not require large upfront investments, prescriptive training or expensive software; nor does it call for a one-size-fits-all formulaic rollout. It requires top-down senior-management support, but Lean can begin in a small group and expand naturally as it grows and as the business needs it. This ease-of-adoption is why Lean has been so successful in small and medium-sized enterprises, as well as larger organizations — and even within operating units of large companies.

- ✔ **Lean isn't a Western-style system.** Take note of this key point: Lean may be very much different from what you're used to. Unlike most Western-style tools and techniques, Lean is not a quick-hit, big-bang, upside-the head, technology-enabled, silver-bullet solution to fix yesterday's problems right now, today. In fact, it's quite the opposite. Lean is a continuous, steady, long-term, everyday approach to building the flexibility and adaptability that enables you to address tomorrow's challenges as they happen. Kaizen events and Lean projects often reap significant near-term benefits, but don't look to Lean as an overnight sensation. Lean is very much a long-term deal. And to sustain the gains, you must develop a culture of respect for people and continuous improvement beyond a project mentality — arrive at every day Lean.

What makes Lean so special?

Companies, organizations, and government entities all know that they must do something — present circumstances just will not allow any of us to sit still. Long gone are the days of doing things the same old way and being successful regardless — or of just being smart, working hard and hoping for the best. Aggressive, unrelenting economic and demographic pressures are forcing everyone to embrace some type of dependable approach and strategy for performance management and improvement. It's now a given that you're going to do something to improve — so what's it going to be?

The Lean approach is increasingly popular, because it offers organizations a sensible, proven, and accessible path to long-term success. Unlike so many of the alternatives, Lean is something that everyone can understand, everyone can do, and everyone can benefit from:

- ✔ **Lean is proven.** The principles and techniques of Lean have been practiced successfully by thousands of organizations of every type and size in every industry worldwide, spearheaded by over 50 years of continuous improvement by one of the world's most successful corporations.

- ✔ **Lean makes sense.** In an era of mind-boggling complexity, Lean is a solid foundation for addressing all kinds of challenges — simply. Lean is broadly applicable in any situation, combining old-world logic and reason with new-world tools and constraints. Lean helps you focus on what your customer wants and how to deliver compelling customer value more effectively.

- ✔ **Lean is accessible.** Lean is accessible to anyone, with any budget. Lean is a serious commitment, but isn't expensive, exclusive, or difficult.

- ✔ **Lean is "hands on."** One of the secrets of Lean is its hands-on approach. From the leaders of the organization to the people working on the front line, everyone understands how to contribute and improve where they can help the organization create value.

- ✔ **Lean is for everyone.** Many performance improvement solutions are strictly tailored for specialty disciplines, or isolated in specific functions or departments — requiring advanced skills and knowledge. Not Lean. Lean is so powerful in part because it is so easily learned and applied by everyone. Lean excludes no one.

The Lean Pedigree

While the specific assembly of principles and practices known as *Lean* date from the late 1980s, the origins of Lean are much older. Lean has a deep pedigree. Historians cite King Henry III of France in 1574 watching the Venice Arsenal build complete galley ships in less than an hour using continuous-flow processes. In the 18th century, Benjamin Franklin established principles regarding waste and excess inventory. Eli Whitney developed interchangeable parts. In the late 19th century, Frank and Lillian Gilbreth pioneered the modern-day understanding of motion efficiency as it related to work. In the early 20th century, Frederic Winslow Taylor, the father of scientific management, introduced the concepts of standardized work and best-practices. (The legendary Shigeo Shingo cites Taylor's 1911 seminal work *Principles of Scientific Management* as his inspiration.)

However, it was in Henry Ford's revolutionary mass-production assembly plants where many practices first emerged. In 1915, Charles Buxton Going, in the preface to Arnold and Faurote's *Ford Methods and the Ford Shops,* observed:

> Ford's success has startled the country, almost the world, financially, industrially, mechanically. It exhibits in higher degree than most persons would have thought possible the seemingly contradictory requirements of true efficiency, which are: constant increase of quality, great increase of pay to the workers, repeated reduction in cost to the consumer. And with these appears, as at once cause and effect, an absolutely incredible enlargement of output reaching something like one hundred fold in less than ten years, and an enormous profit to the manufacturer.

Henry Ford also explicitly understood many of the forms of waste and the concepts of value-added time and effort.

Both the United States and Japan developed new practices during the industrial buildups that preceded and then supported World War II. In the United States, quality leaders like W. Edwards Deming and Joseph Juran refined management and statistical concepts in support of war production. The Training within Industry (TWI) Service formalized practices in management, training, and production, while emphasizing methods and relationships. In postwar Japan, Deming and Juran worked with Japanese industrial leaders to apply these practices to national reconstruction.

Toyoda and Ohno

The Toyoda Automatic Loom Works was founded by Sakichi Toyoda in 1926, where he pioneered the practice of *jidoka* — automation with a human touch. Ten years later, the company changed its name to Toyota and Toyoda's son, Kiichiro, and engineer nephew, Eiji, began producing automobiles with parts from General Motors. Japan's entry into World War II in 1941 diverted its efforts to truck production; during postwar reconstruction, the company nearly went bankrupt.

Meanwhile, Ford regularly invited managers and engineers from around the world to visit Ford plants and observe his mass-production systems. In the spring of 1950, Eiji Toyoda participated in an extended three-month visit to Ford's famed Rouge plant in Dearborn, Michigan. At that time, the Rouge plant was the largest and most complex manufacturing facility in the world. Toyota was producing about 2,500 cars a year; Ford was producing nearly 8,000 a day.

Eiji returned to Japan, and with Toyota's production manager, Taiichi Ohno, concluded that the way Ford's system of mass production had evolved would *not* work for them in Japan. The domestic Japanese automotive market was too small and too diversified, the workforce demands were different and the capital requirements for facilities were too high. Toyoda and Ohno set out to develop an entirely new means of production, including engineering, manufacture, supply, assembly, and workforce management.

The Toyota Production System

A number of the world's leading corporations are known for developing unique, competitive business systems. Some are legendary. General Electric developed Workout. At Hewlett-Packard, there's the HP Way. P&G has IWS — the Integrated Work System.

And then there's the Toyota Production System. It's so famous that it's referred to simply by its abbreviation: TPS. TPS is perhaps the most studied system of production and operations management in the world. Countless companies have visited Toyota and observed TPS in action. Dozens of books have chronicled its successes and hailed its methods (see Chapter 19). It is the foundation for what is now known as Lean.

Lean and Toyota's US challenges

In 2008 – 2010, Toyota Motor Company faced a perfect storm of issues. First, to the great dismay of American industrialists, Toyota had become the world's largest automaker, dethroning the U.S. titan General Motors. This put Toyota in the crosshairs. Then, the Great Recession created a challenging business environment globally for all automotive manufacturers, including Toyota. But throughout these years, Toyota continued to follow their corporate culture (The Toyota Way) and production system (TPS). During the recession they did not layoff any permanent employees or close plants, which is counter to the traditional Western response to such business conditions. Instead, they had their people focus on eliminating waste; they invested in continuous improvement activities and trained their employees more profoundly in both The Toyota Way and TPS. Toyota also worked with their suppliers, whom they consider long-term strategic resources, to help them weather the recession by supporting kaizen activities and implementing creative inventory strategies. Even in a difficult business climate, Toyota stayed true to its culture and way of conducting business.

Just as the recession began to ease, the perfect storm strengthened. In August of 2009, in San Diego, California, a family was driving a Lexus loaned to them by their dealer while their vehicle was in service. The loaned vehicle had the wrong floor mats installed. When the accelerator pedal became stuck to those floor mats, the car sped out of control, crashed, and the family perished. As a result of this accident, Toyota became the focus of a media storm and then government scrutiny. Other accidents and incidents were identified and lumped into a broad category; people began questioning Toyota's legendary product quality.

Fueled by inaccurate and sensationalized reporting in the U.S. media, many people began to lose faith in Toyota and question the company's commitment to its customers and product quality. The response from the company was not what the public and the government expected, based on their preconceptions of how Western companies should act in similar situations. Akio Toyoda, Toyota's president, did not blame others or name scapegoats, but rather apologized to all customers affected by the floor mat issue. The U.S. media perception was that Toyota was not doing enough or acting fast enough. This fueled greater suspicion of Toyota and an increase in vehicle complaints for other quality issues. By February of 2010, Toyota had issued recalls for several quality issues, including aftermarket all-weather floor mats that could cause accelerator pedals to jam, sticky accelerator pedals, Prius brake pedal "feel" issues, and the unconfirmed issue of electronic throttle control system failure. In the past, they would have issued service bulletins for these issues per industry standard because they were not inherent design-quality issues, but because of the negative public opinion and the risk to the Toyota brand, they issued recalls.

What really happened? Did The Toyota Way and Toyota Production System fail? What did Toyota learn as a result of this experience?

After all of the data was in, the analysis — including an analysis by NASA and NITSA — confirmed that Toyota did not have a systemic product quality issue. Toyota did have a public perception issue. In the short term, they had to contain the issue and work to win back customer trust. They were able to redeploy people, who were trained during the recession, to focus on solving problems and fortify customer relationships. In the long term they had to understand the true issues within their organization that caused or contributed to their handling of the crises — both the recession and the customer quality concerns.

Central to TPS and The Toyota Way is deep reflection (*hansei*) to understand the true problem so you can continuously improve the right situation, rather than waste efforts solving the wrong issue. The Toyota culture is one of improvement and understanding, rather than blame. Toyota leadership has always expected the organization to continually improve how it functions, even when it isn't in crisis. True to its culture and practices, Toyota identified several key factors that contributed to the crisis and is steadily working to improve these conditions.

Some of the key findings:

- Rapid growth of the organization resulted in less investment in the training and inculcation of The Toyota Way and TPS across the global organization.

- Centralized decision making and engineering in Japan caused bureaucracy and a disconnection to the voice of the customer. (Fundamental to TPS is the idea that people go to where the action is to fully understand.)

- Information from the dealer networks and customer service centers did not effectively flow to all areas of the organization.

- Cultural differences between the United States and Japan resulted in miscommunications and a lack of understanding of the cultural and contextual impacts of the situation.

- Globalization strategies needed to include trusted, empowered, national leaders.

- Success had caused a drift away from the rigorous adherence to the basics — TPS and Toyota Way.

Toyota has turned this crisis into a learning and improvement opportunity, one not directly related to the manufacturing floor. The TPS and Toyota Way are how Toyota does business in every part of their business. The long-term impact of these challenges is yet to be determined, but the short term data indicates that Toyota has made things right with their customers and has kept their loyalty. Did TPS and The Toyota Way fail? The analysis says not; they were actually the foundation used to move beyond the crises.

For a more detailed analysis of this topic, see *Toyota Under Fire: Lessons for Turning Crisis into Opportunity* by Jeffrey K. Liker and Timothy N. Ogden (Mar 14, 2011).

TPS was principally architected by cousins Eiji and Kiichiro Toyoda and Taiichi Ohno. History credits Ohno as the Father of TPS. He led its development, extension to the supply base, and integration with global partners from the early 1950s through the 1980s. By the time Lean was introduced to U.S. manufacturing, Toyota had been evolving and applying TPS successfully for over 40 years. In the 2000s, Toyota explicitly defined The Toyota Way, which put into words the culture that supported their long term success.

Toyota built the first model House of TPS (see Figure 1-1), depicting graphically that Toyota's quality sets on the combination of just-in-time, built-in quality, and highly motivated people. All of this stands on a foundation of operational stability and kaizen, bolstered by visual management and standardized work.

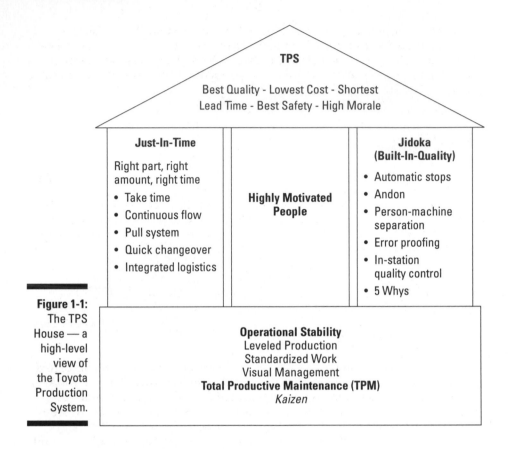

Figure 1-1:
The TPS House — a high-level view of the Toyota Production System.

TPS

Best Quality - Lowest Cost - Shortest
Lead Time - Best Safety - High Morale

Just-In-Time

Right part, right amount, right time
- Take time
- Continuous flow
- Pull system
- Quick changeover
- Integrated logistics

Highly Motivated People

**Jidoka
(Built-In-Quality)**
- Automatic stops
- Andon
- Person-machine separation
- Error proofing
- In-station quality control
- 5 Whys

Operational Stability
Leveled Production
Standardized Work
Visual Management
Total Productive Maintenance (TPM)
Kaizen

Lean and the World of Continuous Improvement

We've been awash in business and process improvement programs for decades. It's been an alphabet soup of initiatives. Remember TQM, BPR, MBOs, and QITs? Well, now we also have the likes of TPM, TOC, GMP, QRM, ISO, Six Sigma, LSS, BPM, and BPE. They're all part of continuous process improvement (yet another acronym: CPI!). It's all very confusing — and somewhat on purpose! Some have come and gone; others have morphed into something else. This section focuses on the ones beyond Lean that are currently well known in business.

Because all these initiatives, methodologies, and "systems" focus on the same basic issues, they have a lot in common. They share some of the same tools and techniques. They claim similar results. But they also have significant differences — critical differences — in focus, scope, application, investment, and return.

Six Sigma

Motorola first developed Six Sigma as an internal quality initiative. Motorola won the inaugural U.S. Malcolm Baldridge National Quality Award in 1988 as a result. Six Sigma hit the national stage following its successful adoption by General Electric in 1996. By 2006, nearly 90 percent of the global *Fortune* 500 companies were practicing Six Sigma in some form, and the estimated combined savings is well in excess of $100 billion!

Six Sigma helps an organization identify and control variation in the processes that most affect performance and profits. Following a prescriptive methodology, trained practitioners known as *Black Belts* analyze root cause and implement corrective action. Black Belt projects typically take four to six months and can return hundreds of thousands of dollars in value.

Note that many of the tools used in Six Sigma are common to Lean. Six Sigma techniques, and its famous Define-Measure-Analyze-Improve-Control (DMAIC) problem-solving methodology, are applicable within a Lean framework as a subordinate toolset for eliminating waste from defects and reducing process variance. (Read *Six Sigma For Dummies,* by Craig Gygi and Bruce Williams, and the *Six Sigma Workbook For Dummies,* by Craig Gygi, Bruce Williams, and Terry Gustafson [both published by Wiley], to find out everything you need to know about Six Sigma.)

Many people mistakenly believe that Lean excludes statistical methods. In Chapter 2 you understand the types of wastes, which includes waste due to variation. In Part IV you learn some of the specific tools that are included in the Lean toolbox. People who truly understand Lean realize that statistical methods — from the simple to complex — are fundamental to successfully transforming to a Lean organization.

Lean Six Sigma

Many large enterprises attempt a "best of breed" approach and implement a combination of Lean and Six Sigma. They believe they can get the best of both worlds by uniting the deployment structure (Black Belts, Green Belts, and so on), the project focus, the DMAIC process and statistical depth of Six Sigma with some of the waste elimination, pull and flow techniques of Lean. You will find many of these initiatives are now called "Lean Six Sigma" (LSS, or L6S).

For those that first implemented the Six Sigma approach, they can discover the benefits of Lean's more accessible techniques. Lean enables greater balance with a more inclusive approach through improvement events, as opposed to the specialization and hierarchy of the belt structure with Six Sigma. Also, where Six Sigma concentrates on solving in-depth localized problems, Lean guides the enterprise towards a solution perspective that includes larger processes. In addition, Six Sigma practice seeks "breakthrough" projects, whereas Lean helps you focus on incremental continuous improvement.

Generally speaking, Lean Six Sigma in practice is more about tools than it is about people and culture. You won't typically find much on Lean's "respect for people" in Lean Six Sigma. Some companies are using independent training to try to compensate for the cultural and people void in LSS.

LSS is really neither Six Sigma nor Lean. Combining Lean and Six Sigma into a single uber-initiative is tricky business that usually has people concentrating mostly on improvement tools. But Lean Six Sigma initiatives often miss out on the key elements required for long term sustainability, achieved through both daily continuous improvement and respect for people. Lean and Six Sigma reflect vastly different cultural approaches to nearly every aspect of leadership and management. You can't just mash up cultures or cherry pick pieces from Lean's decades of maturity as an integrated philosophy and set of principles and methods.

Business Process Management (BPM)

The term *Business Process Management* (BPM) refers to activities performed by businesses to optimize and adapt their formal processes — particularly those processes controlled by automated systems. BPM is often most directly associated with technology and software systems that implement extensive integration and management of process data and information. BPM tools include process modeling, data integration, workflow, and the monitoring and control of work through Process Intelligence (PI). BPM can be significant enabler for Lean, and directly facilitates Lean goals and practices through:

- ✔ Modeling tools that help define and categorize standardized work

- ✔ Data-integration capabilities which capture critical supplier, inventory, cycle time, status, delivery, and other value-stream characterization parameters

- ✔ Activity-monitoring tools to regularly check the performance of processes against controls and limits, alerting people or other processes if key indicators trend improperly

Chapter 2

The Foundation and Language of Lean

. . . .

In This Chapter

▶ Understanding the foundation of Lean

▶ Learning Lean terms and expressions

▶ Identifying waste

. . . .

*I*f you've ever closely watched an elite professional — an athlete, actor, or artist — perform their craft, you're amazed by how natural and effortless they make it seem. Sometimes, what they do just doesn't seem humanly possible — just ask any weekend golfer or home do-it-yourselfer. What these professionals will tell you is not only how long it's taken them to achieve their status, but also that they're never done — they can always get better.

When you undertake a Lean journey, at first it may feel like you're trying to become a ballet dancer or an auto racer. It's new, different, and uncomfortable. The practices may seem strange or even counterintuitive. But with time, education, disciplined application and understanding, you'll become a Lean professional. To start your Lean journey, in this chapter you'll learn about its principles and unique terms.

Understanding Lean Basics

Chapter 1 explains the context of Lean: what it is, where it came from, and how closely aligned it is with the Toyota Production System (TPS). As you come to understand Lean even more, you'll learn that there's not a single concise definition. Lean experts and practitioners don't even agree on a single set of standard principles. There is a generally accepted framework and tool set for Lean, as well as, foundational beliefs and leadership models. Collectively, they form the broad practice known as Lean.

Creating the foundation

Six basic principles of Lean include: customer value, value-stream analysis, everyday improvement, flow, pull, and perfection. Lean always starts and ends with the customer; it is the customer, — and *only* the customer — who defines and determines the *value* of the product and service. Further, the *value stream* is used in Lean to describe all of the activities that are performed — and the information required — to produce and deliver a given product or service. To create value in the most effective way for the customer, you must focus on improving flow, applying pull, and striving for perfection. (More on this in Parts III and IV.) And you implement Lean through people who are respected, engaged, innovative, and empowered.

It's always all about the customer

The underlying reason for being in any business endeavor is to serve a customer successfully. Your customers are your focus: Without your customers, your business effectively doesn't exist. Your customers define what they value and what they don't. The customers set the expectations, and they respond to your offerings with their wallets and their opinions. The fundamental premise for all Lean organizations, and the first step of any Lean undertaking, is to identify your customer and what they really value — what they want today and tomorrow.

Customers are always changing. Technology, markets, and demographics change your customers' behavior continuously. Think about how differently people interact, work, produce, eat, play, and travel compared to 5, 10, or 20 years ago. Most industries and consumer markets have been in a constant state of reinvention since 2000. Events like the Internet boom, the housing bust, the emergence of social media, and various global economic crises have changed consumer habits significantly.

Everything you do in a Lean organization is ultimately focused on serving your customer in the most effective way. All of the organizations that comprise the value stream must understand what their customers want, translate that into a product or service that the customers will buy, and provide it at a price they are willing to pay.

In Lean, *only* the customer can define what behaviors in the value stream add value. To be *value-added,* any process, task, or activity acting on the product or service in any way must meet all three key criteria:

- ✔ **The customer must be willing to pay for it.**
- ✔ **The activity must transform the product or service in some way.**
- ✔ **The activity must be done correctly the first time.**

You can find more about customers, consumers, and tools to understand them in Chapter 6.

Scrutinizing the value stream

When you go into your local supermarket to buy groceries, have you ever stopped to think about all the activities that had to occur, in just the right sequence, in order for you to readily buy what's on your list? Consider produce, for example. You can now find about any fruit or vegetable in your market year-round. Looking in the produce section, you'll find products from around the globe. The produce has more frequent-flier miles that you do! From the fields, through transport, to your store, and ultimately to your table, hundreds of events have occurred precisely the right way and at precisely the right time in order for those blueberries to be available to you at a price and a freshness level that you'll buy.

Delivering value to customers occurs through what's called *the value stream*. In an ideal or perfect world, the value stream consists of only value-added activities. That ideal is what you aim for, but in reality, nothing's perfect. Some waste exists in every process. (We introduce you to the various types of waste in the "Waste not, want not" section, later in this chapter.)

When analyzing the value stream, you identify all the activities and events that occur to get the product or service to your customer, along with the corresponding information flow. These activities and events may occur at your facility, or they may be earlier in the value steam at a supplier facility or later in the value stream in distribution or delivery. Generally, a business begins its improvement efforts with what it controls directly, and later expands beyond its organizational boundaries.

In Lean, you use a tool called a *value-stream map* (VSM) to capture and specify the activities, information, timing, and events in the value stream (value-stream mapping is an important activity, and we cover it extensively in Chapters 7 and 8). First, you scrutinize and map the value stream in its *current state*: How does it all work today? Then you envision the *ideal state:* How would the value stream look if you could do it all perfectly? This Ideal-State value-stream map enables you to visualize and understand what the value stream would look like with no waste — only value-added activities — perfection.

After you've defined the current and ideal-state value-stream maps, you work to close the gap between the two states. Usually a Lean team conducts *kaizen* (continuous improvement) activities to identify and implement the *next future state* moving you closer to the ideal state. Everyone from the organization in and around the value stream is involved in *kaizen*, both as individuals and as part of teams. Initially, most organizations begin their Lean implementation with *kaizen* in a workshop environment. Teams of people use Lean tools to significantly improve a segment of the value stream quickly — typically in a three- to five-day period. In a mature Lean organization, *kaizen* is part of daily business activities. (Chapter 9 addresses *kaizen* in detail.)

For you to design, develop, or deliver any product or service, you need *information* — lots of information! You need it the right way, at the right time, in a flow that effectively supports the flow of the value stream. You identify this information right in the value-stream map. For example, when a consumer buys something, you decrease inventory. To maintain product flow and replenish the inventory, information must flow from the retail outlet to the suppliers. Companies like Coca-Cola, Staples, and Ahold use Business Process Management (BPM) systems so that from the moment of purchase, the information triggers replenishment.

Keep it flowing

Customers and end consumers want their products and services fully finished. They don't want a bunch of in-process, partially finished anythings. They don't care about what's in process, and they don't care about your internal machinations! One of Lean's central principles helps you deliver smooth, continuous flow.

The ideal state of the value stream in Lean is single-piece flow, in every process, with no stoppages anywhere. Multitasking, inventory stoppages, broken equipment, and batching are all inhibitors to flow and must be eliminated. When you have flow, everyone keeps the system moving at just the right speed to deliver the right amount at the right time to the customer.

In the Lean world, you apply the concept of flow to everything, including and especially discrete products and services. Ideally, from the time the first action is stimulated in the value stream, products and services never stop until they reach the customer. From the moment of customer demand, they continuously make their journey through a set of only value-added activities until they reach their destination.

Think about that for a moment: What would it take for a product or service to never stop — ever — in the process of moving through successive steps from first creation all the way to consumption? Imagine a medical facility where the patient never had to wait for treatment. Or buying the latest techno-gadget on its first day in the market without waiting in line, or finding out it sold out in the first 20 minutes.

In a manufacturing environment, flow requires a system of development and processing that adds value to each component, one at a time, with no interruptions, no standing inventory, no defects or rework, and no equipment breakdowns. Processes are synchronized precisely to the customer's rate of consumption. Parts III and IV show you tools to apply to create flow processes.

This concept of flow is not the way people usually tend to think, nor the way most of us have been trained. People tend to organize things in groups and batches, but in Lean you think in terms of *single-piece continuous flow*. Take a simple activity like bulk mailing, for example. What type of process would you use? Figure 2-1 shows a flow chart for a batch process. Now look at Figure 2-2, which shows that same process in as a single-piece flow. In single-piece flow, the documents are handled less, use less space, and are finished and able to be sent more quickly to their recipient. Yet most people think it's faster to process in batch.

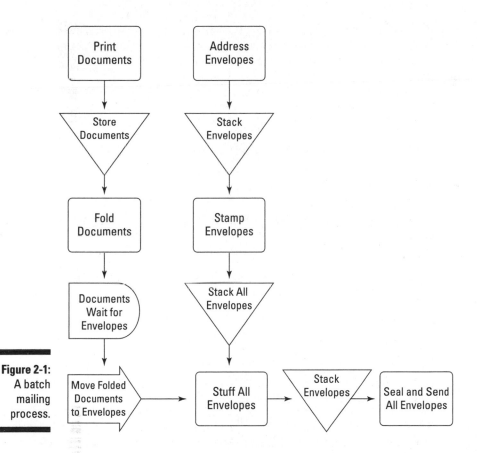

Figure 2-1: A batch mailing process.

Flow is one of those counterintuitive principles of Lean. You actually take less time, use fewer resources, and tie up less money in inventory if you produce your products from a flow perspective.

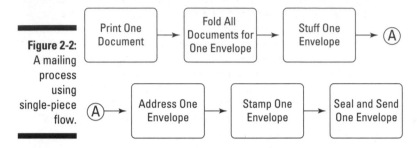

Figure 2-2:
A mailing process using single-piece flow.

Lean requires you to think differently. Throw out your preconceived notions about job boundaries, departments, organizations, or any other blocks that could prevent the implementation of Lean practices.

For *continuous flow* to work, you must reduce variation and eliminate all defects, equipment breakdowns, rework, and outages of any type. These impede flow, whether you're running a manufacturing, retail, service, medical, or support operation. The key to your success is in identifying and eliminating these barriers within the context of your world.

Pulling through the system

Think of products and services being *pulled* through a system as a result of customer demand, rather than being pushed through from previous process without any relationship to consumption by subsequent processes or the consumer. This is *a pull system* — a hallmark of the Lean enterprise.

The classic candy-factory scene from the old television show *I Love Lucy* is a perfect example of an unbalanced push system. Lucy is working on a line where chocolate candies arrive at her workstation on a conveyer belt, and her job is to put them into packages. At first, the chocolates arrive at a slow pace, and Lucy is doing fine. But then the belt mysteriously speeds up, going faster and faster. Lucy wants to do her best, and she tries to stay on top of it. But the inventory has no place to go. When it gets to be too much, she begins stuffing the candy down her shirt, in her mouth, wherever she can, so nothing passes her station. Finally, it all hilariously crashes to a halt. Waste, uneven flow, excess inventory, defects galore — all from pushing too much material at poor Lucy. Why the belt sped up, the audience never knows. What we do know is that this was *not* a Lean process!

In Lean, you use *level scheduling* practices to keep the system operating at a steady and achievable pace. You begin scheduling with the process closest to the customer. As the customer consumes a product or service, each step in the rest of the system is successively triggered to replenish what the next subsequent customer has consumed. In Lean, the pace of value-stream production is known as the *takt time* (see Chapter 7).

One of the most common examples of a pull system is your local supermarket (in fact, the supermarket was the source of inspiration for the pull system). A shelf space has a label that contains information for a given product. A specified amount of the product will fit into the allocated space. When the level runs low, the empty space acts as the signal for the stockperson to replenish the product. The tag contains the information about the product that belongs in the space.

This same idea governs Lean manufacturing. Instead of building up an excess of what's called work-in-process (WIP) inventory, the customer's demand for the product or service pulls goods through the system. The key notion is you only produce as the customer consumes. Think of it as "take one, make one." A pull signal, known as a *kanban,* triggers the need for replenishment. *Kanbans* can come in various forms — a card, a light, a bell, an email, a container, or an empty space. Regardless of the form, the *kanban* signal contains the product information and quantities required for the replenishment of inventory. (More on this in Chapter 11.)

A rule of thumb for equipment availability in a pull system is that the equipment should be available for production 90 percent of the time and down for changeovers and maintenance 10 percent of the time.

When successfully implemented, in conjunction with flow and perfection, pull systems result in higher inventory turns, reduced floor space, faster customer response, and improved cash flow.

Traditional sales and marketing practices need to be in step with the steady-state flow of the Lean enterprise. Sales incentives and seasonal campaigns, like inventory clearance sales or Independence Day sales, drive up demand and cause products to be sold at lower prices. This artificially bullwhips the supply chain. The concepts of level selling and steady-state pricing support a more effective enterprise.

Striving for perfection

Your ability to effectively provide value to your customer relates directly to your ability to eliminate waste and keep it away, permanently. This means that Lean is a never-ending journey. Although it may sound onerous, especially in a goal-driven society, the reality is that there is and always will be something to improve. As you scrutinize your processes, you'll discover wastes that you didn't know existed, because they were masked by bigger wastes. It's like draining ponds or swamps: You never really know what's lurking beneath the surface until you're brave enough to look — and then you have to do something about it. Lean divides the broad category of waste into seven categories and three classifications (we cover these in the "Waste not, want not" section, later in this chapter).

Constant incremental improvements are achieved through *kaizen*. (We cover *kaizen* in depth in Chapter 9.) In its simplest form, *kaizen* means that you improve something every day. It is both a philosophy and a methodology. *Kaizen* improvements are generally not intended to be radical, earth-shattering improvements — instead, they're regular incremental improvements that eliminate waste, here, there, and everywhere, bit by bit.

Companies just beginning a Lean journey often use what's known as *kaizen events*. *Kaizen* events most often begin with workshops that offer a significant opportunity for the organization. This opportunity could be a visual impact through the use of what's known as *5S* (see Chapter 11), or it could be a customer-related opportunity like significantly reducing a specific quality defect. You can also use a *kaizen* event to take on an "it can't be done" challenge and break through a barrier. An example of this is the reduction in equipment changeover time from hours to minutes.

When improvement is on a radical enough scale, it is known as *kaikaku*. When you think *kaikaku*, think "Throw out all the rules." It may come in the form of multiple, simultaneous *kaizen* events (also known as a *kaizen blitz*). Alternatively, the term *kaikaku* may imply a complete change in technology or process methodology. You still use all the same tools of Lean (see Part IV), but you apply them to loftier goals.

Whether it's through *kaizen* or the more ambitious *kaikaku*, the aim is the same: Strive for perfection through improvement. Eliminate waste in all that you do. Create a sustainable, thriving business for the long haul. Continually seek ways to better serve the customer.

Learning from TPS

Because Lean evolved from the study of the Toyota Production System (TPS), you might expect that the principles of Lean and TPS are similar. They are very similar, but they're organized in a different way. To understand Lean, you need to understand a little about TPS.

Keep in mind that Lean and TPS are applicable across many industries, well beyond the automotive manufacturing environments that form their heritage. (This is the subject of Part V.)

Highly motivated people

Traditional organizations often operate with a "shut up and do your job" mentality. This is not the case in the TPS environment. In TPS culture, people are expected and encouraged to engage fully, not just to perform their daily job functions, but also to contribute to daily improvement activities. People use their creativity and provide important and useful suggestions to eliminate problems and improve the value stream. It is through the people — workers and managers — that improvement happens. The people use the tools, the people devise solutions, and the people implement improvements — it's all about the people!

In TPS, people work both in their individual job assignments and also as part of broader teams. The teams may be natural workgroups or may be formed for special projects. As part of natural workgroups, team members are routinely cross-trained to expertly perform multiple job tasks across the team's span of responsibility. Whether acting as individuals or as part of a team, everyone regularly and routinely eliminates waste as part of their normal work.

The approach of man-and-machine interfaces is philosophically different in TPS than in traditional Western-style environments. In TPS, machines are always subordinate to people. This means that processes are designed so that people don't wait on machines — machines wait on people. Western approaches value the resource costs of people versus equipment and may conclude that the equipment is more valuable than the person, but this is never so in TPS. People are always most important. Machines, equipment, and systems are tools used by people as they add value.

Many practitioners have mistakenly focused on the tools and equipment of Lean and neglected the *Respect for People* aspect. Your success only happens through people! Without the people, changes are not sustainable.

Operational stability

The foundation of the TPS is *operational stability*. Operational stability means that variation within all aspects of the operations is under control. To have unobstructed flow, orders must be timely and accurate, schedules must be stable and leveled, equipment must run as planned, qualified staff must be in place, and standardized work must be documented and implemented.

One of the common mistakes that companies adopting TPS make is to not understand how TPS is a complete system, and how important holistic practices are to overall success. They think that implementing *kanban* is the answer — but without level and stable schedules, for example, *kanban* doesn't work very well.

Visual management

Visual management enables people to see exactly what's going on and respond to issues very rapidly. One method of visual management is known as *andon* (a signal to alert people of problems at a specific place in a process). The organization responds according to the signal shown; the response follows the documented standardized work practice. TPS leaders expect workers to trigger an *andon* anytime they have an issue; this enables the leadership to better understand barriers to the standard and to address problems quickly. They know that no *andons* is a problem, and it will lead to missed opportunities to improve. See Chapter 12 for more information.

Other aspects of visual management include cross-training boards, production tracking, customer information stations, communication displays, and tool boards. (We cover the tools of Lean in depth in Part IV.)

Just in time

Just in time (JIT) is the most well-known pillar of the TPS house. JIT means making only what you need, when you need it, and in the amount needed — no more, no less. If you're supplying JIT, you synchronize your entire system with the customer's demands. This is where takt time comes in to play. A JIT environment is almost like an ecosystem where everything is working in concert with each other. If one element is out of balance, then the whole system responds and adjusts. For example, if a major quality or supply issue arises, a JIT system will cease overall functioning until the issue can be resolved.

To operate to JIT, you apply several techniques and practices, including

- **Producing to takt:** Use takt to connect the rate of production to customer demand.
- **Standardized work:** Create consistent methods and standard ways of working to reduce variation and provide a baseline for improvement.
- **Quick changeover:** Develop the flexibility to produce a broader range of products over shorter timeframes.
- **Continuous flow:** Create a steady stream of products or services that flow continuously to the customer.

↙ **Pull:** Use customer demand to trigger the replenishment activities throughout the system. Note that the systems of pull and continuous flow in TPS map directly to the concepts of pull and flow in the Lean framework.

↙ **Integrated logistics:** View all aspects of your supply chain as a system, and manage them as a whole. (See Chapter 11 for ways to do this.)

Jidoka

The term *jidoka* means that you build in quality at the source. Recognize that quality cannot be "inspected in" — after the work has left its station, it's too late. When practicing jidoka, accept no defects, make no defects, and pass no defects.

The philosophy of *jidoka* says the person producing work within any given step has the responsibility for the quality of job they are performing. If a problem exists, that person is responsible for resolving it. If the person can't resolve the issue, then he is responsible for stopping the process in order to get it fixed.

The broader definition of jidoka includes root cause analysis techniques like the *5-Whys* and mistake-prevention techniques like *poka yoke* (see Chapter 11 for more information) where you implement solutions to physically prevent mistakes from happening. Visual management techniques like andon boards are also part of a *jidoka* practice.

Building on the foundation

Beyond the basic ideas of customer value, the value stream, flow, pull and perfection are additional principles of Lean, when coupled with the learning from TPS, lead to the mindset, methods, tool sets and techniques of Lean. When you truly get this wisdom, you get Lean.

Respect for people

Fundamental in Lean is a respect for people that does not exist in most traditional systems of management and leadership. Lean organizations are learning organizations. They effectively support their members through safe work environments, open communications, extensive training, and, in some cases, employment guarantees. Employee cross-training develops the employees, while at the same time adding depth to the organization. People are rewarded for making improvements to systems. People who are knowledgeable about multiple aspects of the value stream enable the organization to minimize variation due to absenteeism and turnover.

In a Lean environment, employees are expected to use their brains for the betterment of the customer, the value stream, and the organization as a whole. They engage in the environment, contribute to improvement, learn from their mistakes, and expand their knowledge base.

People always have more value than machines. In traditional manufacturing environments, it isn't uncommon to see a person standing at a machine, watching while the machine cycles. Lean views this as a waste of the most precious resource — a human being. The Lean view is to implement appropriate technology, so that people can do more valuable work. This is part of the practice of *autonomation* (automation with a human touch). It isn't the belief that people can be replaced with machines; rather it's the practice to add intelligence to machines to detect defects, prevent issues from being passed along the value stream, and automatically unload parts, so people don't have to waste their time and brain power watching a machine.

Make it visual

Transparency helps you eliminate waste. When you can quickly see what's going on, you don't waste time, energy, or effort trying to figure it out. If there is a place for everything, you can quickly see when anything is not in its place. The old adage "a picture is worth a thousand words" cannot be truer in Lean. Through a picture, a graph, a trouble light, process intelligence tools, and other visual techniques, you can quickly and easily understand information, respond to events and improve the process. (We cover more about visual management in Part IV.)

Annually, countless thousands of trees give their lives to become large reports that few people read — but not in Lean. Thick reports are waste. Because the purpose of reporting is to provide information for people to actually use, in Lean, you use a single-page format (also called *A3 reporting,* in a reference to the international paper size) to easily see the truly critical and necessary information, such as a description of the issue, actions, data, and resolution. This way, the reader can put their time into action, rather than digesting data.

Long-term journey

Lean does produce instant results; you see immediate improvement. In fact, you see improvement faster than almost any other way. But Lean is not a fad diet for your business. To sustain that improvement, you must be in the game for the long haul. Lean is a lifestyle change that requires diligence. If

Lean were a race, it would be more like the tortoise, not the hare: steady incremental improvements over the long term. This is not to say that you don't experience a burst of speed along some stretches; this will happen when you conduct multiple improvement workshops simultaneously (known as the *kaizen blitz*). Anyone with some data, analysis tools, and control charts can always improve something in the short term; the key to Lean is the sustainability and incorporation of changes into the normal daily business routine over the long term.

Simple is better: The KISS principle

Life has become so complex that you practically need an advanced degree to change the oil in your car or to program the TV remote. Does all this complexity actually add value? When everything is working well, it seems to — but when it isn't, well, that's a different story. Because everything has become so complex, it doesn't always work so well.

The easier something is, the easier you can learn it, and the easier it is for you to deal with it when problems occur — whether that something is a product, a service, or the process that creates it. Simplicity is one of the beauties of Lean. It doesn't mean that you don't solve complex issues, but it does mean that you strive to find simple solutions to them. Lean improvements don't necessarily cost a lot of money. If you can error-proof something equally well with a block of wood and duct tape versus a computer-controlled apparatus, Lean tells you to tend towards the wood-and-duct-tape solution. Consider the solution that's quicker, faster, and cheaper, both in the short term and the long term.

Quality at the source

Have you ever put on a new pair of jeans and found an inspector tag? Does that add value to you, the customer? Do you feel like the pants have any greater level of quality because an inspector left a tag that you had to pull out of the pocket to throw away? "Certified by Inspector Number 12" was a slogan that the marketing gurus used to make people believe that the product they were buying was somehow better (or at least acceptable) because Inspector Number 12 was on the job. The reality is that by the time Inspector Number 12 sees the product, it's too late: The quality is already there, or not.

You can't inspect quality *into* a product — ever. Many companies use inspectors to try to catch defects before they're released to the market, but the act of inspection doesn't change the quality of what's already been produced. People also use containment, which is the excuse to inspect while you keep producing suspect product. In Lean, you create a quality product at each step of the value stream. If defects occur, the product or service element doesn't leave the current process step, either because the person doing the job caught the error or there was autonomation that detected the issue. Meanwhile, the next operator in the process may check key characteristics of a product. If they find an issue, they send the product back to the previous operation. The person who performed the transformational step owns the responsibility for the quality of his work. Now everyone is an "inspector," and quality at the source becomes a reality.

Not all inspection is necessarily bad, but all inspection is, by definition, non-value added. Inspection does nothing to transform the product or service. Inspection is deemed necessary when the risk of the product or service advancing beyond that stage of the value stream will put the customer at risk or have a great financial impact; it could be a point of no return for repairs, for example. If you require separate inspection stations, be sure they follow a clearly defined, standardized work process.

Measurement systems: reinforcing Lean behaviors

People respond to how they're measured. If your measurement system supports the Lean principles, you'll reinforce Lean behaviors. Also, if your measurement system facilitates a change towards Lean, you'll see the change happen.

One of the main challenges to effective Lean implementations is that most traditional measurement systems in place today do not support Lean practices.

One common example of a measurement system that does not support Lean is the traditional cost accounting system. Traditional accounting for equipment and direct labor actually encourages waste. Under such systems, equipment absorbs overhead, so supervisors run equipment to make their numbers look better, whether they need to produce or not. This leads to one of the seven forms of waste — overproduction — which we discuss in the "*Muda, muda, muda*" section, later in this chapter.

Additionally, cost-accounting environments overemphasize the impact of direct labor. When cost-accounting systems were originally established, labor made up the majority of actual costs; now direct labor can be a minority of the cost. Companies have purchased automated equipment to eliminate direct labor, only to find that they have the same number of bodies supporting the equipment as they used to have performing the work! The difference is that those bodies are now *indirect* labor, and, ironically, they're usually more skilled and, therefore, working at a higher pay rate. However, the accounting system still sees this as a benefit because of the measurement system. Ouch!

In addition to changing business practices, successful Lean organizations know that they need the right measurement systems to reinforce Lean behaviors. One tool that these organizations use is a Balanced Scorecard (see Chapter 13). The Balanced Scorecard tracks aspects of the business beyond the traditional financial measures. Areas like safety, people, quality, delivery, innovation and cost are measured to show the overall health of the business and identify where the opportunities for improvement exist.

No perfect organization exists. Even Toyota, the pinnacle of Lean success, has had its issues. Although the original Toyodas and Ohno are gone, they left behind for all of us a legacy of reflection, learning, and unrelenting quest for improvement. The new leaders have the charge to continue that legacy by learning from issues and addressing inconsistencies and challenges using TPS foundations.

Learning lasts a lifetime

Learning happens thousands of times a day — every day — in a Lean organization. Learning and improving through observations, experiments, and mistakes is fundamental to *kaizen*. In Lean, after a lesson is learned, the knowledge is institutionalized via updated work standards. And then the cycle repeats: Observe, improve, institutionalize. Individuals learn; teams learn; collectively, the knowledge of the organization increases. Every instant of every day is the right time to learn and grow.

Waste Not, Want Not

As an individual, if you've ever tried to get in shape, you know that you have to change the way you diet, exercise, hydrate, and rest in order to have long-term success. In your diet, you have to take out the empty calories and highly processed foods that do not add nutritional value. When you start paying attention to what you put in your mouth, you realize how much garbage has been unconsciously passing your lips.

When you start on a Lean journey, one of the key ways to improve the health of the value stream is to eliminate waste. Like the empty calories of junk food, you'll find that a lot of non-value-added activities have crept into the diet of your value stream. Waste in Lean is described by the three *Ms* of *muda* (waste), *mura* (unevenness), and *muri* (overburden). Muda is divided into seven forms of waste, which we cover in the following section.

Muda, muda, muda

Waste is all around you, every day and everywhere. You waste your time, waiting in line, waiting in traffic, or waiting because of poor service. In your home, you may have experienced walking into a room looking for something that wasn't where it was supposed to be — wasted time and effort. In your kitchen, you may have had to throw out science experiments from your refrigerator — again, waste. Doing things over? That's waste, too.

By now, you may be wondering what "waste" or *muda* exactly is and isn't. Taiichi Ohno categorized waste into seven forms. These seven forms are: transport, waiting, overproduction, defects, inventory, motion, and excess processing. Table 2-1 provides a summary of the seven forms of waste.

Table 2-1	The Seven Forms of Waste	
Form of Waste	*Also Known As*	*Explanation*
Transport	Conveyance	Any movement of product or materials that is not otherwise required to perform value-added processing is waste. The more you move, the more opportunity you have for damage or injury.
Waiting	Waiting or delay	Waiting in all forms is waste. Any time a worker's hands are idle is a waste of that resource, whether due to shortages, unbalanced workloads, need for instructions, or by design.
Overproduction	Overproduction	Producing more than your customer requires is waste. It causes other wastes like inventory costs, manpower and conveyance to deal with excess product, consumption of raw materials, installation of excess capacity, and so on.

Form of Waste	Also Known As	Explanation
Defect	Correction, repair, rejects	Any process, product, or service that fails to meet specifications is waste. Any processing that does not transform the product or is not done right the first time is also waste.
Inventory	Inventory	Inventory anywhere in the value stream is not adding value. You may need inventory to manage imbalance between demand and production, but it is still non-value-added. It ties up financial resources. It is at risk to damage, obsolescence, spoilage, and quality issues. It takes up floor space and other resources to manage and track it. In addition, large inventories can cover up other sins in the process like imbalances, equipment issues, or poor work practices.
Motion	Motion or movement	Any movement of a person's body that does not add value to the process is waste. This includes walking, bending, lifting, twisting, and reaching. It also includes any adjustments or alignments made before the product can be transformed.
Extra processing	Processing or overprocessing	Any processing that does not add value to the product or is the result of inadequate technology, sensitive materials, or quality prevention is waste. Examples include in-process protective packaging, alignment processing like basting in garment manufacturing or the removal of sprues in castings and molded parts.

You may be thinking that some of these wastes are truly beyond your control. Regulatory demands, accounting requirements, or natural events may be causing these. For this reason, *muda* is divided into two classifications:

- ✔ **Type-1 muda** includes actions that are non-value-added, but are for some other reason deemed necessary. These forms of waste usually cannot be eliminated immediately.

- ✔ **Type-2 muda** are those activities that are non-value-added and are also not necessary. These are the first targets for elimination.

All in the family

Beyond the general forms of *muda* are two other cousins of the waste family: *mura* and *muri.* As with the forms of *muda,* the goal is to eliminate these types of waste, too.

Mura (Unevenness)

Mura is *variation* in an operation — when activities don't go smoothly or consistently. This is waste caused by variation in quality, cost, or delivery. *Mura* consists of all the resources that are wasted when quality cannot be predicted. This is the cost for things such as testing, inspection, containment, rework, returns, overtime, unscheduled travel to the customer, and potentially the cost of a lost customer. To understand and reduce variation, you can use statistical tools and methods, including Pareto charts and Design of Experiments (DOE). More on these in Part IV.

Many people mistakenly believe that statistics and rigorous data analysis are not part of Lean. Not true. To reduce *mura* and *muda,* you use data. By measuring your process before and after, you verify that you have improved.

Muri (Overdoing)

Muri is the unnecessary or unreasonable overburdening of people, equipment, or systems by demands that exceed capacity. *Muri* is the Japanese word for unreasonable, impossible, or overdoing. From a Lean perspective, *muri* applies to how work and tasks are designed. One of the core tenets of Lean is *respect for people.* If a company is asking its people to repeatedly perform movements that are harmful, wasteful, or unnecessary, this means the company is not respecting the people and, therefore, is not respecting the foundation of Lean. You perform ergonomic evaluations of operations to identify movements that are either harmful or unnecessary.

In addition to physical overburdening, requiring people to work excessive hours is a form of *muri.* Excessive meetings, "cover your back" emails, and the demands of the global business environment all contribute to *muri.* And you'll see *muri* manifested in employee turnover, medical leaves, system outages and downtime, and poor decision making.

In today's environment of "doing more with less" there is a risk that you overburden and stress your people. Stressed people are at a greater risk for making mistakes. Question assumptions, work methods, everything to ensure the activities your people are doing add value, and that you don't have too much *muri* built into your systems and processes.

Lean lingo

Because the foundations of Lean originated from the Toyota Production System, the language of Lean contains quite a few Japanese words. These words have come to represent Lean systems and concepts. In addition, Lean has unique English terms. The glossary at the end of this book contains a thorough list of terms that are critical to your understanding of Lean. Think of these terms in Lean as you would *please, thank you,* and *hello* when learning a foreign language. Pretty soon, you'll be speaking Lean like a native.

Also, you may hear the word *efficient* used in conjunction with the improvements in an organization's operations. However, the aim of a Lean organization is to provide value in the most *effective* way possible. In Lean, the word *effective* is used rather than *efficient,* to avoid the traditional definitions of efficiency associated with batch and queue and other forms of mass production, such as *labor efficiency.* When you're operating *effectively,* you're providing the right thing, at the right time, through an engaged and motivated workforce producing the highest quality level, shortest lead times, and lowest cost.

One of the foundations of Lean is respect for people. Avoid using terms such as idiot-proof or dummy-proof, which are demeaning to people. The proper language is "error-proof" or "mistake-proof."

Part II
The Lean Culture

"We mapped our corporate value stream, Phillip, and your department was such a mudflat that we're going to eliminate everything but the clams and scallops."

In this part . . .

In this part, we focus on the often overlooked Respect for People aspect of Lean. We look at Lean in the organization, including principles, behaviors, and change. We also show Lean and change at an individual level, and examine the organizational strategy and evolution of Lean.

Chapter 3

Lean in the Organization: Principles, Behaviors, and Change

In This Chapter

▶ Probing the cultural climate

▶ Aligning behaviors to Lean principles

▶ Understanding the phases of organizational change

*Y*ou are part of one or more organizations. An *organization* is a group of people arranged and structured for a purpose. It could be for a business purpose (such as, to develop or provide goods and services to customers for a profit). It could be another purpose (such as education, government, or nonprofit contributions to humanity). A family is a type of organization.

An organization's culture and the principles that drive people's behaviors ultimately determine the degrees of an organization's performance, quality, and success. Think about famous organizational cultures — such as Facebook, Nordstrom, P&G, Nike, Toyota, or Goldman Sachs — and how they've performed. In each of these cases — as in the case of every organization — people's behaviors have both steered and been steered directly by the principles and belief systems fostered from within and spread across the organizational landscape . . . for better or for worse.

Organizational cultures are deeply ingrained. The principles guiding the behaviors of the people within an organization are purposefully long-lived and slow to change. Organizational culture has mass: The larger it is and the faster it's going, the more momentum it builds. This trait is a good thing when that momentum is carrying you in the right direction, but not so good when you wander off course or if circumstances dictate change.

Few organizations are born and raised as Lean organizations, so if you're now embarking upon a Lean journey, you're likely in the process of changing course. This means that in addition to applying the methods and techniques described in the rest of this book, you will also be changing the organizational culture by changing principles, leadership styles and individual behaviors. As you begin this journey, you'll need to understand how your organization's current principles and behaviors align with Lean principles and behaviors. The extent of the gap between the two will help you understand what changes are required and how to make them. As with any change, it's in how you change, how often you change course and how you communicate these changes that you will influence the organization's response.

In this chapter, we tell you all about the organizational principles and behaviors that reflect a Lean organization. We show you how to assess an organization's true principles and behaviors versus its stated principles. You will understand how to compare your current organization's principles to Lean principles, and get a feel for a basic organizational change model. Finally, you will see how to move the organization beyond roadblocks. You can combine this chapter with Chapters 4 and 5 for a complete understanding of implementing Lean with your people and in your organizational culture.

Many analysts and pundits use the term *values* in defining and describing organizational culture and principles. In the Lean world, the term *value* is more directly associated with the concept of what the customer values and adding value within a process or work activity. To avoid confusion in this chapter, when we want to refer to organizational culture and principles, we use the word *principles*.

Assessing Organizational Culture

Before you can change your organizational culture, you have to understand the culture in reality. In this section, we tell you how to assess the current organizational climate, compare it to Lean principles, and identify the gap that exists between the two.

Will the real principles please stand up?

Most organizations have both a formal set of principles and an informal set of principles. Collectively, these form the foundation of virtues and beliefs that reinforce the integrity and character upon which everyone — including employees, customers, suppliers, shareholders, analysts, and consumers — depends.

The *formal* principles are often a flowery list of words, hung on a wall or occupying a page on the employee web site. Most organizations address such hallmarks as customer service, trust, teamwork, diversity, honesty, and respect for people in their cadre of principles. No doubt an expensive team of high-level people spent the better part of a retreat session precisely chiseling those idealistic words into a lofty statement of principles — only to find that, in reality, they're mostly unknown or ignored within the organization.

The *informal* principles are often not stated, but people reflect them through their daily interactions. Be careful, because these attitudes, words and actions will influence new hires before they even finish the orientation class! The informal principles are the basis of what really happens in an organization — when management isn't looking. Your goal is to have alignment between the formal and informal, so no matter who is watching, the people drive the culture in the direction you want it to go.

The informal principles may be at odds with the formal ones. This discrepancy causes tension and conflict across the organization. If "Respect for People" is a formal principle, but people are poorly treated or fired indiscriminately, your principles are at odds. If "Trust" is a formal principle, but people are constantly second-guessed and overruled, you have trouble. "Integrity" was one of Goldman Sach's stated principles, but it's pretty obvious that the real set of principles resulted in behavior of a different sort.

Instead of a declaration of lofty principles that largely go ignored, Google, for example, has a set of ten principles that are actionable and consistent, including "Great just isn't good enough." Another one of those principles is "You can make money without doing evil." Now, that's a principle that can really guide behavior!

In an ideal Lean organization, you live and breathe a specific set of principles. They're consistent and powerful, and they have life both formally and informally. Everyone in the organization is in tune. In reality, you may not be able to live up to every one of those principles 100 percent of the time, but you strive for perfection — every minute of every day with each member of the organization. As a Lean organization, you will strive to eliminate barriers that prevent you from living according to your principles.

Getting the culture to the starting line

If you're beginning the Lean journey, you have to know where your organization stands as the journey begins. Identify the current principles and beliefs, and assess what needs to change before you embark. You have organizational baggage accompanying you on your journey. The culture fairy is not going to wave a magic wand and instantly change the entire climate and culture of the organization — you'll have to work at it with every interaction every day.

If you're like most organizations you have undertaken many initiatives before trying Lean. An organization's normal reaction is to resist change, hoping that "this too shall pass." You'll hear people grouse about needing to do their "real job." Keep in mind that these attitudes are part of your current state. Your past track record will influence your organization's acceptance of another new initiative. Begin by assessing the current state of the organization. Then you can identify the gaps that could thwart your Lean efforts.

Identifying the current state of the organization

Taking stock of organizational culture is a squishy task: By its very nature, it's imprecise. Author and poet Hans Magnus Enzensberger once said "Culture is a little like dropping an Alka-Seltzer into a glass — you don't see it, but somehow it does something."

Begin your assessment of the current situation by asking questions. You can use several mechanisms to gather data: employee engagement surveys, observation studies, electronic surveys, organizational network analysis and employing outside observers or interviewers — these are all options to gather information on the current organizational climate.

Here are some questions to start your assessment:

- ✔ What are the officially stated principles and beliefs of the organization?

- ✔ What organizational behaviors support those stated principles?

- ✔ What behaviors suggest a different set of beliefs?

- ✔ Where are the stated and implied principles at odds? Where are they consistent?

- ✔ Describe the relationship between management and non-management employees. Identify behaviors that typify the management/non-management relationship.

- ✔ Has the organization undergone mergers and acquisitions? If so, how many cultures coexist in the current organization?

- ✔ How has the organization handled change initiatives in the past?

- ✔ When is the last time the organization had a significant improvement effort? How long did it last?

- ✔ Are any formal change initiatives currently active?

- ✔ How effective have these change initiatives been?

- ✔ How many members of the current organization have been involved in the change effort?

- ✔ What behaviors support a Lean organization and should continue?

You can't observe and measure any of this from your office. You must go to "where the action" is to see the true picture (see Chapter 13 on *3Gen*). You're trying to identify behaviors to leverage, as well as misalignments and incongruities, before you formally introduce a set of Lean principles. For example, if one of your stated values is "quality first," but you observe defective product being shipped to meet a delivery deadline, this is incongruent. If a value is "the customer is king," yet you notice your employees ignoring or being rude to your customers, you have a gap to close. If "continuous improvement" is another stated value, but every year the organization fights the exact same fires, what does this tell you?

The organization's formal principles may be close to Lean, yet the informal principles may be across a chasm as wide as the Grand Canyon. Knowing your gaps in your credibility will help you formulate a change strategy to support the shift from traditional operations to Lean.

Defining Lean principles in an organization

Remember, the overarching Lean principle is *continuous incremental change*. Foundational to this are two additional categories:

- ✔ Customer satisfaction
- ✔ Respect for people

Many Lean programs and practitioners focus on "customer satisfaction" and forget "respect for people." You must have "respect for people" to be successful; it is as fundamental to the Lean enterprise as customer satisfaction for your efforts to be sustaining and your success to continue. Each area contains subordinate principles, as shown in Table 3-1.

Table 3-1	A Summary of Lean Principles
Continuous Incremental Change	
Customer Satisfaction	*Respect for People*
Perform value-added activities	Ensure personal safety
Operate just-in-time	Foster employee security
Eliminate waste	Challenge and engage everyone
Flow and pull continuously	Celebrate wins
Create quality at the source	Grow and learn continuously
Live standardized work	Communicate effectively

Measuring the gap

To understand your organization's current culture and define what Lean principles mean to you, go observe what is really happening, and make a formal assessment. In addition to the questions found in the section "Identifying the current state of the organization," this assessment should include:

- ✔ What are the current principles?
- ✔ Is each a formal or informal principle?
- ✔ What behaviors reflect or demonstrate each principle?

✔ Is this principle, and the way it is expressed, aligned with Lean?

✔ How specifically does each principle align with Lean?

✔ What supportive actions should stay in the organization?

✔ What new actions and habits must you develop to strengthen each principle?

✔ What mechanisms in your current "people development process" can you use or create to promote the growth of these habits and actions?

✔ How can you measure these cultural elements and actions?

A commonly used graphical tool in Lean for showing progress in several areas to a defined goal is the *spider chart*. In a spider chart, the outside circle represents full compliance or 100 percent attainment, while the center of the circle represents no compliance or 0 percent attainment. The objective is to fill in the circle as performance increases. The spider chart in Figure 3-1 shows progress for cultural transformation. In this example, the organization has rated personal safety at 90 percent and value-added at 20 percent. (See Chapter 13 for more information about spider charts.)

As the organization matures, your definition for each element will change because you and your organization will continually evolve. Your initial scores may decrease as you continue to learn and scrutinize your performance. You also may realize that your initial evaluation was too high or you need to set a more rigorous goal for the organization. The constant quest for improvement in all aspects is more important than the number.

Figure 3-1: This spider chart graphically depicts an organization's progress toward cultural transformation goals.

Toyota's True North

Because Toyota is so widely recognized as the company that created Lean, it stands out as the model to emulate. Outsiders consider Toyota to be truly a Lean company. Yet, Toyota recognizes that its journey is not complete and never ends. It has identified what it calls *True North*. True North represents what it *should* do, not what it *can* do. True North is Toyota's guiding direction, an ideal state — something it strives for but, in the spirit of continuous improvement, will never reach.

In Toyota's vision of True North, everyone engages, every minute of every day, in always improving the current state. The following table illustrates Toyota's principles describing True North.

Customer Satisfaction	*Human Development*
Zero defects	Physical and mental safety
100 percent value-added	Security
1 x 1, in sequence, on demand	Professional challenge

Remember: Define your own True North. Although Toyota's True North may be a good model to follow, your organization isn't Toyota. If you reference their model, translate it into the context of your organization. What is *your* ideal path?

After you've assessed the organization's culture, you'll know where you're strong and where your challenges lie. The nature of the organizational strengths and weaknesses will determine your change initiative. Leverage your strengths and close your gaps. Going forward, periodically assess your culture, just as you would quality, delivery, cost or customer satisfaction.

Changing the Organization

Rarely are organizations naturally prepared to begin a Lean journey. Most often, organizational cultures twist, contort, and usually writhe in outright pain as they grow and mature into a Lean organization. These contortions are recognizable and typically occur in five discrete phases with each turn through the cycle of improvement. As the Lean journey progresses, the organization generally moves through these phases more quickly. Note that everyone in the organization will change how they do their daily activities in attitudes, actions and approaches; more on this in Chapters 4 and 5.

Everyone in the organization progresses at his own pace. Some people are "change embracers," some are "data driven," some are "wait and seers," and some are "resisters to the end." In the process of change, you must treat each of these factions accordingly.

Pay attention to the "respect for people" aspects of change. It may seem too murky, political and time consuming. But if you don't pay attention to it, your Lean efforts will not be successful in the long term.

Going through the five phases of change

Independent of the nature of the change, an organization that's undergoing a transformation will move through five phases — most likely *not* in strict serial order. Because an organization is a collection of individuals, each of whom accepts change in his own time, the organization may sometimes have to go backward to go forward. As you take your next steps in your Lean journey, you'll go back through these phases. The trick for management is to monitor the pulse of the organization to know in what direction it's morphing and evolving. When backsliding occurs, management needs to correct the course.

Phase 1: Recognition and acceptance

Recognition is the beginning of any change, and acceptance completes this first phase. Just like in your own life, an organization must recognize and accept that today's conditions are no longer viable.

Not until the pain of the present is greater than the pain of the uncertain future will an individual or organization embark upon a change of any type. Opportunity alone will motivate only 5 percent of the population. A fear of loss or some other significant emotional connection motivates the other 95 percent. The critical first step in the process is to clearly identify and communicate the need for change until the organization recognizes and accepts the reason.

Recognition usually requires letting go — letting go of a stale dream, an obsolete vision, current work practices, or nostalgia for the past. People are reluctant to let go — many people cling to memories and work practices of the good old days long after they're gone and irrelevant. And the bigger and more established the organization, the more difficult letting go is.

When embarking upon a Lean journey, the organization has to change — continuously. It can't expect to harbor its old ways and at the same time truly implement Lean. How quickly and how readily the organization adapts to Lean depends upon the past, the present, and how far away the organization is from its desired future.

Think about a family that has outgrown its current home. The lone bathroom is overcrowded in the morning, the kids are tripping over one another in the bedrooms, and there's no place to relax or do homework. But the mortgage is affordable, the neighborhood is comfortable, and the memories are many. At what point does the family recognize and accept the need to make a change?

Phase 2: Direction and planning

After a critical mass of the organization recognizes and accepts the need for change, the next step is to determine the new vision and set the direction for the future. Only then can you define the action plan to move the organization into that future.

Sometimes, the very act of painting the future vision helps cement the acceptance for change. When that vision relieves enough current pain and suffering, organizational buy-in improves. Forward momentum begins to build, which attracts support and ideas for the action plan.

Consider the family from the preceding section in that cramped house. After they accept the idea of change, the next step is to paint the vision of their future — a vision where they have enough space and sufficient facilities to meet their needs and better enjoy their lives together. The parents decide that the time has come for radical change — a move to a new house. As they discuss the move within the family, they receive input and considerations from all family members. They create a vision of their new home and set the direction — a target for what and where to buy. After the direction has been set, the detailed planning phase starts. The plans include the full range of activities required when you move into the new residence — from packing and changing schools to utility transfers and meeting new neighbors.

Overall, the family recognizes and accepts the idea of change, and they define the vision and the plan. Yet each member of the family will deal with the reality of the changes in his own way. If Trevor has to leave his baseball team in the middle of the season, or Sara worries she'll have trouble making new friends at a new school, they may quietly hope that it won't happen. Even if the planning accounts for it, in reality, each family member will adapt in his own time.

Organizational acceptance of change is very similar to what the family experiences. The direction comes from the top, but those in lower positions may feel like change is being forced upon them. They may see the potential for long-term benefits, but in the short term, they'll be uncomfortable — if not downright unhappy and skeptical. When you're able to involve people's ideas about how to achieve your vision, you decrease this resistance.

Include the people in your organization who are key influencers — both the supporters and the potential resisters — in the planning process. As they become champions of change, they will positively influence the whole organization.

To facilitate acceptance within the organization, consider three keys when communicating your change in direction. Paint a picture of your long-term vision for how you see the organization interacting and behaving on a daily basis. Show the reasons for changing with a message that engages your audience at an emotional level. Back up these emotional ideas with data, to appeal to smaller data-driven faction of your audience. After you've painted the big picture, communicate the specific next step you want to develop in the organization. For example, if improved root-cause problem solving is what you want, the behaviors you may want to develop for managers are go and see the conditions rather than lead from their office or a conference room and ask probing, open-ended questions.

Phase 3: Charging forward

After organizational leaders set the direction, make the plans and enroll the influencers, it's time to charge forward and begin to execute. If you're helping to lead the change, you'll look over your shoulder to see if anyone is following you. Some will be, but others will be staying put, waiting to see what happens.

When you start to implement Lean, a range of personalities will be present — hiders, naysayers, adapters, wait-and-seers, opportunists, and a host of other characters. They may cause you to retool your best-laid plans. Facilitating organizational change requires

- ✓ **Clear expectations**: The clearer you can create your long-term vision — what will it sounds like, look like, behave like, and so on — the easier it will be to bring people with you. When you have the big picture, clearly identify the next step you want the organization to reach and incorporate into daily life. This will make the long-term vision feel more obtainable.

- ✓ **Proper communications:** The best way through the change is two-way communication — not only listening but being heard. (See Chapter 4 for more about communication.)

- ✓ **Proper behavior:** Actions must match the new direction — this is vitally important. Actions must support the vision, adhere to the principles, and reinforce the plan. Just like in the family in the too-small house (see "Phase 1: Recognition and acceptance," earlier in this chapter), each member may need something different to adapt to the new situation. But by virtue of the move, the parents have said, "There is no going back."

Think about the family on moving day. There are boxes everywhere. The moving van is loaded up. Matt and Michele are hiding in hopes that mom and dad won't notice. Trevor is convinced that there won't be a good baseball team at his new school. Sara is anxious to meet new friends in the new neighborhood. The dog is wondering what's going on. Meanwhile, the parents just want to get it over with!

Phase 4: Turmoil

Your initial Lean implementation is underway. The first work area has finished its inaugural *kaizen*. Despite its successes, the rumor mill starts to churn, full of dire predictions of job loss — doom and gloom — and another failed initiative. The lunchroom conversation is rampant with dark clouds and reasons why "it won't work" or "if everyone just waits five minutes, management will be on to something else." The first crisis hits middle management, and they're tempted to go back to their old ways. Turmoil is underway. Nothing is settled. Many still doubt management's resolve to the Lean undertaking. No one is comfortable.

This phase is like the family starting to sort everything out In their new house. Things invariably don't go exactly as planned. Belongings are misplaced because they don't have a place in the new house. Boxes are mixed up. The kids are wondering if the parents will crack and decide they can go back to their old life. They'll be watching closely how the parents handle the situation. The parents' actions will either enlist or alienate the kids in the whole moving process.

Similarly, in the organization, how management addresses the rumor mill, conducts themselves, and responds in the face of a crisis will either fuel the negative fire or extinguish it to a pile of simmering coals. It is during this tumultuous phase that the tone is set for the rest of the Lean journey.

Phase 5: Integration

Eventually, with commitment and consistency, proper communications and behavior, the organization absorbs the changes and integrates the new direction into its psyche. People climb onboard and buy in to the vision of a Lean organization. Management will have to handle — maybe even dismiss — the small percentage of the organization that refuses to join in.

Particularly because Lean is a journey and not a destination, integration includes an environment of continuous improvement and change. Full buy-in across the entire organization may take years.

Like with the family settling in the new location, unpacking the boxes is really the easy part. Everyone will find a place for their things. How each of the kids adjusts to his new situation will be as individual as the kids are. But with persistence, patience, and communication, eventually they'll all settle into a new routine — until the next change.

Hurdling roadblocks to success

As with any new undertaking, organizational roadblocks develop along the way. Some of them are cultural, some historical, and some situational. All are rooted in the individuals of the organization and their corresponding perceptions, attitudes, emotions, and actions. In the following sections, we discuss some of the common roadblocks to successful Lean implementation and corresponding organizational change.

Roadblock #1: Rules are made to be broken

Lean is based on the implementation of standards and performance to those standards. It is based on processes being repeatable. You can make improvements only if there is a measurable baseline for comparison. The attitude that "rules are made to be broken" is misaligned with the Lean thought process. If the organization embraces a countercultural attitude, you'll have challenges on your Lean journey. Some people feel that standards restrict creativity, but this is not the case. The reality is that standards focus creativity and enable you to use your valuable resources to make concrete, repeatable improvements.

Reframe this old adage to a new one: *Standards are made to be followed and then improved.* Adopting this new adage will go a long way toward mitigating those challenges. You must be vigilant to ensure that people are following the standards. When someone violates a standard, you must understand why, and then eliminate the barrier to compliance with the standard. If it is the standard itself, then revise it in a controlled manner — through *kaizen* or Plan-Do-Check-Act (PDCA) (see Chapter 9). Standards will always evolve in a Lean organization.

Roadblock #2: Cowboy individualism

No man is an island in a Lean organization. Everyone in the value stream is connected in some way. Cowboy individualists who buck the system, for whatever reason, will inhibit everyone's Lean journey. There is room for creativity and individualism when you direct it toward the elimination of waste and improvement of the standards. There is no room for those who, on principle, refuse to operate to the methods of standardized work.

Roadblock #3: Fear of the unknown and job loss

People fear the unknown. As Dr. Deming, the American author, lecturer, and consultant, said, "No one can put in his best performance unless he feels secure." It is management's job to create a sense of security, using PDCA aligned to the long-term vision to move people through the murky unknown. If management has not made guarantees that employees won't lose their jobs as a result of productivity improvements, the Lean journey will be a very bumpy ride. You're asking them to have faith that, by actively participating in Lean, you won't be rewarding them with a pink slip. It's one thing to get them to trust that the concepts will work — it's another thing to get them to trust that it won't negatively impact their quality of life.

Mature Lean organizations have *right-sized* their organizations to customer demand. They make the commitment to their permanent employees, and use temporary employees to handle demand fluctuations. These organizations realize that they have invested time and money to develop their people — the most valuable assets for the organization, and it is vital to keep them within the organization. When downturns like The Great Recession of 2008 happen, these organizations do not lay people off. Instead, they use the opportunity to *invest even more* in their employees via training and to increase efforts to eliminate waste in all aspects of their business, so when demand comes back, they are even stronger and ready to serve their customers even more.

Roadblock #4: Resistance to change — what's in it for me?

In general, people resist change that isn't their idea. They may be fearful when it's their idea, but if they still feel in control, they'll make the decision to change. But when change is foisted upon them, they feel like they have little or no control, and they may be uncertain about the outcome. Their collective resistance rises up like a tidal wave ready to crash down on the organization, stopping all forward progress. When they do not see a personal benefit or incentive to change, they won't.

Be sure to paint a clear picture of what you want to change and impact their emotions to enroll them in the process. Imagine you are a purchasing manager who has identified that your organization buys 40 different kinds of safety glasses from 20 different suppliers at a price range of $0.90 to $15.00. You could prepare a report on reducing the variation and waste. Or you could collect all the different pairs from all the different suppliers, tag them with key information, and show off a huge pile of all 800 to the heads of each organization that uses the glasses. Which do you think will have the bigger emotional impact — the report or the pile?

Some of your employees will fight through; you don't need to worry about them — they'll be your trailblazers. It's the ones who can't overcome their resistance or fears that you'll need to move forward.

Roadblock #5: Been there, done that

A portion of your organization will be waiting for you to fail, especially if your organization has a track record of failed initiatives, flavor-of-the-month programs, or flip-flopped directions. One of the best ways to mitigate this reaction is to hold your managers accountable to new behavior standards, especially in times of crisis. When the organization sees alignment in the words and actions of their leaders, they are most likely to follow. Also, remember to enlist some of the biggest naysayers early on in the initiative. By winning them over early, you create influential endorsers of the Lean process.

Roadblock #6: If it ain't broke, don't fix it

Even when you think your environment, processes and systems work perfectly as is; they are already in a state of decline. The business practices of today are not going to take you to tomorrow. You need to continually invest time to ensure your people, processes, and culture are providing value, are enabling you to understand and meet the voice of the customer and that they are moving in the direction of your ideal future state.

The organization will not move as fast as you want it to. The whole moves slower than the individuals who make up the organization.

Lean State of Mind

Managers in a Lean organization have a different mindset towards what it means to lead. They have and are committed to a long-term vision, as well as short-term (such as quarterly) results. They realize that *how* the organization achieves results is equally, if not more important, than the actual result itself. They understand that they must behave in a consistent manner, congruent with their long-term vision, independent of the short-term conditions. They realize that their job is not only to achieve results, but also to build capability in their people, so that when problems arise the people know how to respond and solve the right problem. Managers become mentors (more on this in Chapter 4). They also realize the importance of a no-blame culture in a continuous improvement organization to create trust and engagement.

The single most powerful attribute of a Lean organization is adaptability. The Lean journey is continuous; *kaizen* is continuous; change is continuous; learning is continuous. By embracing the principles of Lean, the organizational culture develops the inherent ability to constantly adapt and respond to events — both internal and external — in a systematic way. Independent of all the specific tools and techniques of Lean, this agility of the people makes the Lean organization as competitive as any type of organization anywhere.

There are no measures by which the Lean organization can declare itself finished. There is no Lean Land, where all problems have been addressed, everyone's knowledge is complete and all processes are perfect. There is always something else to improve — something better to strive for.

Certain organizational cultures are destination-focused. For them, initiatives are like projects — they have beginnings and ends. The idea that you never finish may be frustrating and difficult for such organizations to grasp. These organizations need to shift their perspective and alter their principles when they commence their Lean journey. They must adopt the cultural predisposition of *kaizen*.

Unlike traditional organizations, Lean organizations understand that blame improves nothing and prevents true problem solving — *kaizen*. Creating a culture of understanding and learning is the only way to create a culture of trust and continuous improvement. When people know that management will not persecute them for mistakes, they are more likely to participate in a continuous improvement environment rather than hide their mistakes. For example, if you are trying to reduce accidents in your workplace, your response when one occurs will reflect your beliefs and ultimately your culture. Do you blame the person who had the accident, or do you ask and go see what were the conditions that created the accident?

Chapter 4

Power to the People

Everything about business comes down to people. Where in business can we escape the impact of human care, human creativity, human commitment, human frustration, and human despair? There is no reason for anything in business to exist if it does not serve the needs of people.

— Bruce Cryer, Re-Engineering the Human System

One of the oldest clichés in business — you've heard it a zillion times — is "People are our most important resource." From the Lean perspective, these words are both critically true *and* utterly false. On face value, it's true that people power an organization more than anything else. Without the people, there is no organizational performance. People are more important than facilities, equipment, capital, or other resources.

But in the Lean world, you don't think of people as a "resource." You don't categorize, value, measure, and manage people the same way you would manage financial, capital, or intellectual resources. In Lean, people are not the most important *resource* in an organization; people *are* the organization. In Lean, you trust and respect people to make the most effective use of resources in order to add value to the customer.

Lean will not happen without the people. Lean affects every single person in the organization — and each has her own unique role and response. Often, when embarking upon a Lean journey, managers and practitioners focus on the tools and techniques of Lean. They spend too much of their time advocating Lean, and not enough time inquiring — checking in with people, getting their ideas and reactions, developing them and bringing them along. Investing time and energy in the human side of change is not only a critical component of success; it also pays long-term dividends when the organization is fully engaged in continuous improvement.

In this chapter, we show you the human side of change, and let you know how you manifest it in a Lean implementation. You discover how Lean managers act and support change at various levels of the organization. You find out about Lean teams. This chapter includes an in-depth examination of the individual's role in the transformation.

The Human Side of Change

Motivation is a fire from within. If someone else tries to light that fire under you, chances are it will burn very briefly.

— Stephen R. Covey

People love to change when change is their own idea — they have a sense of control, the feeling that they're in the driver's seat. Even if the control is limited, the feeling is there. Whether it's a big change (like taking a different job, having a child or moving into a new home) or a small change (like buying a new pair of shoes or upgrading to the latest technology gizmo), when it's your idea, you're motivated. You determine the effort, the risk, and the rewards. You balance the equation — and you're willing to go for it!

Now alter one critical element of the scenario: The change is no longer your idea. Immediately, you don't feel the same sense of participation. You don't feel in control. You're not sure where it will all lead. Fear, doubt, uncertainty, and perhaps even anger are among the flood of emotions you feel. If it's someone else's idea, do you still trust the opportunity?

Fight, flight, freeze, fake, fall in line, or fade away — the choice is yours. Every individual — facing the same situation — will have her own unique response. In the context of a Lean journey, people will experience the total range of emotions — from excitement to resistance and everything in between. They'll experience stress. They need support. They need you to hear them. They need to be educated. They need to develop new capabilities.

Whether you're a practitioner, manager, or participant of Lean in your organization, you have to work through your own reaction to change. You have to adjust your actions and attitudes and evaluate your emotional responses. There is no magical incantation. It takes real work — work that people usually don't like to do. Ultimately everyone has the ability to become a Lean student, actively engaged in continuous improvement and lifelong learning. First, you have to get over the hurdles of resistance that appear as you move down the road of Lean.

Change and the individual

After living with their dysfunctional behavior for so many years (a sunk cost if ever there was one), people become invested in defending their dysfunctions rather than changing them.

— Marshall Goldsmith

As an individual in an organization moving toward Lean, you have choices. It doesn't matter where in the organization you fit, what your title is, or what job you perform — you will experience change. The attitude you choose to adopt is up to you and no one else. You may choose to jump onboard immediately and become a change agent. Or, you may wait and see. You might also choose to leave rather than change. You may play the victim or you may play the trailblazer — or something in between. It's all up to you, but understanding the dynamics and science behind change helps you in the process.

The basics: Change 101

Independent of the circumstances of change, people experience change in their bodies and minds. In this section, we explore the basics of change and stress.

Perceptions are reality

Have you ever gone to a school reunion and noticed that some of your classmates just can't seem to move beyond their time in school? It's as if their lives stopped at age 17. They long for the "good old days." They relive every moment of the big game. They wish they could go back. Other classmates never even think of coming back to a reunion because they're so over it — they've moved on and embraced the future.

What makes one group able to let go and move on while others just can't? The answer is perceptions — perceptions create reality. Figure 4-1 depicts how perceptions completely overlay a situation, causing a person to act, think, and emote in a certain way. People who think (or *perceive*) that their lives were at their best a long time ago will see the reflection of that perception in their actions, emotions, and attitudes. They may not be able to see a way forward, because their perceptions leave them living in the past.

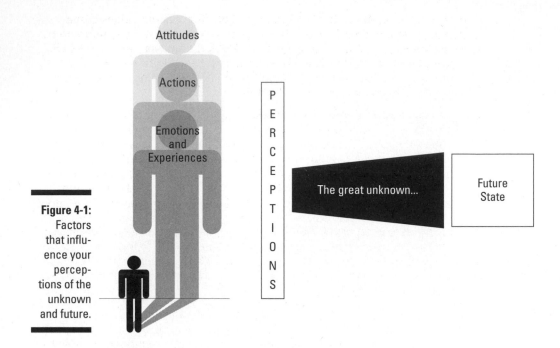

Figure 4-1:
Factors
that influ-
ence your
percep-
tions of the
unknown
and future.

Recognize that people judge situations through their own unique biases and perceptions. Some of the people in your organization will want to hold on to the "glory days"; others will be so committed to change that they run forward without a mere glance back to the old way of doing things. A whole range of people will fall somewhere in between. But eventually, they all need to get on the Lean path.

How people perceive change colors their responses. During an initial communication, many people will check out and won't hear most of the change message. Almost immediately they'll start thinking, "How is this going to affect me? What's going to change? Are they really serious about this? Am I going to lose my job?" How each person perceives the change dictates how quickly they overcome their natural resistance.

The reality of resistance

If you want to create a truly Lean organization, you have to overcome individual resistance to change. Certain attitudes appear — these attitudes are symptoms of resistance. You may recognize some of them:

✔ **"Been there, done that":** If someone feels like this resembles something that failed in the past, she'll resist. She won't willingly jump on the change wagon. Withholding trust, lack of faith, and sarcasm are just a few of the blocks that you have to remove. How? Through two-way communication, demonstrated commitment and consistency, new leadership practices, early results, and reinforcement.

✔ **"A rose by any name":** This attitude manifests in several ways. If the most draconian of supervisors is now anointed a coach or mentor, no one is likely to believe it possible or sustainable. If you've had previous failed attempts at Lean or other continuous-improvement initiatives, you have to show how this time is different. Both of these situations require two-way communication, consistent, active and involved leadership, ongoing monitoring and continual training and development. That supervisor will have to prove that he did more than attend "charm school" to win over the people who work for her — she has to demonstrate her belief that her job is to create capability and ensure standards are followed and eliminate the barriers when they are not.

✔ **"Not invented here" or "Doesn't apply here":** These attitudes will derail a Lean initiative. In the worst manifestation, people may understand how the tools and methods of Lean might apply in some other kind of company, but they don't see how Lean applies in their company. To overcome these attitudes, you must constantly demonstrate how to find and eliminate waste in your processes. This takes creative leadership. You may need to adjust the language or demonstrate a concept to show people how Lean applies in your organization.

✔ **"Fear of failure":** This attitude prevents individuals from actively participating. Being a perfectionist is different from striving for perfection. Perfectionists get scared, stuck or stopped, if you don't reinforce the importance of trying something new — independent of the outcome — to improve the situation. In a Lean culture, when you try something new, it's rarely perfect the first time out. Remember the Plan-Do-Check-Act (PDCA) cycle (see Chapter 9); the Do phase of that cycle is all about trying — testing is part of the process. And improvement is incremental, so the next step is never the final step.

Creating a blame-free culture is the best way to overcome a fear of failure. You do this through the way you respond, guide, and mentor people in the learning process. Encourage them to use the tools of Lean, change only one thing at a time wherever possible, and keep the changes simple. When things don't go as planned, ask questions like "What did we learn?" "What is the true problem we are trying to solve?" "What is the next thing we will try based on our learning?"

It's okay to fail if you learn from it.

Stress: The natural response to change

Stress is a naturally human response to change. It's unavoidable. Stress happens on a continuum, from positive-and-motivating to negative-and-debilitating. In the Lean transformation, the stress you need to watch out for is the negative stuff.

When stress starts to go to the negative side, you may feel tense, anxious, or angry. You may become depressed or frustrated; find yourself easily distracted; become short-tempered or even apathetic. You may also find yourself eating or drinking more than you normally do. And you may not show up where you're supposed to.

You can manage stress in many ways. You can monitor your own behavior, and choose to deal with your stress in healthy ways — through diet, exercise, laughter, and rest. You may also find a friend to confide in and to give support — talking helps you work through stressful situations.

It's a good idea to have a formal mentorship structure in a Lean organization. This may be directly related to the organizational chart, the social network, or you may want to base it on capabilities that you need to create in your people and organization.

Reactions beyond reason

In extreme cases of stress or change, your body can actually have a physiological response — fight or flight. Deep inside your brain is a tiny, almond-shaped cluster of neurons called the amygdala. The amygdala receives a fear or danger signal from the thalamus, which causes it to secrete chemicals in the body, even while the rest of your brain is trying to process the information for the appropriate response. As Daniel Goldman describes it in *Emotional Intelligence,* the amygdala can actually hijack your brain, preventing rational responses.

So what does this have to do with you and a Lean transformation? If you find yourself reacting irrationally to situations — like during a *kaizen* event — you may be a victim of that emotional hijacking. One of the best responses is to walk away and cool down — it can take as long as an hour or more — until your body can actually clear the chemicals and let you think rationally through the situation.

When undergoing any change, it's natural to experience strong, impulsive reactions from time to time. You can learn and grow beyond the knee-jerk reaction. With each change you experience and accept, you train yourself that the situation is okay and the amygdala doesn't need to charge in to save you.

Embracing change the Lean way

In the previous sections we covered the fundamentals of individual change. In the next sections, we show you what the individual can do to embrace the change to Lean.

Know yourself

Assess where you are personally with the changes; this will help you move through the Lean transition. What are you feeling? Are you overcoming your natural resistance? Where can you contribute? What attitudes, emotions, or actions might be getting in the way of participating fully as an individual or a team member? How does working closely around people affect you? How ready are you to learn new things and stretch yourself?

You're the only one who can change you, but how you react to situations can influence a heck of a lot of people — positively or negatively.

Most people are uncomfortable with the unknown. In the absence of information, they anticipate the worst. This "pessimistic" approach is a form of self-protection. *Kaizen* and PDCA help you learn to become comfortable with ambiguity and have the courage within to try something new. Everyone has to go through the phase of letting go of the old and move on to grab the new. When you understand what *new* can be, and begin to make incremental progress towards it, you find it easier to let go of the past. For this reason it is important that top leadership articulate a clear vision of where the organization is going — like Toyota's *True North* (see Chapter 3) — and then create specific, well-aligned, near term targets — measurements and descriptions — that they want the organization to achieve.

Some Lean practices — like taking before and after photos of an area — actually help people let go. Creating ceremonies or events to symbolize letting go can also help. The movement of a monument, burying an old manual, or throwing a party in new floor space — these are all examples of ceremonial letting go. Conducting ceremonies may sound hokey, but it works.

Think about other changes you have experienced in your life that were successful. Identify how you adjusted your attitudes, emotions, and actions to make those situations positive. Build on that track record to propel you forward into the Lean transformation.

When you start to see progress, you'll have an easier time adapting to the changed environment. The concept of Lean will become more concrete for you. This shift in perception usually happens after you've participated in *kaizen* activities — small, continuous improvements in your perceptions will drive you to change your thoughts, attitudes, and, ultimately, your actions.

When you truly start thinking in a Lean manner, you look at life differently. You tend to see ways to improve any situation. You look at waste in a totally different way. You want to make things better — and you know you can! Whether you're standing in line at the money bank or volunteering at the food bank, you have ideas to improve customer wait times or more effectively pack food boxes. Ultimately your actions, attitudes, and emotions will all be colored with a Lean filter.

Personal principles: Alignment with Lean

When an organization shifts to Lean, its principles shift. For an individual to get behind the change, he needs to understand what the impact is on him and his principles. People whose principles are closer to Lean principles will have an easier time making the adjustment then those whose aren't.

How do you align principles? You start by knowing your own principles. Then you identify and understand the organization's Lean principles — both as stated and manifested. When you compare your principles with the Lean ones, you'll see where there is misalignment and how severe it is. Then you can choose how to close the gap.

Although the majority of people enjoy working in a Lean environment, some people may decide that they would rather work elsewhere and choose to leave the organization. That's okay; the people who stay are the ones who want to live Lean.

Speak up, step up: The individual's role

When people are told that there will be a change, they might give their power away. They might not engage, ask questions, or actively participate. Through their actions, they might abdicate their responsibility. What can you do as an individual in a company that's embarking upon a Lean journey?

✔ Ask questions to clarify expectations and understand new roles.

✔ Focus on solutions — how can we make this work?

✔ Stay open and positive, and don't fuel the rumor mill.

✔ Actively learn about Lean tools and concepts.

✔ Identify what you can change in your world; for example, how can you reduce waste?

✔ Request training in topics like PDCA, statistical tools, coaching skills, teaming skills, and change management.

✔ Volunteer to participate in early *kaizen* activities.

✔ Hold yourself accountable to your own thoughts, emotions, and actions.

✔ Commit to following standardized work for your activity

✔ Work with your team leader to identify and improve your work area and remove barriers to performing to standard — daily, if possible.

✔ Ask yourself questions about your perceptions, reactions, and behaviors in the workplace.

✔ Get comfortable with ambiguity. Realize that you can't control the situation or know exactly what is happening all the time.

Managers can help by conducting forums where people can ask questions and voice their concerns. To make these sessions beneficial, keep them real and positive. People need to feel that managers hear them, will help, and will convey feedback and status of their concerns.

Acting Lean

In traditional organizations of all types, people learn to do a task with or without a connection other parts of the organization or to what the end customer or consumer requires. Stockpiling, working in isolation, hiding mistakes, working at an erratic pace, and only bearing good news may be common in a traditional workplace, but such behaviors have no place in a Lean environment.

To eliminate waste or wasteful behaviors, you first must admit that they exist. Have you ever been in a meeting where presenter after presenter discusses dire current business conditions and yet their future trend predicts miraculous recovery? When you venture into Lean, you must accept the current situation and to change your mindset — how you achieve your results is as important as the results themselves.

Many people (including managers) have learned to *create* crisis situations so they can become heroes who fly in like Superman to save the day. Managers reward this type of behavior — sometimes to the point where if the company is not in crisis, no one knows how to act. In a Lean organization, you learn how to thrive without daily disasters and then respond systematically when issues arise. Leaders understand that their job is to foster problem identification and resolution in their people and at all levels of the organization. Managers learn how to reward problem avoidance, root-cause resolution, sound problem solving, working to standards, and continuous improvement.

In traditional environments, people provide information on a need-to-know basis, usually on someone's desk or in files. You can't just walk into an area and know exactly what's going on. People have learned how to hide problems, protect information, and to shirk responsibility. By contrast, a Lean environment is a very open, transparent, and visual environment. It delivers accountability and enforces standards. In Lean, the old saying that "rules are made to be broken" shifts to "standards are made to be followed — *and improved.*"

Team leaders and managers are responsible for ensuring that people are following standards and understanding why, when they are not. When the leaders identify a deviation, they identify the specific condition causing the problem and work together with the people doing the job to eliminate the condition. If required, they should involve appropriate support departments.

Some organizations choose to post the standards facing away from the work area where they are more accessible to the managers, who use them to compare the standards to what is actually happening.

Many organizations are full of individuals who stopped trying to learn after they left school. They don't take classes. They don't really analyze mistakes or failures. After school, they checked the "education box" and they checked out. By contrast, Lean organizations reward and thrive on learning. Like the *kaizen* philosophy of improving something every day, Lean also promotes learning something every day — learning from mistakes, learning to identify the right problem to work on, learning to solve root-cause issues, learning new ways to eliminate waste, learning more about your customer, and learning the capabilities of your organization.

Looking at different learning styles

Not everyone learns the same way — individuals have different learning styles. Most people have a dominant style, but may also exhibit other styles at times. The four common learning styles are

- ✔ **Visual:** They remember what they see.
- ✔ **Verbal:** They remember what they hear and what they say.
- ✔ **Logical:** They conceptualize information.
- ✔ **Kinesthetic:** They learn by doing and explaining what they've done.

Because so many new concepts and changes affect the way you do business in a Lean environment, you have understand your style. The people leading the change and developing training materials need to appeal properly to each individual and to you as an individual learner.

Kaizen events may be a dream for kinesthetic learners, but a nightmare for logical learners. The verbal learners will want to talk about what's happening to grasp the change, and the visual learners may want to hang back and watch the first time, so they get it. When you have a *kaizen* activity, try to identify each of the team member's learning styles. Pay attention to the language the participants use because you may hear cues to their style. You may hear cue phrases like "I think," "I see," or "How can we do" as the teams are interacting.

Learning happens formally and informally along the Lean journey. Formally, you will hold classes, workshops, *kaizen* events, or training sessions. Topics range from team building to problem solving and everything in between. Informally, you will learn from daily actions, individual problem solving, mistakes, and interpersonal interactions.

Appealing to specific learning styles will help individuals learn more effectively and help reduce resistance to change.

Change and the team

In Lean, you rely heavily on teams of people working together to improve the effectiveness of the business. But what, exactly, is a team? A *team* is a collection of individuals working toward a common purpose. If you don't have that common purpose, you just have a group.

Lean environments have many types of teams. There are natural work teams, cross-functional teams, teams that come together for *kaizen* events, teams that include members from upstream or downstream of the organization. The type of team formed and length of time the team stays together is dependent upon the reasons for the team's existence and the performance objectives. The team environment takes advantage of collaboration between individual members to identify better solutions, eliminate waste, accomplish an objective faster, and make bigger gains.

Characteristics of a winning team

Winning teams exhibit certain characteristics. They look a certain way, and they behave a certain way. Although you may define other important characteristics for your high-performing teams, most have the following essential characteristics:

- ✓ **Clear purpose and direction with motivating goals.** Winning teams know where they need to go and why they need to go there. They understand how their part contributes to the success of the whole and how it serves the customer. They have short-term goals that move them in the direction of the long-term goals.

- ✓ **Commitment at both the individual and team level.** They have clearly defined roles, and they develop and maintain healthy relationships. They rely on the diverse talents of each team member. They show mutual trust and support. They resolve conflicts productively.

✔ **Multi-directional, effective communication.** Communication flows effectively within the team and beyond. It is productive, solution-focused and proactive.

✔ **Clear processes, decision making and continuous improvement orientation.** They have and follow clear processes. They are empowered to make decisions and do so in a timely manner. They have a problem-solving and continuous-improvement mentality.

✔ **Demonstrate creativity, innovation and adaptability.** They utilize all of the talents of the team to create new product and process innovations. They learn to adapt to changing market and customer situations while maintaining a commitment to their core principles. They effectively solve problems in a systematic way.

✔ **Quality leadership.** The leadership is from within and it is congruent in words and actions. Managers eliminate barriers, provide direction and mentoring, develop capabilities, and foster growth and development opportunities. They trust the team to perform, and they empower team members to problem-solve and make decisions in a timely manner.

✔ **Celebrate progress.** Winning teams recognize the value of celebration and acknowledgement. They celebrate the incremental successes as well as lessons learned when things did not go as planned.

The most effective teams typically have five to seven people. Each team member is a unique individual, who has something special to offer the team. Ideally, during the formation process, you identify these unique traits.

Many assessment tools — such as the Myers-Briggs Type Indicator (MBTI), the DiSC Classic Profile, the Kolbe A index, or *Now, Discover Your Strengths,* by Marcus Buckingham and Donald O. Clifton — can help a team understand its players and their roles. Be sure to find a qualified person to administer an assessment and help the team interpret the results. The best teams consist of very different types of individuals. You may find it difficult to work with people who think and act very different from your style, but an assessment can help you and the other team members understand how to optimize working relationships, facilitate effective communications, and capitalize on strengths. Assessments also provide a common language, context, and understanding.

Teams must have a variety of perspectives, talents, and types for innovation and creativity to materialize.

Team formation

Dr. Bruce Tuckman, noted psychologist and organizational behavior expert, identified the now-famous five phases of teaming:

1. **Forming:** People join forces to achieve a common goal. Members get to know one another, identify commonality, and begin to develop ground rules.

2. **Storming:** Members are trying to figure out where they fit. Hostilities and emotions may run high as people jockey for position, figure out who they can trust, and claim a role. Leaders emerge.

3. **Norming:** Members learn how to work together. They understand leadership, roles and positions. They establish principles and standards of behavior, and not necessarily the same as the overall organization. They form a team identity — formally or informally.

4. **Performing:** Members work together to get the job done, deliver the outcomes, and generate the results.

5. **Adjourning:** The team completes its work and the either disbands or addresses a new scope of work.

Team leadership is determined during the formation process. Although there may be an official leader, a different leader may emerge as the team matures. Changes to the makeup or direction of the team can cause regression into earlier phases. As your team forms to eliminate waste and improve processes, remember that it will have to develop as an entity. The team will experience these phases. If the team is struggling to get to the performing stage, management may need to provide an intervention — such as facilitation, guidance, change of membership, or clarification of expectations.

External facilitators can help a team get off the ground. A *facilitator* is someone who guides the process of the team and ensures that all members are participating and being heard. Ideally, the facilitator is not a team member and does not to contribute content to the team's project.

Collaboration

For people who are used to working in a hierarchical environment, the idea of such extreme collaboration may seem difficult. The result of a true collaborative environment is the win-win solution. It requires that team members contribute ideas, analyze the situation objectively, and negotiate a best next-state solution. It requires that the individuals let go of an idea or position, if others find better, alternative solutions. It requires that each individual sees a situation not only from his point of view, but from the points of view of others involved — and from the customer's point of view.

In a Lean environment, teams work to eliminate waste. But sometimes, what one person views as waste may be valuable or even vital to another. When individuals within an organization develop collaborative skills, they are able to see both sides of the situation and, with a Lean mindset, propose alternatives that can minimize, if not eliminate, non-value-added activities within the value stream. Ideally, when you collaborate, you gain new perspectives about a situation, which you then use to adjust your perceptions and influence your own attitudes, actions, and emotions.

Multifunctional workers

Lean advocates the development of multifunctional workers, especially in natural work teams. Train each member of the area in the activities of the others. Track training progress and develop a level of competency before an employee performs the task unsupervised. This is easy to envision in a manufacturing environment, but apply the same philosophy in non-manufacturing environments like accountancies, industrial kitchens, retail outlets, or hospitals. By having a well-trained workforce, you're insulated against the effects of absenteeism, vacations, and variations in demand.

Post a tracking chart showing job qualifications and competencies by person (see Chapter 12).

Change and the managers

Managers directly influence the adoption of Lean through their behaviors, decisions, and communications. As the face of Lean leadership, they have the challenging role of leading the organization to success in spite of their own personal reaction to the change. In this section, we discuss what managers can do to make the unknown more known and advance the organization's Lean progress.

Creating the vision

Declaring that the organization will become Lean is easy; actually making the change is harder. Managers should start by creating a clear vision for the organization — not some lofty visionary statement, but a straightforward image of what it means for the organization to move toward Lean. This vision includes performance expectations, timing, expected outcomes, interrelationships to other company initiatives, and commitments to the organization.

In successful Lean organizations, Lean is not an initiative. It becomes the way you do business. Include this as an assumption in your long-term vision.

If you don't want your Lean efforts to look like a Dilbert cartoon of screwy non-performing ideas, you have to pay attention to the human element of change. Management must lead by example and with a constancy of purpose. Eighty percent of change initiatives fail due to human factors, according to studies by noted organizational researchers John Kotter and Daryl Conner.

Engage people early in the process after you make the decision to implement Lean. By involving them in the planning of how to implement Lean, you enroll them in the process.

Communications

People need to be informed and they need to be heard. Make communications clear, consistent, multidimensional, and frequent. One-time declarations don't make a transformation. Develop a communication strategy to support the implementation plan. The communication plan needs to be a two-way effort. One part is what you want to say; the other part is what your employees want you to hear. You're dealing with a collection of individuals, with different needs, learning styles, and perceptions.

Remember the basics of communication when adopting Lean:

- ✔ **Who:** Who is the audience? Is it an internal or external audience?

- ✔ **What:** What is going to happen? What does the audience need to know about it? What do you expect them to do as a result of the communication? What does the audience fear? What could prevent them from embracing the change? What are they saying or thinking?

- ✔ **Why:** Why are you making this change at this time? What are the business conditions that are precipitating the change? Why is this the right method at this time?

- ✔ **When:** When will you communicate? How frequently?

- ✔ **Where:** Where will you make your communication?

- ✔ **How:** How will you engage the audience? How can you solicit input? How will the message permeate all levels of the organization? How can you prevent the message from being changed as it's relayed? How can the company leverage technology to make the communication more effective?

Feedback loops are vital to an organization undergoing change. You need to know how your original message has been filtered by perceptions and misinterpretation. Based on the feedback of the response, you can adjust your message and delivery method in the next round of communication. Figure 4-2 shows a model of a feedback loop.

In the beginning of a change, it's nearly impossible to over-communicate with people. People need to know what they're in for. Supplement the formal communication plan with informal communications. Nothing can derail a change movement faster than misinformation and coffee-pot rumors. In the absence of information, people fill the abyss with speculation and fear.

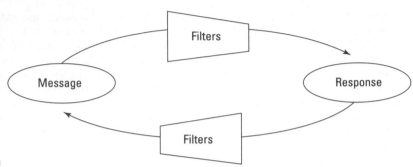

Figure 4-2:
How mes-
sages are
transmit-
ted and
understood
among
people.

Frequently, managers excited about a new initiative fall into the *advocacy trap.* They're so focused on telling people why they should be excited and the benefits of the change that they forget to listen and ask for input. Practicing inquiry is vitally important to your long-term success.

Developing the ability to listen to and truly hear your employees is a critical skill for every manager. People need to be heard. Some may need to vent before they can move onto the new ways of doing business. Providing different forums for communication, including the following, will address the various needs of the individuals within the organization:

✔ **One on one:** Invest sufficient time (at least 15 minutes) with your employees and colleagues to hear what their thoughts, ideas, and concerns are around the change. Use this information to understand where blocks in the organization are happening, to monitor trends in the organization, and to craft follow-up group communication. Strive to have these conversations in or near *gemba* (see Chapter 13).

✔ **Small group:** Conducting regular small-group interactive sessions will help you address larger issues and gather ideas. These groups can be diagonal slices across the organization, functional groups, project teams, or natural workgroups. And remember that people need a mechanism for inputting questions before the sessions.

✔ **Large group:** Make a point to conduct large-group briefings regularly. Recognize accomplishments, show the state of the business and progress towards long-term visions, and recognize both individual and group efforts. Provide a mechanism for people to input questions and concerns.

Communications in action: an example

Assume you're a manager of a large facility who has just received news that your company has won a new contract, but you don't currently have the floor space available in your facility to accommodate the new work. After working with key people in the organization on the right vision and strategy for the new contract launch, you start the communication process. Initially, you gather your organization together, tell them about the new business, and tell them that we'll need to free up 10,000 square feet of floor space in the northeast corner of the facility in two weeks. You tell them that they'll be involved in *kaizen* activities to make this happen and that you expect there to be no negative impact on the customer during these *kaizen* activities. It will require teamwork, commitment, and cooperation. You announce that Pat will be responsible to organize and oversee the activities. You tell them that you will be following their progress closely and that you expect the next gathering will be in two weeks in the newly freed-up area.

Later that day, you go to the northeast corner of the facility and hang a sign saying "Future Home of Whizzo Production." You talk to employees as you walk through the plant, asking them what they think about the new contract and what they think it will take to free up the space. The next day, you and Pat walk the floor again, informally communicating with the employees. You both decide to add a sign showing progress to the 10,000 square feet. You also decide to personally lead or participate in the first *kaizen* activity. After each *kaizen* activity, you meet with the teams, recognize them, and thank them for their efforts. You use a company blog and other social media to communicate the progress, new business updates, and recognize efforts.

Every day you walk the floor to review the progress. At the one-week mark, you gather all your staff and the supervisors in the area to review the status and subsequently make any adjustments to the plan. You record an update that is played in the cafeteria. Finally, at the two-week mark, you gather everyone into the area, recognize their efforts, and announce the next challenge.

Whatever you communicate, be prepared to back up the message with actions. If you say that you're going to do something by a certain date, do it, or explain why it didn't happen. Part of the population is expecting failure — don't let that part win.

Find the best way in your organization to foster multidirectional communication as part of your culture, and make it part of your daily activities. What you should do initially may be different than in the long term, but your long-term vision should guide your short-term actions.

The changing role of management

Two of the biggest challenges managers in an organization face when shifting from a traditional organization to a Lean organization are (1) recognizing how they must do their job differently and (2) recognizing the importance of how the team achieves results is as important as the results themselves. Living in a Lean organization is not like a traditional organization; it requires you to develop different mindset and an updated leadership style.

The following 16 essentials characterize a Lean manager at any level in the organization:

- **Stay true to the long-term focus, even in a short-term crisis.** The top of the organization sets the long-term vision and strategy for the enterprise. You define the long-term vision for your organization, considering as many as ten or more years in the future! When a crisis occurs, like the Great Recession of 2008, the short-term decisions you make must be congruent with your long-term vision. You may choose to invest in further development of your workforce or use the down time to relentlessly eliminate waste in all your processes. Whatever action you decide must be consistent with the long-term vision and investment in the organization.

- **Maintain unrelenting commitment to delivering customer value through elimination of waste in all aspects of the business.** Understand that your organization exists to deliver value to its customers: what they want, when they want it and how they want it. Always do it in the most effective and consistent manner possible.

- **Provide servant leadership at all levels.** Serve your teams; help them break down barriers to eliminate waste and better deliver customer value. Challenge, ask questions, show respect, lead from knowing and understanding and never be satisfied with the status quo.

- **Focus on both process *and* results.** How you and your organization achieve results is as important as the results themselves. Put your efforts into developing sound processes, ensuring people meet the standards, and are relentlessly improving these processes — ultimately leading to the achievement of the results you require.

- **Maintain integrity and congruency in words, actions and vision.** Create long-term and short-term visions. Independent of the circumstances, lead consistently. Be the same person, whether people are watching or not. Through your leadership, create an environment of trust.

- **Engage in deep reflection; understand "why;" accept mistakes, and pledge improvement.** The Japanese call this *hansei*. Whether things are going well or not, reflect to understand why a situation is as it is. By understanding cause, you can direct even more your improvement efforts. Especially in this 24/7, crazy-busy, global business climate, this reflection is vital to success. If you do not understand what worked — or didn't — and why, you cannot repeat success or learn from your efforts.

✔ **Attract and retain talented, willing people.** Focus your hiring processes on finding the right people for your organization. After you've hired them, treat them as a long-term asset, not just a body filling a role.

✔ **Lead by *going and seeing (genchi genbutsu).*** Do not delegate understanding; go to where the action is (to *gemba*) to understand the true nature of problems or solutions. From this knowledge, you guide and direct problem solving. (More on this in Chapter 13.)

✔ **Be nonjudgmental and blame-free.** Do not expect perfection; Murphy's Law is a statement of probability. How you respond when people make mistakes or when solutions don't work determines how well you respect and engage your people. You must create a blame-free culture and never make failure personal. Focus on what can be learned and what is the next thing needed to deliver value or achieve the target.

✔ **Build capability in the people by mentoring them through problem solving.** Because Lean leaders go and see, they have a better understanding of the situation. This doesn't mean you necessarily have the answers or solutions, but you will have foundation for directing the problem solving. (Ideally your managers have matured through the organization and have firsthand knowledge of how to do the work.) You may point an individual where to go look, but do not tell people how to solve their problems. Use Socratic methods — open ended questions — to guide people to find their own solutions. Insist on rapid, simple, systematic solutions first; change one thing at a time. See PDCA in Chapter 9.

✔ **Challenge the organization in a constructive manner.** See the vision as achievable. With this as a foundation, question the organization. How can we achieve this? What do we need to do to eliminate this barrier?

✔ **Build long-term partnerships with your customers, people, suppliers, and community.** Recognize that you are part of a greater community. By creating long-term productive, supportive, and challenging relationships, you can create broader change. Consider the long-term consequences of your decisions and legacy, beyond the time you are in your role. Guide your supply partners to improve and be successful in the long term.

✔ **Never be satisfied with the status quo.** Even if you have the best cultures and processes, they will decline if no one invests in them. Adapt the mindset that "there is always a better way" to move your organization toward your long-term vision. When you have no problems, you have a problem!

✔ **Treat the long-term vision as attainable and a given; eliminate the barriers that block progress to the vision.** Traditional-style managers waiver; they don't believe a long-term vision is achievable. This ultimately causes chaos in the organization. You must accept the long-term vision as a given, and guide people to make short-term, systematic actions that close the gap. Shepherd your organization through the unknown, using PDCA to break down barriers to achieving the long-term vision.

✔ **Oblige a safe and clean workplace.** A clean, safe workplace is non-negotiable. Your respect for people obligates you to ensure their safety. Eliminate unsafe or potentially harmful conditions in processes and environments. Use 5S (see Chapter 11) to create a clean workplace and facilitate the identification of waste.

✔ **Ensure people follow standards and eliminate barriers when they are not.** Accept that you are responsible for ensuring that people follow standards. Without standard conditions, you do not have a platform for consistency or improvement. Nonstandard actions are signals that something is amiss. Understand the nature of the nonconformance. Don't assume that it is a training issue; investigate the root cause to learn what's causing the problem and the singular countermeasure that will create a standard condition. (See the Lean toolbox in Part IV.)

Now that you understand the characteristics of a Lean leader, it is time for some deep reflection on yourself: To what degree have you developed these characteristics in your leadership style? What is the next most effective area where you can develop and grow your leadership ability? What do you need to do or to learn to develop yourself?

Bringing people along

Motivation is the art of getting people to do what you want them to do because they want to do it.

— President Dwight D. Eisenhower

Bring individuals along by addressing their needs. Every organization, team, or department contains individuals who all have their own needs, filters, perceptions, and timelines. To move the entire organization down the path of Lean, meet each individual where he is. Table 4-1 shows some of the differences to consider in your communications activities, strategy development, and implementation steps.

Table 4-1	Organizational Development and Strategy Considerations to Evoke Change
Aspect of Change	**Impact on Change**
Cultural/organizational	People's perceptions are influenced by all the groups that they've belonged to — from family units to other business organizations. Respect that this will color individual beliefs about the "right way" to do things and influence the willingness to change.
Generational	At least four generations are currently in the workplace, each with different values and guiding principles. You must get them to work together and communicate effectively within a Lean environment. People may resist change as they progress in their careers and in position. Fear of loss becomes greater.
Educational	Your organization may have a broad range of people — from those who cannot read to those with PhDs. You may not even share the same first language as your coworkers.
Learning styles	People learn in different ways. When introducing any new concept or change — and Lean is full of them — present in a multifaceted manner.
Personality styles	Understanding personality styles will help you evaluate how best to respond to the needs of the organization and how to get them to respond to the change.
Change motivators	Not everyone is motivated by money. Matching the motivators — such as time off, public recognition, or money — to the individual will help bring people along.

Among employees' biggest fears is the fear of losing their job. Some companies implementing Lean have learned to guarantee that no one will lose his job as a direct result of performance gains made by implementing Lean improvements. This guarantee goes a long way to allay fears. If you make such a policy, be clear that it is only in effect for Lean-based improvements, and ensure managers live up to the promise. Be certain people are very clear in their communications and open with information, because if they aren't clear, they'll cause a credibility and trust problem — and create another unnecessary impediment to change.

Be careful not to succumb to thinking, "Why do I have to baby people and go to all this effort?" If you want to succeed, you must address the needs of the individuals. What is the price of success? It is worth investing time in your people for the long-term payoff!

Chapter 5

Go Lean: Implementation Strategy, Startup, and Evolution

• •

In This Chapter

▶ Preparing for implementation

▶ Starting the transformation

▶ Moving past the starting line

• •

A journey of a thousand miles begins with a single step.

— Lao-tzu

As you know by now, Lean is a journey. It is not a prescription, where you follow steps 1, 2, and 3 and — *voila!* — you're there. It is not a one-size-fits-all continuous-improvement methodology. Lean is like the quest for perfect health: Your pursuit is multifaceted — nutrition, exercise, rest, beliefs. It requires discipline. It's a way of life.

No two people pursue health in exactly the same way. Each person considers how his lifestyle, age, goals, and starting point set him up for pursuit of perfect health. Each person may consult with experts to develop a plan that will work for them in the short term and over the long haul. Everyone must continuously learn about new exercise options and health trends. As all these new developments occur, each person has to discern if the new information is relevant to his personal path. Ultimately, each person's success requires discipline, a change of mindset, and the incorporation of healthy practices. Everyday healthy choices will lead to small incremental improvements. Although "perfect health" is an ideal state to strive for, staying the course moves you in the right direction.

An organization's Lean journey is similar to this kind of quest. You have to assess your present state and determine the right Lean strategy, based on your specific goals, objectives, experience, and the current state of the organization. You change how you approach leadership in both mindset and actions. To be successful, the organization develops new disciplines and healthy practices. You may hire a *sensei* to start you on the right path to change.

When forming your strategy, don't just copy someone like Toyota. Although Toyota's history serves as a good reference, it's not an exact blueprint for anyone else. You have to follow your own path, make your own adjustments, and find your own way.

In this chapter, we offer strategies and tips to help you begin your journey. You figure out how to prevent the "program-of-the-month" trap. And you see how to evolve from your starting point to a place of living Lean.

Preparing to Go Lean

Going Lean is rigorous, to be sure, but it's more of an *evolution* than a *revolution*. Lean focuses on the means to achieving results just as much as it does on results themselves. You don't solely measure your improvement progress by quarterly profit performance, although, over time, you experience improved performance in your financial measures as well as improvements to the other quadrant measures of the balanced scorecard.

Lean is a very action-oriented methodology; it includes the projects, *kaizen* events (see Chapter 9), and continuous learning. The planning process for a Lean initiative doesn't require an elaborate production, but you must develop it to the point where everyone in the organization receives and is aligned to a clear, consistent vision and message about where they're going and how they'll be getting underway.

As you begin your Lean journey, you need to put a few things in place. The most successful organizations have top leadership own, live, lead, and encourage Lean, and expand it to all levels and corners of the enterprise. They also must put people, policies, resources and vision in place to ensure a successful journey.

Lean is easier than many other approaches because you don't have to follow a singular prescribed rollout. You have a lot of latitude and leeway in your approach. But for the same reason, Lean can be more difficult than other approaches, because you don't have a firm prescription to follow and a precise roadmap to fall back on. You need to chart your own course and find your own way. The good news is that, with Lean, finding your way tends to happen naturally. Start where you can have the biggest, most positive impact on your customer or where you can eliminate a significant issue or waste in your organization.

Starting from the top

Lean succeeds in the long term if and only if the management team is dedicated to the journey and has established and communicated a clear vision of where they want to take the organization. You may start Lean in any part of the organization, but if you want sustainable results beyond a small portion of the company — and who doesn't? — the senior managers must endorse and actively participate in the effort. People respond to the cues they get from leadership at all levels — such as recognition, performance standards, and acceptable behaviors — especially in crisis situations.

Senior managers must understand the tools of Lean, the role that the people and culture play in sustainability, the importance of leading from *gemba* — where the action happens — and the philosophy of *kaizen*. They must practice Lean themselves in the course of their regular work routines. They must set a vision and communicate the messages of Lean. And they must follow up by performing Lean management actions (see Chapter 13).

Applying standardized work from the top down

Everyone in a Lean organization has standardized work. For people like the factory-floor assembler or call center employee, most of their work is standardized. Senior managers spend much of their time responding to interruptions, crises, and exceptions — and the rest of their time they spend brainstorming how to have fewer interruptions, crises, and exceptions! But senior managers have standardized work, too — not as much as the frontline worker, but they have it nonetheless. Lean managers use standardized methods such as Plan-Do-Check-Act (PDCA) when they respond to issues. They develop capability in the organization by understanding the issues thoroughly through knowing firsthand what's happening, asking probing questions, and guiding problem solving. Their job is not to give solutions, but to guide their people to find the best solution.

Examples of where standardized work applies in senior management include *gemba* walks (see Chapter 13), standard reports, and the conduct of routine meetings, briefings, and structured reviews. This kind of work may amount to less than half the senior manager's time, but when standardized, it enables the managers to work more effectively, freeing up time and resources for more value-added activities throughout the organization.

Focusing on the message and vision

Staff, directors, shareholders, analysts, suppliers, customers . . . all these constituents must know that you're embarking on this Lean journey. You can't take the journey by yourself and not tell anyone — they'll all wonder where you've gone! You must set the vision for your new path and articulate the mission. Take the time to craft these messages, and convey them to the audiences as the journey begins.

You are starting a journey. Your messages need to inform and reflect that this is a change for the *long term*. There is a danger in flooding the organization with new buzz words and slogans. Be careful not to inadvertently fuel the program-of-the-month rumor mill by presenting Lean as the "next greatest thing." Balance buzz with action.

The beauty of Lean for executives and senior managers is that it provides a toolkit with methods and techniques to back-up management's classic platitudes. Some of these are:

- ✔ **We're customer-centric!** Management's been touting this for years, but how could they really make it happen? Lean gives the executive the techniques to examine added value throughout the organization and conduct business operations from the customer's point of view.

- ✔ **People are our most important resource!** That's the one you're used to hearing right before the next round of layoffs. Lean teaches executives about true respect for employees, and provides the toolkit for safety, security, engagement, celebration, and growth.

- ✔ **Think win-win.** Unfortunately, without a method, this one's been only half-true: management's win for themselves. Lean techniques enable managers to create a win for all parties.

- ✔ **Do it right the first time.** (Also known as *Quality is Job #1* — or, as they say in the software industry, *Quality is Job 1.1* — i.e., fix the bugs in the next release!). But, how do you actually do it right the first time? You can't test and rework products into submission. Lean, using statistical methods, *poka-yoke* (see Chapter 11), and other tools provides the basis for making this real.

Leading by example

In addition to performing standard work, the senior managers must also lead by setting the example. Managers translate the foreign and abstract concepts of Lean into practical behaviors that everyone can observe and emulate. They must change the way they think and react, especially in times of crisis. People will be watching to see if the managers are committed to the change to a Lean way of operating or if they're just giving it lip service. Managers must also use visual controls. Charts, graphs, trends, and reports should be highly visible and apparent to everyone. The manager's job is to reinforce the standard, notice non-conformance, investigate what is its root cause, and eliminate barriers to success.

Managers must exemplify discipline and accountability. They must perform to the expectations they set for others. They must hold themselves accountable, just as they expect everyone else to hold one another accountable. People will follow the leader — be sure you're leading them in the right direction.

One of the most powerful showcases for Lean behavior is in meeting management. Managers should prepare for meetings and have a firm well-defined agenda, with the outcomes articulated explicitly. They must always arrive on time and finish on time — standardized work! When possible, conduct the meetings where the action happens — *gemba.* Consider stand-up meetings and challenge the "hour meeting" mindset.

Managers must also conduct the same Lean practices that they expect of everyone else, including going to *gemba,* developing and analyzing value-stream maps, participating in *kaizen* events and *kaizen* improvement projects, partaking in continuous training and learning, and overtly demonstrating regular, continuous improvements.

Creating the Lean infrastructure

Although there's no standard recipe for a Lean deployment, you'll need to put in place a framework of support elements before you begin the trip. You must acquire certain specific Lean expertise (see Finding the Master and Developing the Students in the next section). You need to disseminate Lean knowledge across the organization in a controlled manner. You must also bring in cooperative human resource practices, set up certain financial and accounting practices, and put in place some specific IT infrastructure. This support framework is critical to a successful rollout.

Adjusting the people policies

When moving into Lean from a traditional environment, you much change numerous personnel policies and practices in order to align with the people-centered principles of Lean. For example:

- ✔ Incentive, recognition and reward systems traditionally focused on the individuals will have to expand to include individuals and teams.

- ✔ Policies must support the realignment and reassignment of employees displaced due to productivity improvements.

✔ Organizational structures and labor agreements, if applicable, will have to be adjusted to support a Lean environment. Frequently, this includes a reduction in the number of organizational levels, the consolidation of job categories, the ability to cross train, and flexible work rules.

✔ Promotions will have to be based on performance, knowledge, and capability. The company may establish standard path progressions for multi-functional workers.

Acquiring training materials

Lean courseware includes formal training on the practices of *kaizen* and the Lean toolkit (see Parts III and IV). Additional courses are available on organizational development, coaching/mentoring, communication skills, and change management. These courses are offered by numerous practitioners and training and consulting firms (see Chapter 19 for recommendations).

Most training firms typically prefer to perform the training for you, rather than license the training materials to you. If you're embracing Lean fully and organically, you want to own the materials and have the ability to adapt them to your organization to use in a variety of settings and formats. But if you're just sticking your toe in the water, you can either send people to training or bring the trainers to you.

Putting the people in place

To initiate the Lean effort, you have to put in place the logistical support pieces. People at all levels of the organization will need training. In addition, *kaizen* events must be scheduled and tracked. Outside resources like trainers, consultants, materials, and software tools will also need coordination. A core group of people will assemble to perform this work.

Make sure that you have the support resources to handle the volume of changes generated by the *kaizen* activities. You may need to pace the events so you don't create *muri* or over stressing support departments like IT or maintenance.

Putting the support tools in place

The Lean practitioner uses software application tools as part of his optimization work. These tools include process mapping, value-stream mapping (VSM), statistical analysis, process orchestration and graphical mapping and charting tools. Some of these are individual desktop-computer tools, whereas others are shared by workgroups. The IT organization must include these in its cadre of applications support. Other software tools include programs for facility layouts and graphics packages for visual aides.

In addition to software tools, the Lean practitioner uses more traditional tools:

- **Markers and flip charts** to record idea generation and team sessions.

- **Video cameras** record the processes, enabling the team to analyze the film for improvement.

- **Digital cameras** record before and after shots of the areas, particularly in conjunction with *kaizen* events.

- **Stopwatches** establish and verify performance standards; use this data for line balancing and takt time (see Chapter 7) comparison.

- **A toolbox** full of screwdrivers, wrenches, and hammers may come in handy for creating display boards, hanging visual aides or other improvement activities. And don't forget the duct tape!

If your organization's policies permit it, use your mobile devices to take photos or videos of the area. Be sure to transfer them from your mobile device to a centralized place where the team can access them.

Finding the Master and Developing the Students

One of the most famous *sensei*-student relationships was in the movie *The Karate Kid* (1984). Daniel, the new kid in town, is getting his butt kicked by the local karate bullies. Mr. Miyagi, a handyman and karate master, steps in and saves Daniel by fighting off the whole lot. Later and after much pestering by Daniel, Mr. Miyagi agrees to become his *sensei,* or teacher. When the lessons begin, Daniel does not understand Mr. Miyagi's unconventional methods. His lessons include washing Mr. Miyagi's car ("wax on, wax off") and painting his fence ("brush up, brush down"). After Daniel blows up in frustration because he feels like he's not learning anything, Mr. Miyagi points out to Daniel that he has been learning karate while doing these tasks. As a *sensei,* Mr. Miyagi has knowledge, experience, and his own unique way of passing on the knowledge. Mr. Miyagi demands that Daniel complete tasks in a precise way — focusing on the "how." He also has the understanding that karate is not just the external techniques and moves, but also the internal belief in the heart and mind.

Lots of great references and books on Lean are out there (you're reading the best introductory one, of course!), but you can't gain the necessary experience from a book. Successful Lean organizations find a *sensei* or a master, not unlike Mr. Miyagi. The Lean *sensei* teaches, challenges, and guides the organization on their path to Lean implementation. The organization may not always understand the *sensei's* methods at first, but eventually, with the right *sensei*, everyone in the organization finds themselves living Lean. In this section we tell you about the Lean *sensei,* and Lean students.

The Lean sensei

The Lean journey does not mandate a Lean *sensei*, but if you want to be successful, having a *sensei* is highly recommended. Many companies have found it beneficial to bring in an external Lean *sensei* when starting the Lean journey. A Lean *sensei* has knowledge of Lean principles, methods, and implementation. They guide and teach. Like Mr. Miyagi's methods, their methods may be unconventional by traditional business standards. They also have a broad understanding that Lean is more than just the external techniques — to truly get Lean, you must change your attitudes, perceptions, and actions.

Identifying the role of a sensei

The *sensei* teaches the principles of Lean and guides the journey. The *sensei* lives where the action is in the organization. The *sensei* guides and teaches through *gemba* walks with individuals and small groups of managers. By questioning practices and processes, pointing out what is un-Lean in the process and focusing on waste elimination, the *sensei* teaches. *Senseis* may lead *kaizen* events, and don't be surprised if you find them rolling up their sleeves and getting dirty with the details. They oversee — but do not own — the short- and long-term vision. Think of the *sensei* as the wise master, who will do just about anything to teach a point.

What are the benefits of having a Lean *sensei*? A *sensei* will

- Jumpstart your initial Lean implementation.
- Ensure your Lean efforts stay on course.
- Offer a broad view of the organization to ensure constancy of purpose.
- Customize the approach and materials based on the organization's particular situation.
- Provide tactical direction in support of the long-term vision.
- Set high expectations, allowing your organization to achieve more than it thought possible
- Produce results faster.
- Serve as an independent observer and advisor.

Hiring a sensei

The Society of Manufacturing Engineers, the Association for Manufacturing Excellence, and the Shingo Prize have joined together to create a Lean Certification, but there is no unique credential for a Lean *sensei*. So how do you find a *sensei*? You can find candidates by contacting consulting companies (Shingijutsu Co., one of the sources of *senseis* in Japan, also operates globally), hiring a former employee from a Lean company such as Toyota, asking other Lean companies for references, and even searching the Internet. You will find an abundance of potential *sensei* candidates whose talents range from hack to expert. To find the one who is right for your organization, be clear about what you are looking for and how much you can afford to pay.

Before hiring a *sensei*, your company must understand its expectations and the background of the prospective *sensei*. Here are some questions to ask of yourself and the *sensei*:

- ✔ Is our long term vision clear so the *sensei* can help us work toward it?
- ✔ What are our expectations of a *sensei?*
- ✔ Where did the *sensei* receive his training?
- ✔ What experience does he have?
- ✔ What expectations does the company have of the *sensei?*
- ✔ How long does the company expect to rely on an outside resource?
- ✔ What is the company willing to spend on a *sensei?*
- ✔ Does the company intend to develop an internal *sensei?*

How many *senseis* do you need? It depends on the size of your company or operating units. You're better off starting with one *sensei* and at one location. As your efforts increase, under the *sensei*'s guidance you may want to bring on more *senseis*. If you have more than one, make sure they're in alignment. You don't want too many cooks in the kitchen.

Organizations truly committed to Lean understand that they must continuously learn, stretch, and grow. To ensure that happens, you need a teacher and guide to show you the next step in the journey. Over time, is that teacher the same person or always an external resource? Probably not. You will likely find that your organization responds better to a different *sensei* as the journey progresses — not unlike your school experience where your kindergarten teacher was different from your high school teacher.

Agree upon performance expectations of the *sensei* as part of the original contract (for an external resource) or part of the performance appraisal (for an internal resource). At the end of the day, you're looking for performance improvement in your operations. Connect the *sensei's* activities with the organizational performance metrics.

Set up a formal mentoring process within your organization and build your own leadership capability to reduce your reliance on outside resources over the long term. As Lean becomes the way your organization does business, transition to having everyone own Lean as the way they do their business activities.

Senseis in the organization

Following the philosophy, "you can't be a prophet in your own land", a *sensei* is usually external to the organization — especially during the initial phases of implementation. In some cases, the *sensei* is a member of the management team who has a broad and deep knowledge of Lean. The *sensei* may also have experience from other companies or have previously been under the tutelage of an external *sensei*.

If the company sources its *sensei* internally, they must be granted proper authority and the backing of the management team. Don't just deem a functional manager as *sensei*. Focus the *sensei* solely on Lean, and have them report directly to the highest levels of the organization.

Lean students

Every member of the Lean organization is a student of Lean. In an unending quest to improve, everyone must learn — constantly. But you won't spend hours in a classroom — the majority of learning happens where the action is — in *gemba*. Every place becomes a classroom, and every situation becomes a class.

All levels of your organization will learn new skills as the Lean journey progresses. You will learn from classes, workshops, books, interactions with a *sensei*, on the job, from trial and error, from mistakes, from online blogs or other resources — the sources are endless.

To stay fresh and make daily improvements, everyone must continuously seek out knowledge. Particularly once you have worked in the same job or in the same area or with the same people for an extended period of time, you need fresh perspective, because you can easily get comfortable and stagnate. As a student of Lean, your responsibility is to seek knowledge daily. You may learn a new job, apply a new technique, learn about a different part of the value stream — learning is all around you!

You'll know when you're an advanced student of Lean: You will not only start applying Lean concepts beyond the workplace, but you will also look for Lean in everyday life. When you've taught your kids how to 5S their room and conduct gemba walks around your house, you'll know that you've changed your thinking.

The ongoing Lean curriculum

The curriculum of a Lean student is not fixed. Sure, you need to learn the basics — like value-stream mapping, *kaizen*, elimination of waste, 5S, visual management, *poke-yoke, kanban* and all the other tools found in Parts III and VI of this book. But if you stop there, it's like dropping out of grade school.

To become a Lean student, you must have knowledge and competency in at least four skill areas:

- ✔ **Technical skills** in applying the tools of Lean, from *kaizen* to *kanban*, and everything in between

- ✔ **Leadership skills** including coaching, empowerment, collaboration, service, conflict resolution, negotiations, teaming, and self-awareness

- ✔ **Strategy and planning skills** including project planning and management, goal setting, and problem solving

- ✔ **Applied skills** including demonstrated competency in the *real world* — where theory and practical application meet

As time passes, you may add pieces to the puzzle. Remember that your responsibility is to be a lifelong learner.

Lean certification

Although several types of Lean certifications are available, there are no standard industry certifications in Lean knowledge, skill, or demonstrated mastery. The whole notion of "Lean certification" is still developing. The Society of Manufacturing Engineers, the Association for Manufacturing Excellence, and the Shingo Prize sponsor lean certifications (see Chapter 19). Note also that Lean Six Sigma consultants have applied "belt" certifications based on a Six Sigma-style structure, but it's not strictly Lean.

Lean certification is a mildly controversial topic. Not all Lean practitioners agree to the value of certification. After all, Lean is life-long learning. A certificate alone does not make you a Lean expert. In the end, only you can determine the value of a certificate. You may belong to an organization that esteems certificates and credentials, in which case certification may be of value.

If you select a certification program, choose one that has both theoretical and practical criteria. Lean knowledge is gained more from practical problem solving application than theoretical, classroom knowledge.

Most certification programs focus on the application of tools. Recognize that tools are only part of the equation. You need additional development in the culture, people, change, and leadership — Respect the People — part of Lean.

Beginning the Journey: The Lean Rollout

You can start Lean anywhere, in any place, and at any time. There's no special magic place to begin. A common way to start the process is by performing a 5S (see Chapter 11) or a *kaizen* event (see Chapter 9) in an area of need or interest. This action begins the journey; then you ensure the journey is progressing by executing to a plan or a framework. Don't make the rollout a big deal or burden it with bureaucratic management — keep it straightforward and simple. It is Lean, after all.

Minding the big picture

True Lean is a process of small, incremental improvements. Sounds simple enough, except that these improvements are happening all over the enterprise, involving the entire organization, across multiple value streams, simultaneously. If you aren't careful, things can get out of control. In this section, we share strategies to keep your Lean efforts on track.

Understanding the enterprise value streams

Within the context of the high-level value stream of the enterprise, most companies have many, many internal value streams. They also may have single areas, or monuments, that services multiple value streams, such as a large piece of equipment or a hospital lab. When the organization understands the many different value streams it has, and how those different value streams interrelate, the organization is better able to coordinate the improvement efforts and avoid *sub-optimizing* (improving one part of the enterprise at the peril of another).

Avoiding the Kaizen blitzkrieg

Especially in the beginning of the Lean journey, people are motivated to get something done — and now! Many organizations respond to this urgency by hosting as many *kaizen* events as they possibly can. They may set a metric for the number of *kaizen* activities performed. In response, everyone runs right out and checks off the "I did a *kaizen*!" box — without coordination, without a larger scale vision, without connection.

When all these blitzes are happening at once, you may minimize the results or create *muri* in the support departments, who try to assist everyone at once. One area may free up floor space, but it may be too small or in the wrong location to be useful or to amount to a true savings. In another scenario, one area may move the *muda* (see Chapter 6) to another part of the facility or value stream, without truly eliminating anything.

Don't turn your *kaizen* blitz into a *kaizen* blitzkrieg — where instead of improvement, you leave only devastation behind. Build into your process ways to coordinate major *kaizen* activities, so that you yield overall improvements.

Kaizen events are a great way to start, but they need a proper scope, vision and tie to the performance objectives of the organization. If the events are random and have little positive results on the organization's goals or positive impact to your customer, you can actually demoralize your organization, fuel the resistors, create a culture of negativity and doubt, and derail your progress.

Connecting the pieces

The Lean toolbox has an array of different tools (see Parts III and VI). The organization must understand how, when, and why the different tools are used. If you're trying to level schedules and implement *kanban* (see Chapter 11), and yet your changeover times are still counted in days, you're implementing the wrong tool at the wrong time. By understanding each tool in the toolkit, you'll better match the implementation of the techniques to your particular situation.

Most organizations have other initiatives already occurring across the organization. These initiatives may be continuous-improvement initiatives or large-scale projects like an Enterprise Resource Planning (ERP) computer system implementation, or acquisitions of other organizations. You must define how all these things fit together.

Neglecting to connect the dots for the organization will cause confusion. Some people in the organization will be waiting for Lean to fail and will jump to the conclusion that Lean is just another program of the month. Showing the organization how it all fits together will help minimize the impact of these naysayers.

Keeping your finger on the pulse of the organization

As we discuss in Chapters 3 and 4, communication is the lifeblood of the Lean transformation. You need to take the pulse of the organization, continually.

If people start reverting backward to un-Lean behaviors and tendencies, or moving off course, you need to be aware and correct it.

Communication activities should be two-way. Make them visual. Remember also to appeal to multiple learning styles, appropriate for the situation.

Enlist volunteers from various parts of the organization to act as a communication advisory team. This strategy will help you keep the message real, keep the movement consistent, and keep you connected to the pulse of the organization.

Picking the starting point

As an actor studies a role to bring art to life, he asks the question, "What's my motivation?" When you're bringing Lean to life in your organization, you, too, should ask yourself this question: What's your motivation? Identify where you have the greatest pain points or the greatest opportunities that will impact the organization in a strategic manner or help you to serve your customer more effectively. Find your greatest motivation, and you've found your starting point.

Impact on the customer

The first place to look is where you have the greatest impact on the customer. Evaluate where you have strained customer relationships or value-creation, and identify the potential sources of the issues. Thoroughly define the problem by exploring potential causes and continue to refine the problem definition to focus your resources on the right problem. Use PDCA (see Chapter 9) to implement the first solution. Continue this process until you have closed the gap with your customer. Build the customer relationship through action and communication.

5S and the enterprise

5S areas where you can reduce waste or improve customer value (see Chapter 11). 5S is a powerful tool, and it helps people begin their Lean journey by "getting the house in order." But be careful not to overdo it and go on a 5S blitz, or everyone will think you're just a crazy compulsively neat person. That's because 5S by itself is just a tool, and it's most powerful when used in combination with other tools or in conjunction with a greater vision.

Quick visual improvement

To build momentum for a Lean initiative, apply measurement and visualization — creating transparency and providing feedback. Find a work area where visualization has an impact, and is quick and relevant, such as:

- ✔ Removing an inventory warehouse or storage
- ✔ Reducing setup times from hours to minutes
- ✔ Reducing repair time for vehicles needed to support soldiers in the field

Wide-open spaces

If your motivation is to create space in your facility to accommodate new business, eliminate unnecessary real-estate, or bring workgroups together, you'll want to create wide-open spaces. Free up large concentrated spaces in your facility. Start by conducting a series of coordinated *kaizen* and 5S activities to create the right space in the right location.

Creating awareness

In the beginning of your Lean journey, you want to create a buzz, get people excited, and engage them in your Lean efforts. As you progress, you want to keep the organization motivated and involved in the Lean transformation. Ultimately, you want your organization to live and breathe Lean. For this to happen, people need to know what's going on and why it is important. In this section, we tell you how to create the initial buzz, improve communication and engage people for the long haul.

Communicating the reason(s)

Before describing the principles and practices of Lean, or why Lean has been selected as the approach to improvement, people need to know why the initiative is necessary. They need to hear and understand that something's wrong with how things are working today, and that there are consequences if we don't change our ways. They need to know what the consequences are; the risks of inaction. These reasons for change must be critically important, undeniable, and fundamentally impactful to everyone in the organization.

Leading by listening

Before rolling out a plan or approach, you need to know that people understand the reason for change and believe they must support a change initiative. Listening is the most powerful communication skills you can use. Whether you're on an intentional *gemba* walk or hanging out at the water cooler, listening will enable you to gauge the pulse of the people. Figure 5-1 depicts an effective listening model.

Your ability to ask probing, open-ended questions will enhance your understanding and your people's understanding.

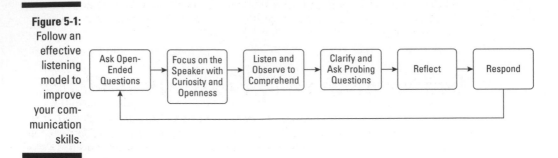

Figure 5-1:
Follow an effective listening model to improve your communication skills.

Ask Open-Ended Questions → Focus on the Speaker with Curiosity and Openness → Listen and Observe to Comprehend → Clarify and Ask Probing Questions → Reflect → Respond

Identifying the approach

Communicate your intention to implement a Lean approach to the organization. Describe why Lean is the preferred way to address the organization's challenges. Make it personal for people; explain how Lean will affect them and make a difference in their lives. Be sure to communicate that this is a change in the way you are doing business, and that it's not just a short-term special event. Maintain credibility by backing up your message up with consistent and congruent actions.

Highlighting progress

Create momentum from early progress by communicating successes. Let people know what has happened, why it's important to them, what will happen next, how the next change is relevant for them, and reinforce the organizations long-term vision.

Highlighting progress is an on-going activity. Many organizations start strong when communicating progress, but lose their momentum over time. If people don't hear about Lean advances, they may think you have abandoned your journey.

Reinforcing the long-term view

Constantly keeping the motivation and long-term vision in front of people will make Lean real for them, even if their area hasn't yet started implementation. The message to the organization is that this is not about a *kaizen* here and there — Lean is about the long-term sustainability and viability of the organization as a whole.

Lean by doing

The best way to create awareness and understanding of Lean is to get involved. Get on a *kaizen* team, 5S your workspace, learn a new technique, and find a pertinent application for it. There is no better way to grasp the concepts of Lean than by actively participating and implementing improvements every day.

Avoiding program-of-the-month syndrome

Since the beginning of continuous-improvement time, battling program-of-the-month syndrome has been a challenge. As long as there are consultants, they will innovate and introduce new methodologies into the market. Or when movements lose steam, clever consultants and opportunists will repackage tools and techniques with a twist. Amidst these ebbing and flowing tides of methods and systems, companies committed to the Lean journey maintain their focus, keep the journey invigorated and determine how best to adapt to changing business conditions. In the following sections, we give you tips how to avoid the program-of-the-month syndrome.

Continuous communication

Communication remains important along your entire Lean journey. People need to know that you are truly committed, and that the organization is committed. They also need to discuss what's happening, and how it affects them. If you do not communicate commitment, people will make things up, start rumors, or do nothing in hopes that "this too shall pass." (See Chapter 4 for more about the importance of a communication strategy to help people change.)

Great expectations

By setting expectations with the staff, customers, stakeholders, and others, you support the Lean principles and establish the behaviors and tone for the organization. When you're clear about the performance and behaviors you expect, and when you hold all the people in the organization accountable, they know that Lean is here for the long term and isn't just a passing fancy. When you connect the dots for them in terms of Lean, you reinforce that Lean is the foundation. Communicate other activities or initiatives in the context of Lean.

Measurable outcomes

When you continually show measurable progress, you build momentum in the organization. As the momentum builds, you increase your progress. Staying the course with Lean — and keeping the momentum going — will show the organization that Lean is not just here for the short term.

Put the outcomes in terms that any individual can see and understand. Translate the impact to a personal level. The outcomes are not necessarily direct financial measures; they could be freed-up floor space, decreased time to serve a customer, a reduced approval chain, or anything that the individual can observe and use to verify the longer-term performance.

Walking the walk

If yesterday, you hailed the TLA (Three-Letter Acronym) improvement program, today you cheerlead the Charge 4 Lean, and tomorrow you're touting The Ten Thetas, you'll feed organizational frenzy. You'll doom your improvement journey to a certain death at the hands of the cynics and naysayers — and you'll deserve it. You must remain a serious practitioner and leader of a Lean process initiative. If you're inconsistent and noncommittal, Lean will be just another bygone program of the month. As a practitioner, build capability through asking quality questions, guiding problem-solving, and understanding what is really happening in *gemba*.

Separating the wheat from the chaff: Handling new initiatives

New ideas and approaches emerge regularly. Don't ignore them. Become familiar with them and develop a process to characterize them and determine your response. In many cases, "new" ideas are really just repackaged old ideas, so fundamentally, they offer nothing compelling. Technology is disruptive, so new whiz-bang IT solutions can offer speed, scale, and extensibility beyond local boundaries and manual effort. Most often, the new offerings are new tools that you can accommodate effectively into the Lean toolkit. As you evaluate the potential for new initiatives, ask yourself the following questions:

- ✔ Does this initiative have potential relevance to the organization? If so, where in the organization does it fit?

- ✔ Are there activities currently underway in these areas — within the organization and elsewhere? If so, what can we learn from them?

- ✔ Is someone offering something fundamentally new, or is it a repackaging of what we already know?

- ✔ How does this fit into Lean? Does our Lean initiative accommodate this?

Measurements: The enterprise at a glance

As you begin your Lean initiative, determine the relevant measurements for your organization. This may require you to measure things that you have not measured before. Most organizations commit the majority of their measurement focus to internal financials, but Lean practice compels you to balance your attention across a broader set of measures. These include customer, people, and process metrics.

Develop measurement capabilities in the following categories:

- ✔ **Customer:** Satisfaction, net-promoter score, and measures across the value stream between them and *their* customers
- ✔ **Safety:** Lost-time accidents, near-miss incidents, and repetitive-motion or ergonomic risk
- ✔ **People:** Learning, proficiency, satisfaction, absenteeism, turnover, certifications or course work
- ✔ **Quality:** Defects per million opportunities, defects by type and source, spills, rework, scrap
- ✔ **Delivery:** On-time delivery, premium freight, total shipping cost per product, customer wait time
- ✔ **Value-stream costs:** Inventory turns, cost per unit, cost per service hour; days outstanding, supplier payments

Tie your Lean implementation metrics to overall company performance metrics, to make the Lean implementation metrics meaningful from a business standpoint. A double-digit savings in floor space is great, but if you don't have work to put in it, then the freed up floor space doesn't mean much to the business.

Be sure that your metrics and incentives don't conflict with one another, where meeting one objective is counterproductive to the achievement of another.

Localized within a value steam, add other measures — both process and outcome metrics — relevant to Lean implementation. Example metrics include:

- ✔ Percent of team cross-trained
- ✔ Performance to takt
- ✔ Actual setup reduction versus target
- ✔ Percent of *kaizen* events complete versus planned
- ✔ Number of work orders completed to plan

A Lean leader must care and focus on both the results and the methods of *how* the people are creating the results. If you are getting results, but creating a lot of waste in the process, you are not implementing Lean.

Make information visual by delivering data in graphical form. Make the postings broadly visible and accessible. Post graphs of these metrics in communication stations across your facility and via your intranet.

Living Lean

After your Lean initiative gets its legs and begins to run, you've changed your organization forever. The positive effects of Lean are contagious, and the mindset of *kaizen* has a certain dogged determination and undeniable inevitability to it. As a result, over time, your enterprise Lean initiative will evolve into an ongoing, sustaining phase. This is when you know you're *living Lean*.

The Lean evolution

The evolution of a Lean initiative begins with the rollout phase and moves into its sustaining phase sometime after you've trained everyone, performed *kaizen* events across the enterprise, and the positive results have occurred widely enough and consistently enough that everyone begins to believe in its power.

What happens then? Are you "done"? Have you "become Lean"? Can you now put the Lean techniques and methods and tools aside — *thank you very much* — and move on with your business? Absolutely not! You don't put anything aside. You focus even more on your culture and the mindset you have created for your organization.

The minute you declare your organization "Lean" is the minute you've lost your way!

Inwardly Lean

The first Lean activities begin with training and *kaizen* events (see Chapters 9), usually in a selected department, program area or workgroup. Successful events give rise to larger improvement projects. These projects address a specific challenge area in a particular value stream, and involve time and effort on the part of a project team and the Lean *sensei*, who together apply the Lean toolkit to improve the process and outcomes. After a few projects have been successful and the positive results become visible, the participants begin to internalize the value, and they understand the power of the approach. Others begin to notice. People start initiating small projects in their work areas and as part of their workgroups.

The next step in the Lean evolution is to develop an enterprise project-oriented mindset, where you address challenges with Lean projects on a broader scale — both within their value streams and in concert with other value streams. Integrated enterprise value-stream activities will begin between organizations like marketing and IT or between design, operations, and customer service.

This is the point where everyone is "doing" Lean stuff. It's a very exciting time: The organization is growing and learning, people are improving their work processes and environments, and the results are showing — in improved business productivity and performance. Figure 5-2 shows how Lean organizations evolve over time.

In a large organization, it takes years to reach a level of ubiquitous enterprise-wide Lean practice.

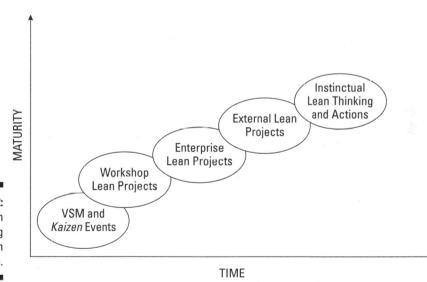

Figure 5-2:
Phases in the maturing Lean organization.

At some point, someone in the organization climbs the next rung on the evolution ladder. Instead of creating a project team to approach a challenge, he improves his part of the value stream on his own. No fanfare, no project team or official results — he makes the Nike marketing team proud and "just does it." At this stage, the mechanical formalities begin to drop away and the mindsets begin to change. People begin to see the world through different eyes. They're acting on instinct. PDCA is a habit. People's performance is judged on Lean actions and progress. Lean is in their DNA.

Outwardly Lean

After people within their own work areas become comfortable with internal projects, they begin examining the cause-and-effect conditions that give rise to the waste in their segment of the value stream. Very quickly, this leads to an expansion of view: They begin to look outside their own world.

Groups begin to look up and down their value stream. They begin to suggest projects with suppliers, and other projects with customers. Eventually, this may lead to integrated value-stream projects involving suppliers, customers, and even the customers' customers. Meanwhile, groups within the enterprise have begun to explore the relationships between them more fully.

All these are examples of outward Lean behavior. Outwardly, Lean is important because it represents the emergence of a systems view, the more holistic view of the organization and its life in the value chain. The external view provides the objectivity needed to adjust how the enterprise fits into the world. It promotes *adaptivity* — the ability to adapt and survive in the economic gene pool.

This adaptivity leads to a decrease in what's known as *functional suboptimization* (a phenomenon where a lot of time and effort is spent fixing problems in a function or area that doesn't matter in the bigger picture).

Functional sub-optimization is a symptom of inward focus, where you think your world and your problems are the only ones that matter. Don't be mistaken: Improving any area and removing waste from any value stream are the right things to do, but diverting enterprise resources to further strengthening a strong link in the chain when there are weak links all around isn't a smart move.

Eliminating waste is just that: elimination. It's not moving waste. Using logistics tools like postponement, third-party kitting, distribution centers, and topping up to move your waste to someone else is nothing more than sweeping dirt under the rug. Sure, your room looks clean, but the dirt is still there. Don't move *muda*; eliminate it.

Growing through mergers and acquisitions

One popular way companies decide to grow and expand is through mergers and acquisitions. When a new team joins your company, you will be starting your Lean journey again. You are blending cultures, business practices, and people. If you are the acquiring company, start communication of your principles on Day One and *kaizen* activities as soon as possible to bring the new team on board (see Chapter 16). Have key leaders lead these events to show how committed your organization is to your Lean journey.

One mistake companies frequently make in these circumstances is failing to recognize the strengths of the company being acquired. Learn from the new organization; don't assume that they don't have anything to offer just because they were purchased. You may know how Lean can apply, but they know their business. You may find that they have great improvement ideas, but they were unable to implement them under the former owner due to a lack of resources or a different management philosophy.

If your organization is acquired by a non-Lean organization, you may have to educate your new leaders and fight to stay your course. Do everything you can to communicate the power of Lean to your success as an organization. The risk is that the new management, through a lack of understanding, will dismantle everything you have built and then wonder what happened to performance several months down the road.

Practically Lean

Lean practice compels you to define your ideal state and continually work towards it. But be practical about how you approach your journey. You want to provide the best value to your customer, and you will have to challenge traditions and the traditional mindset of your organization to make progress. If you find your "next right step" for the organization seems contrary to pure Lean principles, but at the same time, it moves you in the right direction without creating excess waste, don't stand on ceremony. Remember that no step or state is ever your final answer; it's just the next right step. Establish the new standard, measure the outcomes, and conduct your next *kaizen*. Continually reassess to see how you can improve the solution — again, and again, and again.

Turnover due to high retirement levels or rapid changes in emerging markets may also be a reality. You need to apply a practical strategy as a leader in these situations. For the retirees, motivate knowledge transfer to build capability. For the high turnover in emerging markets, error-proof the processes and retain your key people.

Natural disasters are statistical probabilities, so be practical and plan for them. Don't build excess inventories around the world — remember inventory is a form of waste and products in inventory are at risk to the same disasters. Work together with your suppliers, whom you have developed as long-term partners, to create contingency plans, especially on long lead-time or critical items.

Mature Lean organizations especially rely on Lean principles when crises arise. Organizations just beginning a Lean journey risk reverting to old behaviors when the going gets tough. When *stuff* happens, leaders must focus even more on the Lean culture and application of the Lean tools and principles. Use Lean principles and practices in crisis management planning from the beginning of your Lean journey.

After a crisis or disaster situation has passed, reflect on the people, processes, and outcomes, and improve your response plans for the future, based on what worked and what you learned.

Unleashing the mindset of kaizen

Vision is not enough; it must be combined with venture. It is not enough to stare up the steps; we must step up the stairs.

— Vaclav Havel

Lean learning is always performed in concert with application. The power of understanding is released by putting it into action. The Lean organization's thirst for knowledge is complemented by the equally strong hunger for improvement. Lean organizations turn knowledge into progress.

Unleash the continuous-improvement mindset by fueling people's thirst for more, and by providing comfort in the notion that no matter where we are or what we've achieved, we can always accomplish something better:

✔ We can always know and delight our customers even more.

✔ We can make our value chain even more effective.

✔ We can create greater capability in our people and partners.

✔ We can always find and remove more waste.

✔ We can work to standards more consistently.

✔ We can better balance the cycle time to the takt time.

✔ We can remove more defects, reduce variation, and improve quality.

✔ We can improve our application and leverage of technology.

Continuous improvement isn't a death march. It's not tireless drudgery. This isn't an assault on Mount Everest. The maturing Lean organization doesn't feed off Herculean victories; it thrives on constant progress. The Lean mindset, therefore, never has the need to rest on its laurels because it never tires out.

The Lean organization is like a long-distance runner, rather than a sprinter. Lean is a sustainable aerobic movement, leveraged through fitness, disciplined through training, maintained by momentum, fueled by balanced nutrition, and spiced by endorphins.

Facilitating with finance

The finance and accounting functions directly support the Lean journey by providing financial measures of the benefits and effectiveness of processes and operations as they're transformed. This role is similar to the role of finance in a Six Sigma initiative, where improvements are independently measured and validated for their bottom-line financial impact.

There's nothing like financial incentives to move the mountain. When Lean processes make money, everyone notices. The finance and accounting function is responsible for working with the Lean practitioners across the enterprise to define the key metrics that demonstrate the financial benefits that accrue from Lean process improvements.

Standard accounting practices and systems don't capture, manage, analyze, or report financial information according to Lean practices. You need to develop specialized applications first, and then tune the financial systems over time, in order to implement financial practices that align with your Lean initiative. You can find many books in the market about Lean accounting to guide your development of these new practices.

Because Lean operations cut across traditional functional boundaries and generate new types of metrics, traditional accounting systems and measures don't facilitate the Lean organization. Not having the right metrics can be a real problem. Remember the part about how the finance organizations are slow to change? When you ask them to change how they count the beans, you may encounter some resistance.

Now I am the master

Over the long term, as the Lean initiative progresses, everyone in the organization develops Lean abilities and masters certain tools and techniques. Over time, the novices become the masters. Expertise develops naturally from within.

As the initiative matures, the organization continues Lean principles and behaviors more by momentum and cultural predisposition than by impulse. It's not a matter of who carries the torch, because everyone is carrying his own torch. Lean behaviors become ingrained, and, because organizations are slow to change, those behaviors don't disappear. Continuous learning and improvement become cultural mainstays.

Still, management must maintain leadership and continue the Lean direction. They must continue to exhibit Lean behaviors, build capability and ensure the organization stays on course.

An enterprise doesn't need to maintain a significant organizational entity to support the long-term Lean initiative. However, a core group is required:

- ✔ To maintain, improve, guide, and focus the organization's Lean practices.
- ✔ To integrate Lean practices into other organizations — such as new suppliers, merger or acquisition partners, and new distributors.
- ✔ To stay abreast of Lean developments and trends in other industries.

In the years to come, as you become a mature Lean organization, you must continue to invest in the people and the organization. People will flow through your organization; the new ones need to develop the same capabilities and cultural awareness as the old-timers, and the old-timers need to keep their skills fresh. Even the most successful organizations experience drift naturally over time. To minimize the drift, invest in your people, reinforce your culture, keep close to your customer, relentlessly look for ways to reduce waste, measure what you value and always remember for the long term where you ideally want to go — your ideal state.

Part III
Understanding Flow and the Value Stream

The 5th Wave   By Rich Tennant

"Something I can help you with, sir?"

In this part . . .

Now that you know the basics, it's time to get started. At the heart of Lean is a focus on the customer and a spirit of continuous improvement. In this part, you figure out how the customer defines value. You discover how to analyze your business today and create a vision of the future. You also find out how to eliminate waste through continuous improvement of kaizen.

Chapter 6

Seeing Value through the Eyes of the Customer

In This Chapter

▶ Understanding the concept of value

▶ Identifying what customers value

▶ Differentiating customers and consumers

*Y*ou may think the concept of value is pretty straightforward, but the reality is that everyone has their own perception of what constitutes value. What people value and how they value it changes with circumstance and time. But, as mutable as the criteria for defining value may be, Lean provides a framework for understanding what customers and consumers value, and then helping you understand how to provide that value in the most effective way. As you define what your customers value, you also define the very nature of your activities and actions: what you should be doing, how you should be doing it, and even *if* you should be doing it.

Consider this: When the coffee-shop barista writes your name on the cup for your double latte, is he "adding value" to your drink? When you check out at the grocery, is the full-service checkout "adding value" to your purchasing experience? When you fill out the form at the doctor's office for your annual checkup, are you "adding value" to your health? Maybe — and maybe not. It all depends on how you define *value*.

Defining "value" is important because it forms the foundation upon which you build Lean processes to deliver that value and satisfy your customer. In this chapter, we provide the basic definition of value, and show you the Lean standard definition of value. You discover how to distinguish customers and consumers and learn ways to understand what they value.

What Is Value?

Simply stated, *value* is the worth placed upon something. That something can be goods, services, or both. The worth can be expressed in terms of money, an exchange, a utility, a merit, or even a principle or standard.

Who determines the value? *Customers determine value.* And there are billions of them — individuals, businesses, social groups, and other organizations.

Although Lean provides us a standard definition of value, what is more difficult to understand is what these customers deem worthy and then how to create, apply, measure, and translate their definition of value. What are the actions and activities that actually create value? How does a person or organization come to value a particular product or service? What determines how much a person is willing to "pay" for it — with their time, money, or other resources? In addition, how do they exchange value?

Value isn't absolute — it doesn't occur in isolation. Value is relative to such factors as location, place, time, timing, form, fit, function, integration, interactions, resources, markets, demand, and economics. But in all cases, *value is defined by the customer.*

The process of *value creation* — the act of developing and delivering a product or service that the customer desires and is willing to invest in having it — is usually lengthy and complicated.

Consider the complexity involved in the process of creating value in something that many people regularly take for granted: autonomous, personal mobility in the form of the automobile. In this case, value creation involves not just the design and assembly of the thousands of parts in a car, but also the highway system, the petroleum refining and distribution system, the maintenance and repair industry, the insurance industry, and the knowledge and conventions enforced in the millions of other drivers out there that you have to interact with in order to move about with some degree of certainty. Every driver antes up, in the form of sticker prices and insurance payments, gasoline and maintenance fees, highway and other taxes, greenhouse gases and environmental damage, personal risk, and, of course, lots and lots of time. Autonomous, personal mobility is an extremely high-value item, and each of the previously mentioned elements contributes a critical piece to that total value.

The cycle of value means that, in any endeavor — large or small — all of the activities, actions, and steps involved must lead to an end-result that has value for whoever is consuming it. And they must easily perceive that value, be able to readily quantify it, and willingly exchange for it. Meanwhile, the providers must deliver that value for some net benefit or profit.

To Add Value or Not to Add Value, That Is the Question

Every activity in your organization either adds value or it doesn't. In Lean, you analyze each activity in every process for its contribution to value, as defined by your customer. In the ideal state, every activity directly meets your customer's criteria for value — and if it doesn't, you don't do it.

Makes you think, doesn't it? Everyone and everything in the process doing *only* what creates customer value? Well, ideally that's what Lean is all about!

Think about this principle in the context of what you do for your customers, whoever they may be. How much of all the time, people, resources, capital, space, and energy consumed around you and by you is directly creating value for your customers? Now put on the other hat, and think about it from the customers' point of view. When you're paying for a product or service — with your valuable time, money, and effort — how much are you spending to get what you really want . . . and *only* what you really want?

In this section, we fill you in on Lean's strict definition for *value-added* and *non-value-added*. You will understand non-value added according to the three *M*s — *muda, mura,* and *muri*. Some activities in your process do not add value according to the customer's definition, but they are unfortunately necessary for your processes to function. We will tell you what to do in those cases, too.

Defining value-added

In Lean, always define value from the customer's viewpoint. The customer is the one — and only one — who defines the value of the output of a process. For an activity to be *value added,* you must meet *all* three precise criteria:

- ✓ The customer must be willing to pay for the activity.
- ✓ The activity must transform the product or service in some way.
- ✓ The activity must be done correctly the first time.

This strict definition applies to everything. To add value in a process, all actions, activities, processes, persons, organizations, systems, pieces of equipment, and any other resources committed to the process must meet all three criteria.

You can easily spot value-added activity:

- ✔ At the carwash, it's when someone actually washes the car.
- ✔ At the hospital, it is when the patient receives treatment.
- ✔ On the assembly floor, it's when someone is actually putting parts together.

In each of these cases, it's clearly what the customer is paying for; it's transforming the product or providing the primary service; and as long as it's being done correctly the first time, it is by-definition contributing directly to customer value (that is, it's *value-added*).

Defining non-value-added

In Lean, if an activity does not meet all three value-added criteria (see the preceding section), then it is deemed officially to be *non-value-added*. Either the customer isn't willing to pay for it, or the activity hasn't transformed the product or service in any measurable way, or the activity wasn't done correctly the first time. In other words, from the customer's perspective it's wasted time or effort.

At the carwash, it's the order-taker, the car-mover, the cashier, the queuing time, the excess water, and the customer waiting lounge. At the hospital, it's the check-in time, the wait time, filling out forms, inconclusive tests, and yummy hospital food. On the assembly floor, it's the parts bins, the travel time, the setup time, the inspections and testing, the conveyors, the supervisors, the bad-parts reject basket.

In each of these cases, the item or person wasn't something the customer wanted to pay for or the activity didn't directly transform the product or service, or something wasn't done correctly.

Wait a minute, you say: Some of those things are important, even necessary! Customers have to pay for what it takes to provide a product or service. Employees need supervisors. Forms convey important information. Customer lounges keep people happy — you can't just make them wait outside, right? And bad components have to be removed — after all, isn't it a good thing when you catch a failure and don't ship a bad product to the customer?

Sorry to burst your bubble, but if the activity in question doesn't meet all three criteria, it's just not adding customer value. The customer lounge is nice, but it doesn't get your car washed better. Filling out forms may get you admitted to the hospital, but it doesn't directly contribute to your treatment.

The reject basket means you caught the failures, but they're a living example of something that wasn't done correctly the first time. None of this means that you might not want or even need to do these things based on your existing process model, but it *does* mean that those activities are not directly adding value for the customer.

In Lean, non-value-added activities are further described by the three *Ms —* *muda, mura,* and *muri:*

- ✔ *Muda* **(waste):** *Muda* is an activity that consumes resources without creating value for the customer. (We define the seven standard forms of waste in detail in Chapter 2.) There are two types of *muda:*

  - Type-1 *muda* includes actions that are non-value-added, but that are for some other reason deemed necessary. These forms of waste usually cannot be eliminated immediately.

  - Type-2 *muda* are those activities that are non-value-added and are unnecessary. These activities are the first targets for elimination.

- ✔ *Mura* **(unevenness):** *Mura* is waste caused by variation in quality, cost, or delivery. When activities don't go smoothly or consistently, *mura* is the result. *Mura* consists of all the resources that are wasted when quality cannot be predicted, such as the cost of testing, inspection, containment, rework, returns, overtime, and unscheduled travel to the customer. You apply variation reduction techniques to eliminate *mura*.

- ✔ *Muri* **(overdoing):** *Muri* is the unnecessary or unreasonable overburdening of people, equipment, or systems by demands that exceed capacity. From a Lean perspective, *muri* applies to the design of work and tasks. For example, tasks with *muri* have movements that are harmful, wasteful, or unnecessary. You perform ergonomic evaluations and detailed job analysis of operations to eliminate movements that are either harmful or unnecessary.

As a Lean practitioner, you strive to eliminate all non-value added activities. If you can't immediately eliminate them, then continuously reduce them until you eventually do eliminate them.

When non-value-added seems like value-added

By their very nature, processes are full of waste that masquerades as value creation. Many activities may seem as though they're necessary or value-added, but upon closer examination, and through the eyes of the customer —according to the three criteria listed in the "Defining value-added" section earlier in this chapter — they're not.

Muda, particularly type-1 *muda* (see the preceding section), is usually created because of current facility or technology limitations, government regulations, or unchallenged company business practices. Oftentimes, *muda* is so insidious that the organization is blind to it. Identifying *muda* is particularly difficult when *muda* is programmed into computer systems.

Seeking out and eliminating *muda* takes effort — it requires someone to challenge the status quo. Sometimes people don't think they have the time or energy to do that level of work. Sometimes they don't feel like they have the tools or authority to change the current state. Sometimes they don't know where to begin. And sometimes, they just don't want to change. Yet the fact of the matter is that when you put in the effort to identify the *muda,* you will find a gold mine of opportunity.

Common examples of type 1-*muda* include the following:

- ✔ Bureaucracy, such as forms, reports, traditions, and approvals
- ✔ Administrative activities, such as supervision, accounting, and legal
- ✔ Product support, such as product testing, critical inspection, and transportation

Type-1 *muda* includes all the things that surround or support the value-added functions, but they don't actually do any direct transformation themselves.

You may insist, "These activities are necessary for the business!" And you may even be right — maybe they *are* necessary. But whether they're necessary or not, it doesn't change the fact that they are non-value-added. Here are some examples:

- ✔ **The admission process at a hospital:** Surely it must be value-added. After all, how else can you get in to the hospital to be treated — what could be more value-added than that? Not so. Nothing in the admission process directly contributes to the treatment of a patient; therefore, it is not adding customer value.

- ✔ **The in-line inspection station in the automobile manufacturing industry:** You need to ensure operations are performed correctly; you must protect your customer. Although this is may be true, you cannot transform a product through inspection, you can only mitigate risk. The most well-choreographed inspection station, while seemingly necessary, is always non-value added.

✔ **Staying late and pushing extra hard to get a job done and meet a deadline:** The job has to get done, and people will rise to the occasion, right? Yes, but consider the cost. Not only do people tend to make more mistakes when they drive too hard without rest, but burned-out people leave and take critical knowledge and experience with them. On occasion, working in this manner may seem necessary, but no matter how you look at it, it's a waste.

Understanding How the Customer Defines Value

Who is this elusive customer — the one who defines value? If you're like most people, you're thinking it's the person at the retail end of the line — the one who buys the product or service, who walks into a store, gets out his wallet, pays for something, and leaves with it. Actually, that person is a special form of customer known as the *consumer;* we cover the consumer in the "Understanding How the Consumer Defines Value" section, later in this chapter.

The *customer,* as far as Lean is concerned, is the person or entity who is *the recipient of the product or service you produce.* For many, the customer is another business. For others, the customer is someone inside their own business. Sometimes the customer is a specific individual; other times, the customer is a group or team. In any case, the customer is the one who places the value on your output.

Uncovering the elusive customer

The world has grown so complicated that sometimes it's difficult to determine just who anybody's customer really is. So many functions, supply chains, outsourced providers, contract distributors, and channels are part of the mix. In the Lean world, this question — "Who is your customer?" — is fundamental because the customer is the one who matters. The customer is the *only* one who truly defines the value of what you produce.

Your customer is likely not the consumer — the end user of the product or service you provide. You're probably part of a supply chain or network for some set of designs, materials, products, information or services that are combined in a complex series of processes to provide that end-item solution to a consumer somewhere. Your customer is therefore most likely an individual (or set of individuals) within a group who pays for the products and services you generate.

In Figure 6-1, we show you a SIPOC (suppliers, inputs, process, outputs, and customers) diagram that lists the suppliers and inputs to a process on the one side, and the outputs and customers on the other. Considering the process itself as a black box for the moment, focus on what outputs you produce and who receives them. This recipient is the elusive customer you're looking for. The SIPOC diagram is a standard tool in process management that helps identify and characterize these key driving influences on a process.

Figure 6-1: A SIPOC diagram.

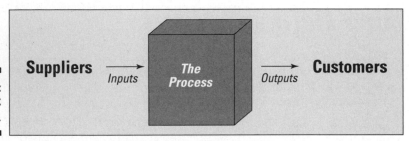

Every process — no matter how large-scale and all-encompassing, or small and focused — has a customer or customers. Large-scale processes, such as order entry or production, have a broad spectrum of many types of customers. In small processes, such as screen assembly for the latest mobile phone or the daily setup of a jewelry department in retail, the customer is much more narrowly and specifically defined. But in every case and at every level in any organization or endeavor, processes have customers.

As you consider who receives such process outputs in your own organization, consider these tips:

✔ **When you're improving a small process within the overall process, recognize its role in the larger scheme of things.** Many sub-processes — each with their own customers — make up the larger process of creating the total product or facilitating a complete service.

✔ **Your process may produce outputs for multiple customers.** Every customer has their unique characteristics, and you'll regularly need to adjust your process according to requirements, attributes, and situations for each one.

✔ **Recognize how your process output serves the end consumer.** If your process does not directly supply the consumer, then your customer is a middleman. Your direct customer may be adding, filtering, interpreting or changing how the end consumer defines value. Your direct customer has different motivations and needs from the consumer. Make sure that you are meeting your direct customer's needs, but don't lose sight of the consumer's expectations and definition of value.

✔ **Don't become distracted by stakeholders.** A *stakeholder* is someone with a vested interest elsewhere in the greater enterprise. Stakeholders may include managers, board members, stockholders, employees, suppliers, family members of employees, retirees, government, or the community. Stakeholders are important, but they are not the customer. Stakeholders have an interest in company performance or results. When a business is distracted by the stakeholders, it may lose the focus on the process and take short-term actions that will actually increase *mura*.

Considering customer value

The customer is the purchaser of your goods and services, and they are the recipient of the outputs from your process. The customer has options, so why would they choose the outputs from your process? What goes into a customer's purchase decision? And how does the customer determine what they're going to pay?

The answers to these questions come down to value. The customer will choose your option when they believe it represents the best overall value for them. The customer has many requirements and decision criteria, and their methods of assigning value may be formal or informal, but ultimately they will place a worth on process and outputs and will select yours when they believe the outputs and the process best fulfill their requirements.

Understanding customer satisfaction

Because the customer assigns value based on the degree to which the process outputs fulfill their requirements, this means that the greater the fulfillment of requirements, the higher the customer's satisfaction, and therefore the greater the customer's attributed value.

Not all customer requirements are created equal. Some requirements are extremely important *must-have*s, other requirements are *nice-to-have*s, and still other requirements fall somewhere in the middle. How the fulfillment of these different requirements translates to customer satisfaction is not always obvious. Don't worry — in this section, we spell it all out.

In the 1980s, Japanese professor Noriaki Kano developed a visual way to understand customer requirements (see Figure 6-2). This model is a graphical plot of fulfillment versus satisfaction. What Kano recognized is that customer requirements naturally come in three flavors, and the extent to which a process fulfills each type of requirement directly affects the level of customer satisfaction and perceived value.

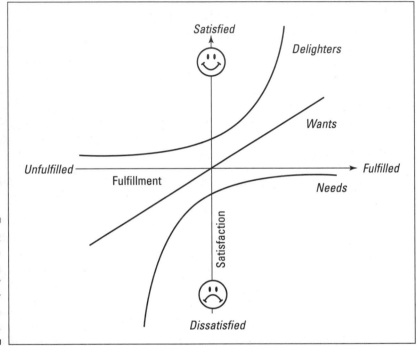

Figure 6-2:
Using Kano modeling to classify customer requirements.

✔ **Needs:** Needs are fundamental — they're absolute requirements. You must fulfill the needs of your customer. If your customer has unfulfilled needs, that very quickly translates to complete dissatisfaction. However, at best, fulfilling your customer's needs results in neutral satisfaction. In other words, meeting your customer's needs is a thankless job, but failing to meet your customer's needs is disastrous.

✔ **Wants:** Wants are expectations. If you don't fulfill your customer's wants, the customer will be dissatisfied; if you do fulfill your customer's wants, the customer will be satisfied. The relationship is linear: No lack of fulfillment of wants will ever create the dissatisfaction that unmet *needs* will, and likewise no degree of fulfillment of wants will ever have the satisfaction potential of the third type of requirement — the delighters.

✔ **Delighters:** Delighters are pure upside. No one really expects them, so there's no penalty if they're missing. But the level of customer satisfaction increases exponentially if the process fulfills these most whimsical of requirements.

Take a moment to ponder the application of the Kano model to your business or organization. Of the many requirements you chase and manage, which fall into each of the three categories? How well do you fulfill them? How satisfied are your customers?

Breaking down customer requirements

Fulfilling the customer's wants, needs, and delighters is the path to customer satisfaction. Kano modeling and Quality Function Deployment (QFD; this is covered in Chapter 10) are two tools that you can use to capture and understand customer requirements.

To understand your customer's requirements, ask them! Talk to your customer extensively. Involve your customer in your planning and development through interviews, surveys, clinics, user groups, design reviews, or online communities.

After you identify your customer's requirements, you can analyze how effectively you're satisfying those requirements. When you understand how effective you are, *then* can you optimize value creation, ensuring you meet all three conditions of *value-added* with your products, processes, or services.

To create a solution and fulfill your customer's requirements, first translate them into product or service *specifications*. Start by documenting these specifications at the highest level, known as the *top level,* the *system level,* or the *A level*; then, successively expand the specifications into subsystems or sub-processes, each of which fulfills a specific role in achieving the overall objective defined by the top-level specification. Within each of these levels, categorize the specifications into the following "spec-types":

- ✔ **Form and fit:** What are the shapes and sizes, the constraints and the tolerances of the way the product or service (or components thereof) must be designed, must align, or must interact?

- ✔ **Functionality:** What are all the things that the product or service must do? How must it do them? How uniquely? The specifications are usually described through a set of action verbs, but they may also describe aesthetics and other physical or operational attributes.

- ✔ **Maintainability:** What are the support and maintenance requirements? Is the customer or consumer required or able to maintain it, or portions of it, themselves? How will it be supported?

- ✔ **Perception:** How are you perceived in the market? What is your brand identity? What has been the customer's past experience with your organization? Have you had any bad press that may affect a purchasing decision? What is the experience you want to create for the customer?

- **Performance:** How quickly, how often, or for how long must the product or service perform its functions?

- **Pricing model:** What is the price that the customer will pay for the product or service? Is the price dynamic (will it or should it change over time)? What is the desired profit margin? What is the total cost picture?

- **Purchase:** What are the various purchasing models and terms by which the customer will buy? What should the purchasing experience be?

- **Reliability:** With what levels of reliability and dependability must the product or service perform its functions? What is the pedigree and what experience do you bring to ensure that reliability?

- **Safety:** Are there safety aspects to the product or service — as related to the suppliers, consumers, maintenance groups, or even the general public?

- **Scalability:** If the customer wants more, how readily should they be able to have more? Do any of the other requirements elements change with scalability?

- **Security:** Security concerns are a separate requirements element. Could the product or service pose a security risk in any way, either directly or indirectly?

These categories of requirements apply during any phase of the product or service life cycle; they apply to the core processes of design, development, delivery, and service, as well as support processes, including sales, finance, legal, marketing, human resources, information technology, and facilities. Every process must reflect these elements to ensure the product or service provided will properly fulfill the customer's needs, wants, and desires. These categories apply not just to the end consumer, but also to your immediate customer and each successive customer in the chain. No matter where your process sits in the big picture, these categories of requirements apply to you!

In today's connected information world, when anyone can express their opinions or dissatisfaction instantly on line, it is even more important to know and delight your customers.

Remember that what your customer values is not static. Customer interests and satisfaction change over time. The Kano model has a "downward migration": over time, delighters become wants, and wants become needs. Having processes that connect you with your customers will help you stay agile and change with their changing demands.

Understanding How the Consumer Defines Value

The ultimate customer is the *consumer*. The consumer is defined as "one who obtains goods and services for his own use," rather than for resale or use in producing another product or service. Consumers are the catalyst in the value chain; their buying action triggers the flow of activities on the part of the many product and service providers whose contributions ultimately fulfill the consumers' requirements and values.

As such, the consumer holds a uniquely important customer position, and it's incumbent on you — regardless of your position in the value chain — to be aware of consumer motivation and behavior. In most cases, you work directly for your immediate customer because they specify your requirements and receive your outputs; however, consumer actions will ripple through the chain to affect you, so you must also understand how the *consumer* defines value.

Recognize, too, that although the entire stream of activity is ultimately oriented toward satisfying the consumer, the consumer's requirements and values do not necessarily align with the processes and agendas of all the many value-stream players providing those goods and services. Your direct customer will likely represent the consumer's needs to you differently than the consumer would, so you must be in a position to understand and balance your direct customer's requirements with those of the end consumer.

Because Lean processes are customer focused, they respond to the requirements of the customer and refine their processes accordingly. Although each successive process may have a unique set of customer requirements, the starting point is with the consumer, because the consumer is the first point of requirements definition. The consumer is the first to assign value and first to vote with their wallet. The consumer kicks off the whole process.

Many organizations are agenda-centric, believing that they can foist their agenda on their consumer market. These organizations are not customer focused and do not practice the Lean art of customer-driven process definition. In recent years, it has become increasingly difficult for such companies to thrive. Customer-centric organizations fare far better.

Responding to the consumer

Organizations of all types strive to understand and anticipate the consumer. The better an organization can predict consumer behavior; the more effectively it can fulfill the consumer's needs, wants, and delighters (see "Understanding customer satisfaction," earlier in this chapter). In some cases, you need to understand broad consumer behavior and then produce products in volume for the general consumer market. In other cases, you have to maintain the capacity to produce a product or deliver a service on demand. In most cases, it's a mix.

Most companies aren't fluid or flexible enough to wait for a customer-demand event to act across their entire supply chain, but many such demand build-to-order models exist at the direct consumer end of the market. Can you imagine a world where all companies operated that way? Can you think of a few who currently do? Here are a few:

- Most fast-food restaurants now build your meal to order. They have the basic ingredients on hand (based on past consumer behavior), and when you order, they prepare your meal to your specifications and deliver it to you in a matter of minutes.

- Eyeglasses used to take days or weeks to arrive, but now some companies have moved the lab into the retail location. Your glasses are now ready in an hour.

- Business consultants wait for the call and then configure their solutions based on the requirements. Consultants are extremely adept at forging new solutions in near real-time, based on the application of their latest knowledge, and quickly preparing a new solution for the client.

In these types of applications, the value stream is closely connected to the needs of the consumer. For example, the disk-drive manufacturer who supplies hard drives to the computer assembler follows the consumer demand market very closely. Similarly, food suppliers to restaurants know what the diner is requesting — organic, gluten-free, and low-carb are recent trends in mainstream dining.

Consumers further influence the market through the unique spin they have on requirements. In addition to the Kano profiles and formalized requirements flow, consumers exhibit specific behaviors and styles. These styles set the stage for how the entire value stream — and all the intermediate processes and customers — will act. Consumers largely fall into one of eight behavior style types, as defined by Sproles and Kendall's Consumer Style Inventory:

- Perfectionism; high-quality conscious

- Brand conscious

- Novelty-fashion conscious

✔ Recreational, hedonistic shopping conscious

✔ Price and "value-for-the-money" shopping conscious

✔ Impulsiveness

✔ Confusion over choice of brands, stores, and consumer information

✔ Habitual, brand-loyal orientation toward consumption

Consider the eyewear shop that promises to deliver your glasses in an hour. What must that store do to live up to its promise? It must have all the materials, processes, and services on site to fulfill the needs of their customers and market. This includes having a sufficient variety of styles on hand to appeal to the variety of consumer interests — they need the designer section, the hip-and-trendy section, and the value section. They must also maintain the right level of inventory of frames and the lens blanks to go with them. They must maintain their equipment locally. They must have trained technicians on site. And they must be conveniently located for consumer access (in shopping malls). All these elements come together to provide the consumer with glasses in an hour.

Not all consumers purchase the same way. Technology and globalization are changing the options for purchasing, but not everyone will adapt to the changes at the same rate.

Online purchasing and mobile Internet devices have changed consumer behavior. Consumers see value in going online, both to check out and to check you out. They relish having the tools at their fingertips to research and make more educated purchases. More than ever, they know what they want, they're empowered by knowing how to get it, and they'll search until they find it. This connectivity is causing companies to become increasingly innovative in the ways they reach their existing markets, as well as penetrate new ones. Some consumers will do the research online, but still want to talk to a human or buy from a store. Other consumers are content to do everything online — from researching to buying to returns. Lean practitioners recognize these new channels represent different value paths with customers and consumers, and that processes must adapt.

Traditionally, Lean applications have neglected to focus sufficiently on many of the processes that the consumer touches directly. These processes include customer service, technical support, warranty, and more. Business reach can be improved dramatically by improving the processes that support these services. When a consumer is delighted by a product or experience, that consumer will be your biggest advocate. Conversely, when a customer is dissatisfied, he can be your biggest detractor — and he'll use the World Wide Web to let everyone know!

Understanding what consumers value

Consumers are customers with a twist. In addition to the behaviors that business customers exhibit across the value chain (the so-called business-to-business, or B2B, group), the consumers have unique requirements and demands. The business-to-consumer relationship (B2C) must interpret these demands and properly manage them — directly or indirectly — back upstream to all the suppliers.

Understanding the distribution of styles in your market is a key step to understanding what your consumers value. Depending on the industry, the product or service, the magnitude of the purchase and other factors, the relationship with consumers through the pre- and post-buying phases ultimately determines the degree of your success. Table 6-1 provides a list of consumer interests. For each interest, the consumer has demands, which place constraints on the processes that support them.

Table 6-1	Mapping Consumer Demands to Process Constraints	
Interest	*Consumer Demands*	*Lean Process Constraints*
Final Purchase Price	Price-point sensitivity Total system or solution price	Price pressures are distributed across all providers, each with their own cost and profit profiles.
Quality	Initial quality Safety/Security Durability Ease of maintenance	Each provider must deliver to quality levels that combine to support the final end-item quality, create no safety hazards and are easy to maintain.
Delivery	Fast delivery Delivery on demand	Every component must be available exactly when required by the processes that build the final consumer product or service. The delivery system must be able to meet the consumer's delivery expectations.
Service	Immediate assistance Friendly service Reasonable terms	Services must be provided at each level — or combined to provide effective consumer service. Timing and completeness of response are critical.

Interest	Consumer Demands	Lean Process Constraints
Purchase Terms	Monthly payments Favorable rates	The consumer's financing and payment terms affect everyone in the supply chain.
Image	Fashion, trendiness Newness, novelty Premium value	Everything is affected — from design to manufacture to delivery and terms — for all component products and services.
Convenience	Open 24/7/365 Brand preference	You must produce and deliver in ways that the consumer values most.
Returns	Unconditional returnability	Reverse logistics processes must meet the consumer's needs — understanding the circumstances of responding to satisfaction issues.
Experience	Environment and amenities	Make the customer experience inviting and delightful. Understand what delighters can be added to perceived customer value with minimal impact on the operating cost.

In simple terms, consumers want what they want, when they want it, at the price they're willing to pay for it, and if something goes wrong, they want accurate and friendly assistance or the ability to return it easily. These demands place tremendous pressure and constraints on each provider of the goods and services that combine to provide that end item to the consumer.

Companies are just now beginning to include the interface between the company and consumer as part of their Lean efforts. Processes from the point the consumer purchases through customer service and technical support are new frontiers for Lean implementation. These processes can make or break your relationship with consumers (not to mention their friends and families!), and are a new spring of improvement possibilities. Eliminating waste and creating a positive, value-added customer experience will increase competitive edge.

Think about how much the morning cup of coffee has changed. Starbucks created the coffee experience — any time of day, people could meet up, work, or just relax in one of their shops. Customers were willing to pay a premium price for a cup of java to delight in the experience. Now, people expect a Starbucks on every corner; they expect their exotic drink quickly, made-to-order, and consistently. The former delighter has now become a necessity.

Food chains like McDonalds and retailers like Target are incorporating the "coffee experience" into their stores with expanded coffee menus and free wi-fi.

Think also about how personal computing has changed. Not too long ago the standard was a desktop system; then it was the laptop. Then Apple introduced the iPad — a light, ultra-portable, powerful, and sexy computing experience — and the game changed again. Established industry players are feeling the challenge to compete with these new customer expectations.

Beginning with the Y2K phenomenon, many companies outsourced call center work to other countries. Some companies have had to rethink their approach, because consumers struggled to communicate with the people on the other end of the line. When the consumer was already frustrated, this made matters worse. True costs increased, because the companies alienated their customer base. The companies failed to understand fully what the consumer values.

The consumer is the ultimate customer. What the consumer values is ultimately what counts. Although you may have intermediary customers who have their own set of values, it is important not to lose sight of the consumer's wants and needs.

Chapter 7

You Are Here: Mapping the Current State

*U*ltimately, all organizations are defined by what they produce. Not only do the most successful organizations produce goods and services that are highly valued by customers or consumers, but they also produce them in a manner that sustains the organization's viability over the long term. In the Lean enterprise, these capabilities are not an accident. They're the result of a very conscious awareness that every activity is really a *process* that adds some amount of measurable value.

Even more, these organizations understand and capitalize on how all of their processes work together to provide value to their customers and consumers. Think of materials and information flowing through a series of connected processes that ultimately deliver a product or service to a customer. Lean organizations call this the *value stream.* And a *value-stream map* (VSM) is the graphical representation of the value stream. The value-stream map has an enterprise focus, instead of a functional focus, because it covers all the activities required deliver value to the customer. It depicts all the steps and highlights any ineffectiveness in the value stream. As a Lean practitioner, you will use value-stream maps to visualize three different "states" of your processes: your current state — the way things are now; the ideal state — the way things would work in the ideal case where all work is only value-added; and the next future state — the state of your processes after your next improvement effort (more on the ideal and next future states in Chapter 8).

In this chapter, you learn more about the value stream. You also learn how to look at your value stream from a macro and micro level. You also see how to create, use, and validate the current state value-stream map.

Introducing the Value Stream

If you've ever stood alongside a stream and watched the water flow, you probably noticed how the water runs and how the current changes. When there are no obstructions, and the volume is just right, the water moves freely and easily. But of course most streams have disturbances. Sticks, rocks, and fallen trees dam and disturb the flow. If there has been a storm, all sorts of debris drifts downstream. Where there are rocks, white water appears. Too much or too little water for the size of the riverbed, and there's more whitewater.

If you liken the stream to a process, the ideal condition is when the process flows unobstructed, like smooth, even water. The sticks and stones in a process are things like variances, defects, inventories, rework, and other forms of waste — the non-value-added activities that block the flow of the product to the customer. Strive to remove the debris and smooth out the flow.

Visualizing the value stream

The term *value stream* is used in Lean as the basis for describing how all activities line up and work together to produce a given product or service. The activities combine to form a process of value creation. The process flow consists of activities that are both value-added and non-value-added (see Chapter 6).

The stream is always viewed from the customer's perspective, ideally from the ultimate customer's (the consumer) perspective. In viewing the value stream, you start where the stream ends, with the consumer's view, and you track it all the way upstream to the smallest tributary — the sources of raw materials and labor. Figure 7-1 depicts a product value stream.

For any product or service, it takes many activities and different types of materials and people all contributing together to make it happen. Organizations bring together materials — sometimes from all over the world — to make products. Likewise, many services are global. As consumers, we experience the final product or what's called "the last mile" because we're at the mouth of the stream, but a lot is going on upriver!

Think for a moment about all the things that have to happen for UPS or FedEx to deliver a parcel overnight. Consider all the events that must be coordinated perfectly and must occur at precisely the right time in the value stream to deliver that parcel to the right address, on time, and in perfect condition. Sorting and handling, trucks, airplanes, tracking information — a staggering degree of logistical sophistication.

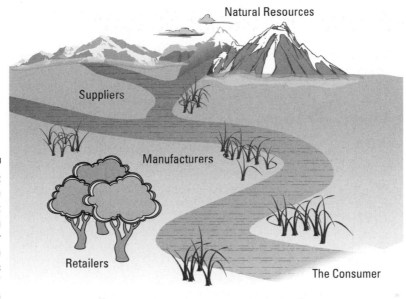

Natural Resources

Suppliers

Manufacturers

Retailers

The Consumer

Figure 7-1:
The value
stream:
Each
contributor
adds value
as products
"flow"
to the
consumer.

The Value Stream

Now, visualize something different: the value stream required to deliver a new automobile to the showroom. Literally tens of thousands of parts must arrive on the manufacturing line — in the right order, of the right quality, in the right color, with the right orientation — for assembly to the right vehicle.

A value stream manager (see Chapter 14) oversees the value stream, but everyone in the organization has a role in the value stream, and each has the responsibility to know how their part interrelates to deliver value to the customer in the best way. Visualize how each part contributes to the overall value stream through the value-stream map.

The Fundamentals of Value-Stream Maps

A *value-stream map* (VSM) is a graphical representation of how all the steps in any process line up to produce a product or service. A VSM also depicts the flow of information needed to trigger the process into action. In the product world, the process may be about something physical, like making a mobile phone, or a car, creating a design, or authoring a report. In the service world, the process may be calling a help desk, buying premade food for dinner, or obtaining a driver's license.

Your initial value-stream map shows the *current state* — the way things are now and how they currently work.

Map reading 101

Figure 7-2 shows a typical value-stream map, drawn to standard conventions. If it looks like Greek to you now, don't worry — just keep reading. We explain everything you see and it will all make sense shortly.

A value-stream map flows from left to right with time — raw materials come in on the left, the process steps line up in order of occurrence, and the finished products or services exit for the customer to the right. The main flow is like the river channel, and the ancillary processes are like tributaries that feed the main process. When constructing a value-stream map, time the process steps — how long does each step take? Also, categorize them as either value-added or non-value-added. So you see that a full value-stream map includes not just the flow of materials, but also the flow of the supporting information.

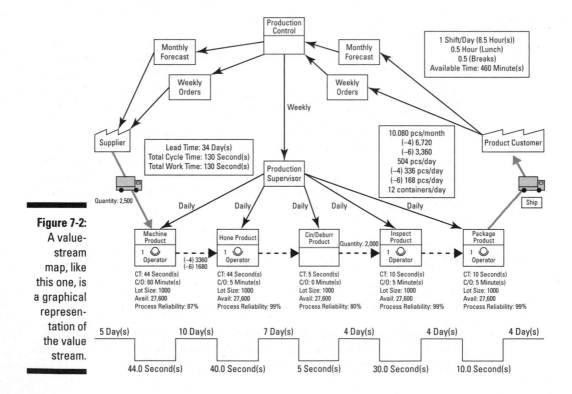

Figure 7-2: A value-stream map, like this one, is a graphical representation of the value stream.

The purpose of a value-stream map

A value stream map is a powerful tool. It provides information that other process diagrams or activity descriptions don't.

- ✔ The VSM always has the customer's perspective and focuses on delivering to the customer's expectations, wants, and needs.

- ✔ The VSM, in a single view, provides a complete, fact-based, time-series representation of the stream of activities — from beginning to end — required to deliver a product or service to the customer.

- ✔ The VSM provides a common language and common view to analyze the value stream.

- ✔ The VSM shows how the information flows to trigger and support those activities.

- ✔ The VSM shows you how much of the time your activities are adding customer value — and how much is wasted not adding value.

- ✔ The VSM shows you where your activities add value and where they don't, enabling you to see what ultimate impedes your ability to supply and satisfy your customer.

After you construct the value-stream map, not only do you see the process from the customer's point of view, but you also see what is required and how long it takes to deliver the product or service to the customer. The VSM shows you the primary activities, as well as the ancillary processes. And the VSM is not limited to the traditional functional perspective — it shows all the contributing activities and processes.

The *customer* identified at the end of a value-stream map is not necessarily the end customer or consumer who buys or consumes the final product or service; it's usually the customer of this process because you often start with a smaller scope for your VSM. It may be another business or even someone or some other function within your own organization.

The people who use a value-stream map

Who uses a VSM? The users are many because it helps everyone involved. Here are some examples of how people in your organization may use the VSM:

- ✔ **Process owners:** They own the cost of the process and the value it creates. In a VSM, process owners can quickly identify the opportunities for improvement throughout the whole value stream.

✔ **Process designers:** They design and help implement changes to improve processes. They use a VSM to focus on internal process steps and minimize non-value-added activities within and among those process steps.

✔ **Process workers:** They work within processes and must understand the context of the process and process changes. They see in a VSM where their own process activities are located, and they can quickly identify ways to improve their process.

✔ **Supply-chain managers:** They must optimize the interfaces with suppliers. They use a VSM to look for opportunities to establish delivery windows, consolidated delivery routes (known in Lean as *milk runs*), and level schedules, as well as other opportunities to improve the logistics of the value stream.

✔ **Procurement managers:** They negotiate relationships with suppliers for the long term. In a VSM, procurement managers find opportunities to work with suppliers to receive incoming products and services in a manner that supports the Lean initiatives in the facility. This sometimes includes bringing Lean principles into the supplier community.

✔ **Information technology (IT):** They manage the supporting information flow. They see in a VSM where they need to develop systems to support Lean efforts and properly link upstream and downstream systems of the value stream.

✔ **Value-stream managers:** They own the value-stream at an enterprise level. They use a VSM at a high level to guide the organization toward improvement opportunities to serve the customer more effectively.

The elements of a value-stream map

The VSM is a snapshot of the value stream at a specific point in its evolution. It's a graphical representation of all the steps occurring in a process. In addition, a VSM contains essential, descriptive process information. When constructing a value-stream map, follow these conventions:

✔ **Process steps:** Show each of the process steps in the value stream, including both value-added (VA) and non-value-added (NVA). Include process statistics like cycle time, NVA time, changeover time, number of operators, number of pieces, amount of inventory, and percent defective.

✔ **Inventory:** Show inventory storage on the VSM, including the amount and movement of inventory within the process.

✔ **Information flow:** Show all supporting information required by the process on the VSM. This can include orders, schedules, specifications, *kanban signals* (a *kanban* is a signal to replenish inventory in a pull system), shipping information, and more.

✔ **Box score:** Include a summary of the key operational metrics of the process on the VSM. At a minimum, include a summary of the total lead time of a process with the value-added and non-value-added times identified. You may also include information like the distance traveled, parts per shift, scrap, pieces produced per labor hour, changeover time, inventory turns, uptime, downtime, and more — it's whatever matters in your business.

✔ **Lead time:** Along the bottom of the VSM include the current lead time performance of the value stream. *Lead time* is the amount of time that one piece takes to flow completely through the process. The time is divided into value-added and non-value-added portions. At a glance, you can see where the major portions of non-value-added time occur.

✔ **Takt time:** Place a box in the upper-right-hand corner of the VSM to show the customer demand rate or *takt time*. This rate is determined by the customer demand and production time available. Ideally, all steps in the value stream should then produce to this rate.

Teams often find it unwieldy to try to map the whole value stream at a detailed level all at one time, so they start with a smaller scope. Start with your immediate customer and map the stream back to the point where you receive inputs from a supplier. Just don't lose sight of where in the overall value stream your process fits.

Pick one *product family* (a series of products or services that pass through the same processing steps) to map. If the product family is processed at more than one location, for instance an eastern service center and a western service center, then focus on one location, but include representatives from the other location on the improvement team.

Pack Your Bags: What You'll Need to Get Started

Before you actually make your value-stream map, you will need to do some pre-work — it's like packing your bag before a trip. You need to make some decisions, get information and go to *gemba* to observe what's happening.

Identifying the natural owner

Every value stream has a natural owner who acts as the hub to make it easier to manage the improvement activities. The natural owner is like the captain of the ship — someone who by her very position or role in the organization manages the value stream. The natural owner is normally *not* a functional boss. This is the value-stream manager if you have one.

If you can't readily identify the natural owner, find someone with influence or authority who can be assigned the ownership role to drive the Lean improvement initiative. Preferably, find someone who is willing to be a change agent.

Gathering the crew

Begin by gathering the cross-functional team that represents all the disciplines involved in the value stream. Bring them together into a workshop setting. Having all these areas represented in the value-stream map improves the quality of the VSM and facilitates conversation between the team members about the "real" process. The workshop setting creates a focused environment where people are away from the distractions of their day-to-day jobs.

The best workshop location is a balance between one that is away from day-to-day activities, and yet is close enough that the team can physically go look at the action in the value stream. Be sure they can confirm the real process, as opposed to what they *think* it is.

Outside Lean experts are also a vital part of the initial crew. They train the organization in Lean tools and techniques, guide the development of initial value-stream mapping and facilitate the initial improvement efforts. They also model and help mentor people in how to think and act in a Lean way.

The ideal *core* team size has five to seven members. Larger teams are unwieldy, and smaller ones are too narrowly focused. You can always bring in support experts when you're analyzing specific value-stream tributaries. Eventually, you'll expand the team to include customers and suppliers as you expand your Lean implementation and VSM scope.

Have someone who is *not* part of the team act as a facilitator to record the value stream. This helps the team to focus on the content, while the facilitator focuses on capturing the value stream.

Using mapping tools

Mapping the value stream can be as simple or as complex as you choose to make it. Whatever method or combination of methods you choose to use, it's important that all participants — in a group setting — clearly see the value-stream map being created and contribute to its construction. Your options for mapping include the following:

✔ **No tech:** Paper stuck to the wall, and markers

✔ **Low tech:** Templates or preprinted formats

✔ **High tech:** Software programs like ARIS, available from SoftwareAG

Even if your plan is to maintain your VSMs in a high-tech tool like ARIS, many Lean practitioners find it more engaging in a team or workshop setting to construct the initial VSMs using "no tech" — paper on the wall with makers or Post-its.

Tools such as ARIS allow you to construct your value-stream maps in layers, which make it easier to visualize parts of the overall process.

When you draw a value-stream map, be sure to follow the conventions for drawing each icon that represents an activity, element, or event. VSM software tools supply these icons automatically. Table 7-1 shows the basic, standard icons used in a VSM. The book *Learning to See,* by Mike Rother and John Shook, is a good VSM reference manual, which includes instructions and a complete listing of VSM icons.

Table 7-1	Value-Stream Mapping Icons	
Icon	*Icon Name*	*Description*
	Process box	Describes an activity in the value stream. Includes a title and description of the process, as well as data, like process time, setup time, and so on.
	Outside source	Indicates and identifies both customers and suppliers.
	Truck	Indicates an outside delivery — either to a customer or from a supplier.
	Information flow	Describes information transmitted along the value stream.
	Electronic information transmission	Indicates that the information is transmitted electronically.
	Manual information transmission	Indicates that the information is transmitted manually.
	Inventory	Identifies stored inventory — either raw materials, in process, or finished goods.

(continued)

Table 7-1 *(continued)*

Icon	Icon Name	Description
	Finished goods movement	Indicates when materials in a finished state are moved along the value stream. This can be a supplier moving its product to a company or a company moving its product to its customer.
	Material push	Indicates material being pushed through the process. The push is usually a production plan or schedule.
	Supermarket	Indicates in-process inventory stored in a controlled environment called a supermarket.
	Material pull	Indicates material movement via a pull signal (kanban)
	Operator	Indicates that one or more operators are present at a process step.
	Kaizen burst	Indicates the need for and description of a *kaizen* activity within the value stream.

If you use a software-based VSM tool, you may find that the icons are different from the ones shown in the table. Choose an icon set that is close to these, and agree as a team how they'll be used going forward.

Gathering supporting information

Capture information about all the process steps at a detailed level. The more detail you have available, the easier it will be for you to uncover the waste — *muda, mura,* and *muri* (see Chapters 2 and 6). Each team member has supporting information to enable the value-stream mapping process. The more information you have readily available during the construction of the VSM, the better the resulting value-stream map.

Supporting information needed to build a VSM may include the following:

✔ The end consumer's requirements and expectations

✔ Kano models and other customer (consumer) information

- A macro-level view of the entire value stream from the consumer all the way back through to raw materials and information

- Customer schedules and demand information

- Process-time studies, including

    - Cycle time (C/T)

    - Lead times

    - Number of operators

    - Changeover time (C/O)

    - Working time, less breaks

    - Photos and video of the operations in their current state

- Standard work instructions

- Quality information

- Equipment uptime and availability

- Product design and process variation information

- Inventory and work-in-process (WIP)

- Batch or queue sizes

- Pack quantities and other shipping information

- Cost data

- Any other information that will help you characterize the process

The best way to understand a process is to go to it and watch it yourself for a significant length of time — go to *gemba*. If you can, video-record the operations. The video will give you an objective perspective — you'll notice things you don't normally see when you concentrate on a specific part of the process over many cycles. People can watch themselves to see what they *really* do, instead of what they *think* they do.

Premade gourmet salads: A value stream case study

Imagine that you're on your lunch break or heading home after working out at the gym. You're hungry, and you want something quick to eat. You don't feel like cooking, and you don't have time for a restaurant. So you pop in to your local grocery and grab a premade, gourmet salad from the deli case.

You expect the salad to be fresh and flavorful. Because you're paying a premium, you expect a gourmet offering of high-quality ingredients, uniquely combined and pleasingly presented. You expect to pay a reasonable price. You want a variety to choose from. And you may be delighted if you tried a salad that then became your new favorite.

Have you ever stopped to think about all the things that have to happen in order to bring that fresh, flavorful salad to you? It seems simple enough — not much more than lettuce, toppings, and a bowl. That doesn't sound too difficult, right? But when you look at it closely, there's much more to it than what you see on the surface.

What's happening behind the scenes? What are all the pieces, who are all the people, and how is it all coming together just right? How much of all the effort, activity, time, materials, and cost involved actually adds value to you, the customer? How consistent is it? Businesses who take the time to map and improve their processes can execute a process like this consistently and effectively thousands of times a day to satisfy discerning customers like you.

If you were on the team analyzing the salad-making process, you would first look at the value stream from the consumer's point of view; in this case, that's the hungry person. Her requirements are indicated in Figure 7-3 via a Kano model.

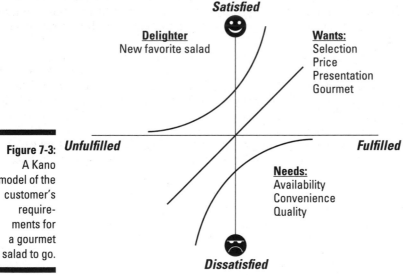

Figure 7-3:
A Kano model of the customer's requirements for a gourmet salad to go.

Next you would map out the high-level flow of all the process steps that must occur across the entire value stream in order to meet the consumer's requirements and expectations. This high-level view is called the *macro-level value stream* diagram, and it's used to capture the big picture and to set the context within which the provider understands how it must operate.

Macro-level value stream diagrams begin with the consumer and show all of the various processes that must occur to support the consumer's demands. Unlike a process-flow diagram, you create the macro-level value-stream diagram from right to left, emphasizing the pivotal role of the customer at each step.

Figure 7-4 shows the macro-level value stream diagram for the salad production process. It starts with the consumer and ends where nature produces wild salmon. This simple chart encompasses a global supply stream — so global that, when taken from its first tributary, raw materials, all the way through to the consumer, it takes years to complete. All for a salad!

Contained within each box in Figure 7-4 are multiple individual processes and different companies that support the overall value stream. By first depicting the value stream at this high level, you can see where the salad company fits into the picture.

Understanding how your part fits into the overall value stream and how you contribute to the consumer's demands is important. Start by creating a macro-level value-stream diagram that shows your contribution to the overall value stream.

You don't need to map everything shown on this macro-level diagram! Start at the level of your contribution, and refine the detail or expand the scope as you dive into the value stream. The waste-devil is in those details — that's where you'll uncover *muda*.

We use this salad company example though the following sections, as we show you how to develop and validate the current-state value-stream map.

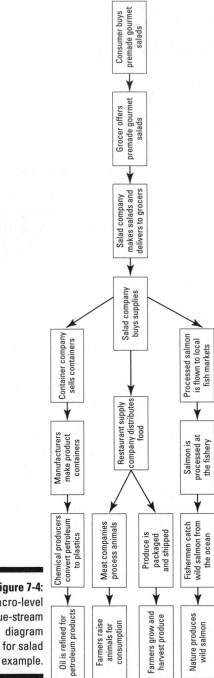

Figure 7-4:
Macro-level
value-stream
diagram
for salad
example.

Hitting the Road: Creating the Current-State Value-Stream Map

After you've identified the captain, assembled the crew of players and participants, and gathered the critical data about your processes, you're ready to create your current-state value-stream map. Begin by capturing how your process works *now* — before any improvement efforts have started. From this initial VSM, you'll begin to understand where you are and where the waste is in the process. Before you start to construct the VSM, it's a good idea to *go to gemba* (go to where the action is, and review the process as it happens every day). This will give everyone a common starting point of reference.

Always construct your VSMs from right to left to maintain your customer focus. Start at the end closest to the customer and record the process working your way to the beginning of the value stream. You'll see what is happening the farther away from the customer you travel.

Identifying the activities

Begin by titling the current-state VSM, dating it, and identifying the major process steps.

Most teams start with the part of the value stream that they own. After you've identified the major process steps, you can use your supporting information to more precisely characterize each step.

In the salad example, the company owns the part of the value stream where the salads are made and delivered to the grocer. With the participation of the cross-functional team, divide this process into its major process activities. This team includes the owner, the lead chef, the sous chef, the driver, the kitchen hand, and an outside observer. The salad company recognizes that it conducts five major process activities. For each salad, these activities are:

- ✔ Preparing ingredients
- ✔ Assembling the salad
- ✔ Labeling the container
- ✔ Packing the container
- ✔ Shipping to the grocer

Start at the right side of the map with the customer. You may choose to show the immediate customer as well as the consumer. For any outside player — including the consumer, customer, supplier, or any other source — use the outside source icon.

Along the bottom, from right to left, are the steps in the process of your part of the value stream. The step on the right side is the final step before you deliver the product or service to the customer. The leftmost step is the first step in your process. In the case of the salad company, Figure 7-5 shows the current-state VSM where the operation on the left side of the value stream is "Prep Ingredients" and the final process, on the right side, is "Shipping."

After you lay out the process steps, connect them with the appropriate connector: Use dashed arrows to indicate material pushed through the system. Use open arrows are for material movement to or from external sources. Indicate where you store inventory in the process — beginning, work-in-process, or end. Use icons for regular inventory, buffer stock, supermarkets, safety stock, and queues. Clearly identify what type of inventory is in process, in addition to the amount of inventory at each location.

TIP

Take your first pass through the VSM at a relatively high level. After you characterize the value stream at this level, you can choose an area of focus, and map that at a greater level of detail. The process for creating any map, though, is the same.

WARNING!

Beware of the dangers of mapping paralysis. Don't get caught up in making the VSM so complete and perfect that you don't proceed to the improvement stage. Make your initial best cut, validate, and move on. You'll have plenty of opportunities to come back and improve your VSM later.

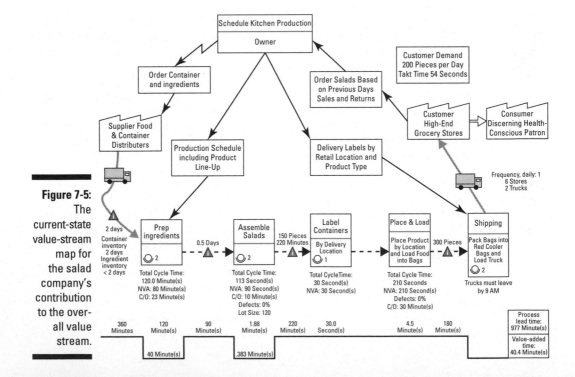

Figure 7-5: The current-state value-stream map for the salad company's contribution to the overall value stream.

Qualifying and quantifying

After you've captured the current-state VSM, it's time to quantify the process and qualify the value-added (VA) and non-value-added (NVA) activities. Cycle time, changeover time, inventory levels, and the number of operators are all types of information you'll use to understand and analyze the process.

Characterizing the process time

When considering process time, there are a number of angles. Use your supporting data and information from *gemba* to answer these questions. For each step in the value stream, evaluate the step by asking the following types of questions:

- ✔ What is the actual time required to perform the task identified in the process step?

- ✔ What is the waiting time before each step?

- ✔ If inventory is involved, how long does it take to deplete it?

- ✔ What is the transport or conveyance time?

- ✔ What is the inventory between the last operation and the consumer?

- ✔ How many operators are active at each process step?

- ✔ How long does it take to change over a process when changing product types?

The VSM is a snapshot in time. Use the best data you have available to get the job done. It's OK to estimate some of the times at first; you can validate the estimates later with actual data.

With your answers, you can assign a time value for each process step. After characterizing the entire process, sum the individual times to arrive at an overall process time for the value-stream map. If you're using a software package, the overall calculation will be done for you, based on the information you enter about each process step.

When the value stream has parallel processes that come together, one stream represents the longest lead time from the beginning of the process (the raw-material stage) through to the product reaching the consumer. This is known as the *critical path*. Identify the critical path on the value-stream map. Any waste eliminated from the critical path flow will positively impact the productivity to the consumer.

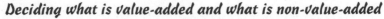

Deciding what is value-added and what is non-value-added

Further evaluate each process step by dividing the overall process time into value-added (VA) and the dreaded non-value-added (NVA) activities.

To be value-added, an activity must meet all three of the VA criteria:

- ✔ The customer must be willing to pay for it.
- ✔ It must transform the product or service in some way.
- ✔ It must be done correctly the first time.

Anything that doesn't meet these three criteria is NVA and is, therefore, a waste of some type.

There are two types of non-value-added steps (defined in Chapter 6):

- ✔ **Type-1** *muda:* Non-value-added but necessary.
- ✔ **Type-2** *muda:* Non-value-added and not necessary.

Designate each step as VA or NVA. For the NVA, note the type: T1 or T2. This information will be handy when you start to identify improvement opportunities.

Don't get hung up on dissecting VA versus NVA classification at this stage. Pick one, assign it, and move on. In the end, you'll improve the entire process. The designation of VA and NVA are guidelines for when you start the improvement activities.

In the salad example, only those steps that directly contribute to the finished salad are value-added. For example, cutting the lettuce, baking the chicken, slicing the chicken, putting the ingredients in the container — these are all VA. These steps, however, are buried in the macro process steps "Prep Ingredients" and "Assemble Salads."

In the salad company example, placing labels on the top and bottom of the container is considered type-1 *muda*. The labels do not directly contribute to the customer receiving her salad, but they are required for the scanning and payment processes at the grocery store. Another example of type-1 *muda* is the weighing of the ingredients during the assembly process. The act of weighing adds nothing to the transformation of the salad, but it does ensure the quality and consistency of the product. Examples of type-2 *muda* are trips back and forth to the cooler for forgotten items or disposing ingredients that are still good.

When the process owner maps the process along with an outside observer, typically she has an idealized perception of the process. However, when an outside observer goes to *gemba* to observe the process with the process owner or team, the findings are often eye opening for all involved. ("Holy cow! Do we really do that?")

Quantifying overall lead time

Lead time is the amount of time it takes one piece to flow though the process from start to finish, including process time, inventory time, waiting time, and so on. In the case of the salad example, it's the time from when the shipment of produce arrives until it's transformed into a shipped salad. In the case of a service, it's the time from when you arrive at the doctor's office until you receive treatment and complete the checkout process. Within the lead time are value-added and non-value-added activities. A detailed time-study analysis will help you to identify these activities — so bring your stop watch to *gemba*.

On the VSM, draw a line along the bottom of the map to represent the overall lead-time for the product or service. The line is segmented according to the lead time of each major step in the process. Where value-added work is done, you can record it below the overall lead time line, to visually see the difference between the lead time and value-added time. (See Figure 7-5 for an example.) You may be shocked at what you find — lots of NVA and little bitty amounts of VA. If you use a software package, like ARIS, it automatically generates the line for you based on the data you provide.

Determining the information flow

Every process requires information to support or direct the transformational activities. This information flow might include any instructions, orders, or messages that occur through the course of the process. Information flow may also include schedules, orders, shipping transmittals, approvals, and more — whatever you need to support and communicate within the process.

Just like in the rest of the process, you want your information flow to be value-added. The right information arriving at the right time, in the right manner, to the right recipients is the information flow. When the information does not flow, it creates waste in other areas. Because the information flow is so critical to the timely and effective execution of the process, you include it directly on the value-stream map. This is a unique feature of the value-stream map. Initially, consider the location, quantity, and frequency of the information flow, using penetrating questions like these:

✔ What information is being transmitted?

✔ When is information being sent?

✔ Who receives the information and are they the right people to receive the information?

✔ Where in the value stream does the information transmittal occur?

✔ How is the information being sent — manually or electronically?

Start with the information that is vital for the value stream to function. You can always add additional information flows to the VSM later. Place the vital information flow on the VSM at the proper location. Indicate information flow using the rectangular information box. Remember that there are two information arrows. Manual transmissions use a straight arrow, and electronic transmissions use a jagged arrow that resembles a lightening bolt. (See Figure 7-5 for an example.)

In the salad example, information flow includes such items as the daily customer order, the production schedule, the order to the suppliers, and the order list for each customer location. Other examples of information flow along the entire value stream include:

✔ The grocery sends orders to the salad company.

✔ Production sheets schedule the kitchen assembly process.

✔ The salad company sends orders to distributors for the ingredients needed and delivery times required.

✔ The salad company sends orders to container suppliers.

✔ Distributors send orders to the growers.

✔ Customs brokers file papers to import produce from other countries.

✔ Suppliers send delivery receipts with produce orders.

✔ The grocery fills out product return sheets and sends these sheets back to the salad company with products that did not sell before the expiration date.

Summing Up the Process

After you develop the initial current-state value-stream map, summarize the key descriptive process statistics and place them in a summary chart directly on the map.

The graphic for this is the *box score*. Think of a box score in sports, like baseball — it contains important statistics on players, the score, hits, errors, runs, and so on. The concept of the box score in Lean is similar.

The box score

The box score is a summary of the critical statistics of a process. At the very least, the box score usually includes the total lead time and the value-added and non-value-added time. If the process includes the physical movement of an object, then travel distance is also normally included. Physical movement refers to any object that is transformed as it literally moves through the process. Typically, transformation is thought of as a manufacturing process; however, transformation also happens in transactional processes. An example of a transformation in an office setting includes the completion of paperwork through several departments of a process.

Box-score contents

The box score contains the summary chart of the key process metrics. You often want to contrast the measured scores against an ideal state, where all process steps are only value-added. (More about the ideal state in Chapter 8.)

In the salad company example, its initial box score includes its portion of the value stream — from receipt of ingredients to shipment of the finished salads. The box score is shown in Table 7-2.

Table 7-2	The Salad Company's Box Score	
Metric	*Current State*	*Ideal State*
Total average VA time	40.4 minutes	40.4 minutes
Total average NVA time	936.6 minutes	0 minutes
Total average lead time	977 minutes	40.4 minutes
Changeover time, between types	30 minutes	1 minutes
Actual cycle time	210 seconds	54 seconds
Takt time, seconds.	54 seconds	54 seconds

In the future, the salad company may need to track other metrics to address other types of waste in its value stream. Some of these metrics may include inventory turns, the value of lost ingredients due to waste or expiration, the number of unsold salads versus shipped salads, or salads as shipped versus salad as priced. As the company dives deeper into the value stream, it will select the measurements that will best gauge improvement efforts.

Additional metrics for a box score

The following are some of the other common metrics that companies may include in their box score:

- ✔ **Parts per shift:** Parts produced during a standard work shift. In a service example, this could be customers serviced per day.

- ✔ **Scrap:** The percentage of defective parts produced.

- ✔ **Pieces per labor hour:** The total number of piece produced divided by the amount of labor hours expended. In a call center setting, this could be calls per hour considering all of the service representatives available.

- ✔ **Change over time:** The amount of time required to convert a manufacturing line from the last good part of the previous product to the first good part of the new product. In a surgery facility, this could be the time to change over operating rooms between surgeries.

- ✔ **Inventory turns:** The number of times a company's inventory cycles in a year (Inventory Turns = Average Annual Cost of Goods Sold ÷ Average Annual Inventory).

- ✔ **Uptime:** The amount of time the equipment is actually producing versus the planned production time.

- ✔ **Cost breakdown:** An evaluation of the cost components at each step of the process.

Takt time

Takt is the German word for "beat." In Lean, it is the pace of production tied to customer consumption. Show the takt time in the box score or as a note on the VSM. The formula is Takt Time = Available Production Time ÷ Customer Demand.

The salad company uses its kitchen to support other value streams. For the premade salads distributed to local groceries, the available production time is 3 hours (or 10,800 seconds [$3 \times 60 \times 60$]), and the customer demand is 200 salads per day (on average). So the takt time is $10,800 \div 200$, or 54 seconds per salad.

Check the Chart: Validating the Value-Stream Map

Have you ever driven the same route to work or home but not really seen what you were driving past? Then, one day, you notice a restaurant or business that has been there for years. You've passed it hundreds of times, but for whatever reason, on that day you noticed it for the first time.

The same thing can happen to members of a team with respect to the value stream where they work. You can walk by a process or an office but not really "see" what's happening. When the team is capturing the first VSM, it's important that there be a common starting point — that all the members "see" the same thing.

Although perfection is not a requirement, you do want the baseline starting point to be as accurate as possible. Real improvements happen from a common leaping point. Maybe the team thinks that standardized work is in place, when it's really not. Or maybe the team assumes one step is in a different place than it really occurs. Information that one team member believes is important to be distributed may not be getting to the "right" people, or it may not be so important after all. In any case, you have to validate your VSM before you proceed to the improvement phase of the game.

Although the team members might think they know what's going on in the value stream, the only way to truly know is to go to *gemba* (go to where the action is happening). It's one thing to walk by the process — it's a totally different thing to observe with intention. When you stand and observe the process over a repeated number of cycles, you open your eyes to what is really occurring.

One powerful tool is video-recording the process and then reviewing the video with the team. The video will create a common foundation from which the improvements can occur.

The key things that you're validating are:

- ✔ Whether the process depicted on the value-stream map is, in fact, the process
- ✔ Whether the process time is correct (particularly if you use estimates)
- ✔ Whether the inventory amounts are accurate
- ✔ Whether the number of operators is correct
- ✔ Whether the process is performed according to a standard instruction

   ✔ Whether the key process statistics are correct

   ✔ Whether all operators are performing the activities in the same manner

   ✔ The number of process changeovers that are performed and how long they take

   ✔ The accuracy of the quality data, and the identification of where the defects are occurring in the process

If your facility has multiple shifts, it is important to validate the VSM across all shifts. Often you will find the operators perform their jobs differently on different shifts.

Work with your core team to construct the current-state VSM. Involve experts to assist you with portions of the VSM. Not every person is going to know every nuance of every process. Seek out experts who truly know what's going on.

After you've identified the discrepancies, the team can update and correct the current-state VSM. The team may also decide that it needs to further refine an activity and map it.

Detail is important. You may start with a higher-level view of the value stream. As the improvement efforts progress, you may take one of those steps and create a more detailed value-stream map for that step. The more detail that is available, the easier it is to uncover waste.

Chapter 8

Charting the Course: Using Value-Stream Maps

*T*o make a change, you need a catalyst. In Lean, that catalyst is the recognition that the current state is not where you want to be. Lean is applicable whether you need to fix something that's broken or prepare for new opportunities to come. So like that "fat picture" that sends you to the gym and juice bar to get healthy, the current-state value-stream map (VSM) and supporting information — like quality data, customer complaints, or financial reports — provide objective reflection that motivates an organization to modify its processes and practices and helps the business regain its health and vitality.

When you decide to make a change, not only do you plan where you're going to go, but you also consider where you *could* go. You ask what's possible. For example, when you decide to get healthy, does *healthy* just mean weighing less? It may also mean better cardio performance, improved flexibility, lower cholesterol, a smaller clothing size, or living one hundred years. In a perfect world, what would a perfectly healthy you look like? The thought process is the same when you decide to make changes in your business. In Lean, use the *ideal-state* VSM to define that perfect world — what your business would look like if anything were possible. You then use the *future-state* VSM to identify the next right step to move you toward that goal.

In your life, you may have several initiatives going at the same time to help you get healthy — a new diet, gym membership, recreational change, and nutritional supplements. Similarly, your business may have several initiatives going to get it healthy. Understanding and communicating how all these initiatives fit together in the process of moving toward improved business performance is important to engage and lead the organization.

In this chapter, we show you how to analyze your current-state VSM to get a real picture of the process. You discover how to develop the ideal- and future-state VSM. Along the way, we answer common questions and respond to common objections about value-stream mapping. Finally, you determine how your future plans fit with other organizational initiatives.

Investigating the Value-Stream for Clues

In Chapter 7, we show you how to create a value-stream map (VSM) for the current state of the business. After this initial current-state VSM is complete, your next mission is to dive into it and understand where you have waste. You first start looking for waste when you qualify the process steps in the stream as value-added and non-value-added. At *this* point in the process, you look for where your value stream isn't flowing.

The current-state VSM, combined with the use of the supporting data, provides the clues where to start looking for improvement opportunities. In Lean, strive to have the entire value stream flowing unencumbered at a rate equal to the customer's demand in the most effective manner (that is, with the highest quality, the shortest lead time, and the lowest cost). You can quantify this customer demand by looking at the demand rate, or *takt time.* By using this metric, you can start to see where blockages to the flow are occurring in the current state. The blockages are evidence of *muda, mura,* or *muri.* You improve performance by resolving and removing the root cause of these blockages.

It is important to define the true root cause of the problem so you do not waste precious resources solving a symptom rather than the problem.

The Lean process is one of seeking understanding. To understand the true nature of your processes and the origins of waste and loss ask questions — many questions — to discover truth and understanding. When you develop your skill to ask powerful questions, you will engage people, improve the quality of analysis and find better solutions.

Rounding up the usual suspects

As you begin your analysis of the current-state VSM, start by considering the most common causes. Look first to your customer. What are their complaints, praise, returns, and actions? Even if the customer voices issues that aren't at the root of the problem, they may give you clues as to what the issue truly is. If you aren't getting any indications from the customer, start looking for evidence of the three *Ms*: *muda, mura,* and *muri.*

While conducting the current stream analysis with the team, mark up a copy or plot of the current-state VSM. Use the low-tech, pencil-and-paper method, with a different color or sticky notes to indicate where in the value stream the improvement opportunities are.

Putting your ear to the street

As you hear feedback, examine the issues and relate them to where they occur in the value stream. For example, are your customers complaining about not getting your product when they want it? Look at the critical path to delivery. Are they complaining about not getting the right mix of product? Examine the material flow and information flow. Are they concerned about the quality of your product? Study the design and manufacturing processes. And if you're lucky and your customers are all singing your praises, you may need to make room for new business.

Also identify what you are doing right, so you don't accidentally change your process and eliminate something that your customer values.

An effective tool for analyzing potential causes of customer issues is the *Ishikawa diagram,* also known as the *Cause-and-Effect* or *Fishbone diagram* (see Chapter 12). With this tool, you can identify where in the value stream the issues originate. Figure 8-1 shows an example of an Ishikawa diagram for our salad company where the issue was late product arrival.

Examine the many possible causes for the delays. Use your supporting information to help you identify the most likely root causes of the delays, and to quantify how late "late" really is. Is the complaint a recent development or has there been a chronic problem? Look in the value stream to find the operations that are sources for the major issues. Ask these types of questions to identify issues in the value stream that are directly affecting the customers:

- ✔ Are the operations running slower than takt time?
- ✔ Are the operations running faster than takt time?
- ✔ Are there deviations to the work standards?
- ✔ Is the product not available for shipment?
- ✔ Have there been material supply issues?
- ✔ Are the drivers leaving late from the facility?
- ✔ Have there been any personnel changes?
- ✔ Have the employees been trained and demonstrate proficiency safely?

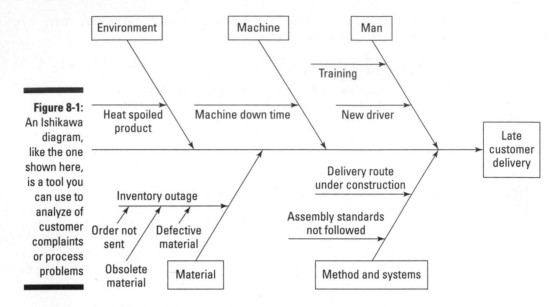

Figure 8-1:
An Ishikawa diagram, like the one shown here, is a tool you can use to analyze of customer complaints or process problems

Focus on fixing the process, not assigning blame. Lean is all about respecting people. Most of the time, you will find a process problem (like a lack of defined standards) preventing people from performing at their best.

Use the *5 Whys* (see Chapter 12). The aim of the 5 Whys is to find the root cause of a problem. When using 5-Why questioning, ask "Why?" until you've exhausted answers and found the root cause of the problem. The number 5 is arbitrary; ask *why* until you discover the true root cause. Practicing 5 Whys is like becoming a curious three-year-old again, when the question "But why?" was the first thing out of your mouth. Here's what this technique looks like in action:

> Are the drivers leaving late from the facility?
>
> Yes. But why?
>
> Because the product isn't ready. Why?
>
> Because the production line was behind. Why?
>
> Because the preparation was not done the day before. Why?
>
> Because ingredients were missing. Why?
>
> Because the supplier was behind. Why?
>
> Because the order was issued late. Why?

You get the idea. In this example, these *whys* would lead you to look at the ordering process and information flow.

Searching for the culprits

You've seen your business through the eyes of your customer and examined the direct causes of customer dissatisfaction. Now you must look within, and find causes of waste occurring inside your business. During the first pass through the current-state VSM, you initially designate process steps as value-added (VA) or non-value-added (NVA). Now it's time to examine these designations more closely.

Refer to Chapter 2 for the precise definitions of value-added and waste.

Lean strives to eliminate *all* forms of waste. Begin with type-2 *muda*, and ask the following types of questions:

- ✔ Does the step create value? If not, why does the step exist in the process and what can be eliminated?

- ✔ Is excess inventory or work in process accumulating along the value stream? (This may be physical product or in a service world, people or paper.)

- ✔ Does the step create scrap or rejects? If so, it's a candidate for improvement and, at the very least, further study.

- ✔ Is the step capable? If not, the step should be improved using statistical tools, like those found in the Six Sigma methodology. (For more information on Six Sigma, see *Six Sigma For Dummies,* by Craig Gygi, Neil DeCarlo, and Bruce Williams [published by Wiley])

- ✔ Does the step perform as designed — to the standard?

- ✔ Is the equipment needed to perform the step functioning and available?

- ✔ Are the materials required available, at the right quality level, and in the right quantity?

- ✔ What is the capacity of the process step? How does it compare to the takt time?

- ✔ Are people waiting for work?

- ✔ When changing from one product or service to the next, how long is the process step not producing? (This question relates to changeover (C/O) time.)

- ✔ Does the process step flow or does it cause a bottleneck in the process?

- ✔ How does the process time of the step compare to the customer demand?

A great place to start is where you find overproduction. Extra parts, material, or information sitting around creates all kinds of problems. Overproduction causes other types of waste and means you have to store things, move them around, handle them, and sort and process through them when you find a defect later in the process, all of which drive excess cost.

Anytime you use *re–* in front of a word, it is a candidate for waste elimination, because, by its very definition, it means you aren't doing it right the first time.

Get a physical layout of the work areas, and create a two-dimensional flow diagram that reflects the physical movement of material or people through the process. This technique is especially useful in manufacturing processes, lab processes, restaurant kitchens, and other places where physical material moves through processes and places. It also applies to the movement of data or information between people and among systems. These layouts are commonly known as *spaghetti diagrams* (see Chapter 10) because after all the movements are drawn out, it tends to look like a plate of spaghetti!

Analyzing from different perspectives

Different players in the value stream bring a different set of eyes and information to the evaluation of the current-state VSM. Whether you're improving an unhealthy business practice or enabling the pursuit of a new opportunity, take the time to examine the value stream through different perspectives. As you strive to find waste, these different views can be invaluable sources of insight.

The VSM team will involve people working in the process who have a daily operational perspective. This will include process owners, including the value-stream owner, and perhaps even the business owner. In addition to these participants, others have a keenly valuable perspective.

Examples in the following sections are oriented more towards the production of a physical product, but they have analogies in the transactional and information worlds.

Lean principles: The Lean sensei's view

The *Lean sensei* is the master and teacher of the Lean principles and knowledge. (For more information about the Lean *sensei* see Chapter 5.) The Lean *sensei* guides and teaches the organization to learn, implement, and embody the Lean philosophy. The lens through which the *sensei* evaluates the current-state VSM highlights the short-term and long-term opportunities to institutionalize Lean in the organization. The Lean *sensei* poses these types of questions:

✔ How closely is the process producing to takt time?

✔ How can the process be more visual?

✔ What will motivate the workers stop the line immediately when quality or other issues arise?

✔ How is the material and information flowing through the process?

✔ Where best can continuous flow be implemented?

✔ Where do supermarkets need to be implemented?

✔ Are standardized work instructions available, being followed, and visible?

✔ How can the workload be leveled?

✔ Where can operations be combined to improve flow?

✔ How effectively are the managers leading problem solving and building capability in their people?

✔ What exists in the value stream preventing the implementation of Lean at this time? How can it be addressed?

Quality

The quality practitioners — whether they're from a formal quality function or other experts such as Six Sigma practitioners or statistical analysts — examine value-added from the perspective of correctness: Does the transformation happen correctly? Is it done right the first time? Is the process capable of producing defect-free results regularly?

Think of debris dumped into a river and what it does to the flow of the current. When quality losses occur in the value stream, it is like debris dumped into stream — impeding its flow. The quality practitioners evaluate the process to identify where it isn't capable of creating good product or service, and where suppliers or downstream contributors create poor quality for the consumer. Analyzing the value stream from a quality perspective will lead you to ask the following types of questions:

✔ Where is poor quality reaching the customer? What are the defects?

✔ How are quality issues reported from the customer, transmitted into the organization, and resolved? What is the response time to address a customer complaint?

✔ How is quality controlled at the source?

✔ What is the fall-off rate at each step?

✔ Where are the losses the greatest?

✔ What is the most common cause of scrap?

✔ What is the root cause of the scrap (design, equipment, training, and so on)?

✔ How are suspect items handled?

✔ How are reworked items returned to the normal flow?

✔ How can the process, design, or equipment be designed to prevent errors? Where can error-proofing create quality at the source?

✔ What is the capability of each step?

✔ Which suppliers are the providers of the poorest quality?

✔ How frequently have quality spills occurred and in what location?

✔ What steps have been taken to quarantine defective product?

Supply

Most processes have inventory — either by accident or by design. Inventory can collect at the beginning, somewhere in middle, or at the end of the process. Inventory acts like a dam to the flow of the value stream. Where there is inventory, there is no flow. Likewise, where there are outages, there is no flow. Balance comes in orchestrating the flow of material supply and processing precisely to customer demand — in other words, matching the cycle time to the takt time.

Ask the following questions to evaluate how materials move through the current state process:

✔ Where is the inventory? Is it planned or unplanned?

✔ What is the inventory turn level?

✔ What is the size of the storage?

✔ Where is the storage? In a warehouse? In process? In transit?

✔ How low can it go? Can you maintain an inventory of one?

✔ How is inventory managed?

✔ Can the inventory spoil? Does it have a shelf-life?

✔ Do you practice first in, first out (FIFO)? How is it managed?

✔ What signals the withdrawals from the inventory?

✔ What are the reorder signals in the process?

✔ Where is material pushed through the system?

✔ Where is the material pulled through the system? Where else can pull signals be used in the process?

✔ Where are shipping costs exceeding plan? Why?

✔ How are the quantities of raw material balanced with the shipping quantities?

✔ How far does material travel in the value stream?

✔ How are the incoming material shipments coordinated?

✔ When a quality issue arises, how is the inventory handled/quarantined?

✔ What is the dollar value of the inventory?

✔ What is the cost of floor space to handle the inventory?

Questions like "If FedEx or elves were moving our material, how would they do it?" can open the team up to creativity and benchmarking when creating the future-state VSM.

Engineering

Evaluate the current-state value stream from the perspective of the engineering disciplines: design, production, and maintenance. The engineering perspective will also help you examine the interfaces of the people, equipment, and processes.

At this juncture, you're evaluating the current state of production processes and practices. Be aware that the designers are meanwhile developing future designs of new products and services. Because the majority of cost is established during the design phase, you want to involve the design engineers during the current-state VSM analysis. You also want to include the production engineers to ensure continuity.

Analyzing the value stream from a **production-manufacturing engineering** perspective, will lead you to ask the following types of questions:

✔ Is the process designed for flow and proper assembly?

✔ Can processes be combined? Can alternative processes be used?

✔ How can operations be laid out to maximize the effectiveness of operators?

✔ How far away is the material or inventory being stored? How far does it travel between operations?

✔ How is material presented into the process?

✔ How are the raw material quantities balanced with the shipping quantities?

✔ How can changeovers occur more quickly? How can concepts like the "Indy pit crew" be applied during changeovers?

✔ What modifications can be done to equipment to prevent errors, facilitate the operation, eliminate workload from operators, combine operations, or facilitate flow?

✔ Is standardized work being followed? How can it be modified to improve quality and eliminate unnecessary processing or movement?

✔ Does the process design cause safety or ergonomic issues?

✔ How can cycle times be balanced with takt time?

Analyzing the value stream from a **design engineering** perspective, will lead you to ask the following types of questions:

✔ What type of product defects occur during the process? Where do they occur?

✔ How can features be built into the design to ensure it is always made correctly?

✔ What issues in the current product, process or equipment design might be in the future designs?

✔ Can the design be simplified to facilitate production without compromising customer requirements?

✔ Are certain design specifications unnecessary for the customer requirements? Where can specifications be eliminated or changed without negatively impacting customer requirements?

✔ Are the design tolerances properly specified to ensure the product could be made right the first time, every time?

Analyzing the value stream from a **maintenance/equipment engineering** perspective will lead you to ask the following types of questions:

✔ What is the uptime of the equipment?

✔ What is the current maintenance schedule? Is it reactive or planned? If planned, is it preventive or predictive?

✔ What modifications can be made to the equipment to prevent defects from being produced?

✔ What pieces of equipment have the greatest maintenance issues?

✔ Are there different brands of equipment performing the same function/ operation? Is there a difference in performance level?

✔ What modifications can be made to the equipment, tooling, and process to facilitate quick changeovers? (See Chapter 11.)

✔ What is the process to notify maintenance? How can it be improved?

✔ When there is an issue, what is the response time for maintenance to respond? What is the time to resolve the issue?

✔ What simple maintenance activities can be transferred to the operators to perform?

✔ What visual controls can be used or improved to communicate the accurate status of the equipment and scheduled maintenance performance?

✔ What modifications, features, or controls can be added to the equipment to enable operators to run multiple pieces of equipment?

✔ What controls can be added to the equipment to automatically stop when defects are produced or equipment problems arise?

Information

The VSM depicts the flow of information that supports the product and material flow. Your analysis of the current state should include a focused examination of the information component. The purpose of this analysis is to find opportunities to eliminate waste or make improvements based on information.

Answering the following questions will help you when determining where waste exists in the information flow:

✔ Does the information flow to the customer, without delays?

✔ Does the information flow from the customer, without delays or filters?

✔ Does the information flow through the organization smoothly?

✔ Is the information flow accurate? Is the right information going to the right people in the right place? Complete? Contradictory?

✔ Does the information arrive at the right time? Is it too early or late? Is there too much or too little?

✔ Are the right people in the information flow and receiving the right information?

✔ Is the information being transmitted in the most efficient way?

✔ Is the information being used?

✔ Are prompt and proper approval chains in place?

Evaluating the evidence: An analyzed example

A small salad company supplies local, high-end grocery stores with gourmet salads on a daily basis. It operates on one shift: The morning is assembly, and the afternoon is ingredient preparation for the next day. The drivers are scheduled to leave the facility by 9 a.m. so that their deliveries will be complete by 11 a.m., in time for the lunch crowd. They conscientiously adhere to health and safety standards for food preparation.

The salad company's direct customers (the grocery retailers) have one major complaint: The deliveries tend to run late. When the salad company reviews its shipping data, it realizes that its drivers are leaving late from its commissary — about 45 minutes late, almost every day.

After reviewing the video from production one morning, the team realizes that several things were causing the product to be late in the morning. However, the main place they need to start is with the salad assembly process. To better understand where the waste happens, the team makes a detailed assessment of that process. The full analysis would be much longer, so only an excerpt is shown in Table 8-1.

Table 8-1   Excerpt of the Salad Assembly Process analysis.

Seq	Process Step	Time (seconds)	Value Added	Waste, but Needed	Waste	Type of Waste
88	Walk to office-end of work area and place dressing in salad	8	Vaue Added		Type -2	Transport
89	Grab large dressing container	2		Type 1		Motion
90	Walk to cooler with large dressing container	30		Type 1		Transport
91	Walk around kitchen looking for balsamic chicken	315			Type -2	Transport
92	Bring balsamic chicken to far end of work surface (wet area end)	25		Type 1		Transport
93	Walk to wet area end of kitchen to get clean, green cutting board	15			Type -2	Transport

Seq	Process Step	Time (seconds)	Value Added	Waste, but Needed	Waste	Type of Waste
94	Bring green cutting board back to work area 15			Type 1		Transport
95	Get clean knife	4	Value Added			
96	Put on gloves	11		Type 1		Motion
97	Slice four chicken breasts; throw away top slice	27	Value Added		Type -2	Excess Processing
98	Place sliced chicken in hand, as much as can carry	4			Type -2	Motion
99	Walk to office end of work area	6			Type 2	Transport
100	Place approximately 3/4 of a breast on salad, fanned out	24	Value Added			

The team observes that the following issues directly contribute to lateness:

- In general, the process was disorganized.
- The work standards were not well defined.
- Considerable time was lost wandering around looking for things.
- They did not consistently complete the ingredient preparation completed the afternoon before.

> ✔ Ingredients had not been ordered on time, causing them to send one of the workers to purchase them at a premium from a retail store.
>
> ✔ Untrained workers were used to help get the product out the door.
>
> ✔ Product flow was backwards causing the finished product to end at the point farthest from the shipping point. This caused unnecessary product movement and employee traffic in the flow.

In addition, they notice other wastes occurring in the process:

> ✔ There was an unnecessary loss of ingredients as a result of the current process. Good product was thrown away. Containers were overfilled, causing ingredients to fall to the work surface.
>
> ✔ Ingredients were not being measured, which could affect the quality and consistency of the product, not to mention contribute to inventory losses and excess costs to the small business.
>
> ✔ The workload was unbalanced. Some operators appeared overloaded and others were waiting on product to process. Drivers were waiting on product to label.
>
> ✔ The number of labels did not match the production sheet causing them to question which was correct.
>
> ✔ The order of production dirtied extra dishes unnecessarily.

This current-state value-stream analysis not only identifies numerous contributors to the lateness problem, but also many other sources of waste. The foundation has now been set for considering improvement options. The first step is to ponder the ideal state — what would be possible if all constraints could be cast aside. Then define the future state, an incremental step towards the ideal state, and set the plan to achieve the first round of improvement.

Painting a Picture of the Future

The current-state VSM is a snapshot in time — it's where you are now. That's an important view, but it's only the first step. After you've characterized the current state, it's important to set your sights on the view of where you're going. In this section, you take the opportunities for improvement that you've identified in your current-state value-stream analysis and turn them into a design of the future.

In Lean, you consider two future views.

- ✔ **The view of the utopian or ideal state:** In a perfect world, with only value-added steps, how could you best meet the customer's requirements? (Toyota's True North is one example of this; see Chapter 3)

- ✔ **The more-grounded future state that you can implement relatively quickly with a focused plan:** In the future state, you make incremental improvements to the current state, eliminating waste and reducing the non-value-added steps. Identify what is the next right step over a defined time period. Define this based on your specific business conditions, focusing first on those items directly affecting your customer.

Creating the ideal-state value-stream map: Long-term vision of possibilities

If your process is in a state of ideal flow, you make one as the consumer takes one. The process is in perfect balance. All activities are value-added. All process steps take the same amount of time. There is no inventory in process. All process steps produce perfectly, without defects. You have the exact capacity needed for the consumption rate, with the precisely correct number of staff, trained perfectly for the tasks.

Ponder this for a moment: a process where everything is exactly right. Don't ruin the thought with the realities of imperfection — that's for the next section. For now, picture utopia. See it all working perfectly.

If you're having trouble with this pie-in-the-sky stuff, it's because you're being pragmatic. You're thinking that you can't achieve perfection, and it's because you've been conditioned to think that way. Don't think about how you would get there; think about where you want to go!

Why define an ideal-state VSM? Why spend legitimate business time and effort considering something that you probably can't have? The reason is simple: Because it defines a consistent long-term vision, sets a direction and challenges you to move the organization toward it. When you allow people to imagine cutting the ties of the past and letting go of the constraints of the present, you raise the collective consciousness and enable teams to engage in radical thinking that often identifies breakthrough opportunities.

Toyota uses True North as a foundation for all changes. They may not know how to get there today, but they know if they keep working in that direction, they will continue to improve and achieve more than if they only focused on what they know how to do.

Frequently, the ideal-state VSM exercise results in dramatic gains. The power of imagination is unbounded. When unbridled, ideas flow freely and great things emerge. The ideal-state VSM produces a vision for the long term and direction for the next step: the future state.

To define the ideal-state VSM, use the same icons and graphics you used to create the current-state VSM defined in Chapter 7.

Stepping closer to perfection: The future-state value-stream map

Now it's time to take all the mapping efforts, the analyses, and the ideal-state visions and marry them to define the future state. The improvements that you select now become the foundation for your planning activities. The future-state VSM is your next increment of performance improvement.

Pacemakers, supermarkets, and heijunka, oh my!

Before you can envision the future-state VSM, you first need to understand several additional Lean concepts. Chapter 2 addresses the principles of Lean. Chapter 6 addresses the concepts of value added, non-value added, flow, and the three *Ms* (*muda*, *mura* and *muri*.) Here is where you put those principles and concepts into action, as well as some of the following new ones:

- **Pacemaker operation:** The pacemaker operation sets the pace for the rest of the value stream. It's the one and only operation that receives the production schedule. The pacemaker produces to the takt time and sets the pace for the operations before it to produce only enough to replenish what the pacemaker operation has consumed. After the pacemaker operation, the process must produce in a continuous flow (unless a storage area or *supermarket* is required for finished goods — see later in this chapter). Balance multiples of pacemaker production to the quantity shipped to the customer. For example, if the shipping quantity to the customer is 60 per container, then you might release 20 at a time to the pacemaker operation.

- **Bottleneck process:** The *bottleneck process* is the process with the longest cycle time.

- **Work modules:** *Work modules* are aggregated operations fit into a compact area, in order to facilitate continuous flow, and single-piece production. Work cells are capable of performing all, or most, of the operations required for the value stream to deliver its product or service. This is wholly different from a traditional functional-department organization.

- **Supermarkets:** *Supermarkets* are stores of in-process inventory used where the process cannot produce a continuous flow. Examples of supermarkets include when one operation services many value streams, when suppliers are too far away, or when processes are unstable, have long lead times, or have out-of-balance cycle times. The supplying operation controls the supermarket and its inventory. Supermarket inventory is tightly controlled.

- **Standardized work:** *Standardized work* is the description of the work being performed, and it includes the takt time, specific sequence or activities and defined work-in-process inventory. It's the standard to which the actual process is compared, and it represents the foundation on which to improve. (See Chapter 12.)

- ***Kanban:*** *Kanban* are the signals to move and produce. In a *pull system,* where material or work is "pulled through" a process by demand, *kanban* is instruction that declares that a withdrawal has been made, so you can produce more. The signal can come in many forms: an empty container, a card, a ball — it takes whatever form best tells the supplying operation to produce. *Kanban* identifies a standard production quantity. (See Chapter 11.)

- **Heijunka:** *Heijunka,* also known as *workload leveling* or *production smoothing,* is the practice of smoothing out the volume and mix of the schedule for what's to be produced. The goal of *heijunka* is to level work schedules to the point where there is little variation on a daily basis. *Heijunka* makes continuous flow, pull signals, and inventory minimization possible. (See Chapter 11.)

- **Pitch:** *Pitch* is the amount of time required to make a standard container of finished product. If the standard container is 60 pieces and the takt time is 45 seconds, the pitch is 45 minutes.

Marking up the current-state VSM

The future-state VSM begins as a markup of the current-state VSM. Don't start with a clean sheet of paper! Make changes directly on the current-state VSM. Identify where and what type of improvements you intend to make. Based on the team's evaluations and observations, indicate what changes will address the issues. The markup technique is to indicate the changes in a sunburst icon called a *kaizen burst.*

Marking all of the areas you want to change doesn't imply that you'll necessarily make all the changes at the same time, but it defines an endpoint and scope for this particular improvement phase. With this picture, you can predict the type and extend of improvement you anticipate from the implementation. By identifying such things as how much NVA time will be reduced, and how much key process times are reduced, you can quantify the improvement goals.

It's important that everyone be able to see markups and make changes easily. Use sticky-notes and pencils if you're in a low-tech environment, or if you're in a high-tech environment, use collaborative tools and track comments and changes ideas.

In the salad company example, the team marks up their current-state VSM with numerous ideas for improvement as a result of their observations and ideal-state brainstorming. Figure 8-2 shows the areas where the team would like to improve. They start with a 5S (see Chapter 11) to clean up and organize the work area. In particular, they identify standard containers and scoops for the ingredients, and improved visual controls in the area. Because they observed that not all team members understood the work standard for the salad line, they review the process and establish formal, written standards; they then post the standards on the line. Because the salad-preparation work was not complete, they evaluate ways to eliminate NVA time and implement pull signals between assembly, preparation and supply. They also reverse the product assembly flow to eliminate the extra traffic in the production area, which is a safety hazard, caused by the drivers retrieving finished salads.

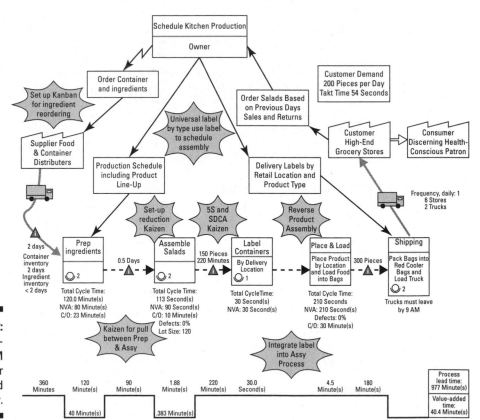

Figure 8-2: The current-state VSM markup for the salad company.

Eventually, the team also wants to improve the inventory management in the value stream. In addition, they want to involve their suppliers in identifying ways to receive more-frequent deliveries and have better stock rotation.

Gazing into the crystal ball: Seeing the future-state value-stream map

As soon as you've identified the candidate changes, create a new picture: your future-state VSM draft — the picture of what the value stream will look like after implementing the improvements. Begin with the current-state VSM and implement the proposed changes. Leave the *kaizen* bursts in place for reference.

Also ask yourself a set of qualifying questions. (See the "Pacemakers, super-markets, and *heijunka*, oh my!" section, earlier in this chapter to clarify any of these questions.) Indicate the answers on the future-state VSM draft, either directly or through the selection of the correct icons for *kanban*.

- What is the takt time (confirming it hasn't changed from the current state)?
- What is the actual cycle time compared to the takt time?
- Where is the bottleneck operation?
- What operation has the greatest variation in cycle time or quality performance?
- Where can continuous flow happen?
- Where can work cells be implemented?
- Which is the pacemaker operation?
- What process will be scheduled to the customer demand?
- Where will you use *kanban* signals?
- Where do supermarkets need to be located?
- What is the right lot size between processes?
- What is the standard shipping quantity for the customer?
- What is the pitch?
- What are the current setup times?
- How can schedules be smoothed at the pacemaker operation?
- How much time, of the available hours, is being used for production and how much is leftover for changeovers?

Answering real questions about value-stream maps

Value-stream mapping is uniquely related to Lean. You typically don't encounter VSMs outside of Lean practice. If you're new to Lean, you'll naturally have questions. In the following list, we answer some frequently asked questions:

✔ **What makes a VSM so useful, as opposed to standard process-flow diagrams?** A process-flow diagram is a valuable tool for identifying resources and interfaces, but that's only part of the picture. A value-stream map is a more complete process flow — and it's customer-centric. The value-stream map, in one place, shows not only how material flows through the value stream, but also the information flow, takt time, bottleneck operations, operator location, size and type of inventories, modes of transportation, as well as the relationship of customers and suppliers along the whole value stream. The value stream is much more comprehensive than a process flow diagram.

✔ **Why create an ideal-state value-stream map?** Creating an ideal-state VSM encourages you to think outside the box, looking at the value stream with an objective viewpoint to identify breakthrough ideas. It opens up your mind to the possibility of dramatic innovation, sometimes referred to as *kaikaku*. Although the main focus of Lean is in making regular, small, incremental improvements, if you never take the time to contemplate or dream of a radically different state, you'll be missing an opportunity for truly innovative improvement. You also create a long-term vision to work toward as you incrementally improve.

✔ **Where is the best place to start with value-stream mapping?** As always, start with your customer. If your customer is not the end consumer, you still start with your customer — but keep in mind how your processes are affected by the consumer. After you've identified the customer's requirements, work your way upstream.

✔ **What is the "right" level of detail?** There is no single "right" level of detail — it depends on your context and condition. The right level of detail is a balance between defining enough detail to find and eliminate meaningful amounts of waste and not having so much detail that you bog down and never move to the improvement phase. Value-stream mapping is an iterative process, so with each pass through, you can add more detail as necessary.

✔ **What is the difference between the macro (or high-level) view of the value stream and the value-stream map?** The macro-level view is a diagram that shows you where your process fits in the overall value stream relative to the consumer and the first supplier of the rawest of raw materials. If you were to try to construct a VSM on a detailed level of the entire VSM, it would be unwieldy and you would never get to the improvement phase. With the simple macro diagram, you gain perspective.

✔ **Which is better: creating a manual VSM or using a software package to create the VSM?** In a team environment, it can be faster to use manual drawings to create initial VSMs, because they're simple, quick, more visual and engaging for a team of people constructing them. After the initial creation, use software tools like ARIS to maintain and control the on-going VSMs.

Warning: Whether you use manual VSMs or plots from a software tool, you need to go to *gemba* when creating, validating or brainstorming processes.

✔ **How do I VSM the same product made in different places?** Start at one location and carry the knowledge to other facilities. As you form the team, include members from the other locations. When you *go to gemba* (where work physically is done.), include the other facilities to observe what variation exists in the process. These steps will prevent the "not invented here" syndrome when you spread the knowledge across the organization. You're also more likely to create a blend of best-practice ideas to implement.

After you've answered these questions and indicated the changes on the future-state VSM draft, you can analyze the map and predict what the future-state process should look like. If you're using a software program, the lead time along the bottom will update as you change the information for the step in the value stream.

Figure 8-3 shows the future-state VSM draft for the salad company. Note the changes. The company will first establish standards and improve the scheduling for the preparation operations by implementing a supermarket and preparing for replenishment. By establishing standards and eliminating the push inventory, the company sees significant reductions in lead time. They move the labeling operation into the assembly process. They use universal UPC codes to eliminate the sorting of labels by store.

As with the current-state VSM analysis, don't get stuck analyzing the potential changes for your future-state VSM to death. Lean is an iterative process. Identify what you want to improve, then improve it, and then repeat the cycle (Use the PDCA for this; see Chapter 9.) The future-state VSM is a snapshot of where you want to go. Make the picture and move to *kaizen* (Chapter 9).

Creating the Mosaic of Continuous Improvement: Setting the Stage for Kaizen

Value-stream mapping is a foundational tool used as part of a cycle and philosophy of continuous improvement. It may sound like it's a big effort — creating a current-state map, then an ideal-state map, then a future-state map draft, and finally a future-state map that you can actually implement. You may feel like you need to command significant resources to bring a team together, analyze all the data, brainstorm all the ideas, and involve all the different perspectives. You may be thinking you're developing a new career in cartography with all these maps! But the role and purpose of value-stream mapping is not about conducting huge efforts, big projects, and long implementation programs. You create value-stream maps in order to document, focus, and guide improvement efforts. Value-stream mapping is a concise effort, typically performed in a short time-span of just a few days — even for a relatively complex process. For simpler processes like the salad making exercise, you perform these VSM activities in a few hours.

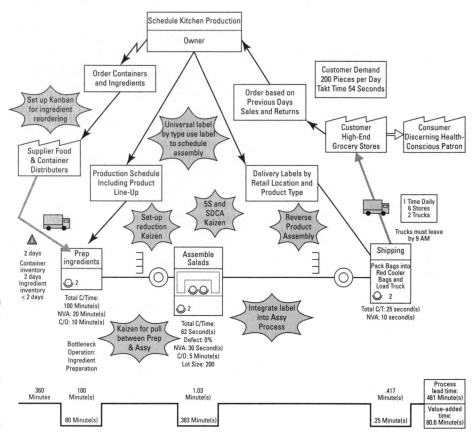

Figure 8-3:
The future-state value-stream map draft for the salad company.

Looking toward the annual horizon

Use the improvements that you identified on the future-state VSM to establish implementation priorities and a plan. The plan should be concise — just a few pages, no frills — it's a brief look at the year ahead. Scope individual improvement activities to days, weeks, or months, depending on the complexity of the activity. The plan should be a list of the projects that you will complete, with timing and responsibilities clearly defined.

To maintain the proper scope and focus of your future-state plans:

✔ Identify a minimum number of key metrics for improvement. Don't try to solve all the problems at once.

✔ Prioritize changes that are most meaningful to the customer first, then look at those most meaningful to the business.

✔ Make the project just large enough to be meaningful and measurable.

✔ Try to change one thing at a time, quickly to see the improvement effect.

✔ Remember that you're going to be doing it again!

How often you revisit your future-state VSM depends on your business cycles; however, do it at least every six months. Validate your ideal-state VSM annually. You don't have to go through the entire Current State-Ideal State-Future State map exercise each time you make a change to the current state. The emphasis is on the improvement, not the mapping exercise. If you have completed all your planned improvements before six months, create a new future state VSM.

Many companies make the mistake of changing too many things all at once. This is a recipe for less-than-optimal results, and it makes it impossible to understand true root cause. Make small, simple incremental changes quickly and frequently. You will gain momentum and have more traceability and control for the results.

Improving just for improvement sake is a waste of time and resources; it can even cause people to disengage if you are not careful. Be sure your improvement efforts directly affect the customer for good or improve the business in a cohesive way — safety, people, quality, delivery, cost and so on.

Future-state implementations

After you have the maps and the plan, you're ready to implement. In Chapter 9, we show you how to implement Lean projects. At this juncture, you may be wondering, "What happens to the maps as I make improvements?"

- ✓ **Update the current-state VSM to reflect the new state as you make improvements.** This is a critically important configuration-management practice. You must show that current state reflects the new standard. You also need the record of where you are in pursuit of your goals. Keep a copy of your first current-state VSM. Two or three years from now, you won't believe how much change you've made. The old maps are also good to have on hand so you can remind people just how far you've come and how you got there.

- ✓ **Compare the new current state to the predictions on the future-state VSM.** If you aren't on track, you may need to adjust your plan.

- ✓ **After all the ideas have been exhausted or you're at the end of a planning period, start the mapping process again.** Use the latest current-state VSM, and move through the exercise of confirming the validity of your ideal-state VSM and building the next future-state VSM.

Chapter 9

Flowing in the Right Direction: Lean Projects and *Kaizen*

Recognize that a value-stream map (VSM) is just that: a map. A VSM of the *current state* shows where you are and, once you analyze it, what needs to be improved; a VSM of the *ideal state* is a vision of what paradise looks like; and a VSM of the next *future state* shows where you're going. But a VSM does not tell you *how* to get there. If you were to take a trip, you would pack your map, but the map alone won't get you out of your driveway. You need to know the *how*s of the journey: the modes of transportation, the number of travelers, available resources, the timing of events, and so on. *Kaizen* is the how. *Kaizen* is the way you improve the value stream; it's practiced through a continuing series of improvement workshops and projects — at both the individual and team level.

Have you ever traveled somewhere so much that you're just as comfortable on the road as you are being at home? Experienced travelers or even commuters reach a point where taking the trip is no big deal. They don't have to think about what they're going to pack, which bag they're going to take, how to make travel arrangements, or any other details. Traveling becomes second nature to them. As you travel down the road of Lean, a similar thing happens: The change is no longer a special event, but rather the very way you conduct yourself and your business every day. You begin to address problems continuously and to act in a Lean manner. You begin to behave in a Lean way. *Kaizen* is this way of life.

In this chapter, we tell you what *kaizen* is, how to practice *kaizen* in your own organization, and how to conduct *kaizen* workshops and projects.

Kaizen: A Way of Life

Kaizen is a Japanese word that translates to betterment or improvement. It has become a Japanese business philosophy. The goal of *kaizen* is to eliminate waste in the value stream. You accomplish this through the application of techniques like organizing work areas (5S, see Chapter 8), achieving standardized work, leveling production, balancing production to customer demand (takt time), right-sizing equipment, reducing inventory and work-in-process, just-in-time delivery, and more. *Kaizen* is how you improve quality and safety and reduce cost.

Although *kaizen* has typically been practiced in the West simply as an improvement workshop or event, true *kaizen* is a way of life. It governs everyday thinking and business. *Kaizen* is a regular, daily activity that considers the process as well as the results. It examines the big picture and takes in the whole of the environment, as well as the immediate issue locally at hand.

To practice *kaizen* is to respect people first. Equipment, facilities, processes, and technology are important tools — and they're subordinate to people. *Kaizen* focuses on humanizing the workplace and eliminating hard — both mental and physical — work. And you don't blame or judge people for the mistakes of the past, because blaming is in itself wasteful.

Kaizen involves everyone, at all levels; don't relegate it to a function or specialty. Ultimately, everyone — from the CEO to the last office worker or factory worker — practices *kaizen*.

According to Masaaki Imai, one of the principle pioneers bringing Toyota Production System and *kaizen* to the West, a better definition of *kaizen* is "Every day, everybody, and everywhere improvement."

Kaizen: The philosophy

Kaizen is a philosophy of improvement that encourages continuous, incremental changes in life across all aspects — personal, social, work, home, play. *Kaizen* means not letting a day pass without some form of improvement. If Western philosophy can be summarized as "If it ain't broke, don't fix it," by contrast, *kaizen* says that even if it isn't broken, it can — and must be — improved. Do it better and make it better. The alternative is stagnation and decline.

As a work philosophy, *kaizen* means continual, incremental change in all areas — large and small, internal and external — to improve the whole organization. Business *kaizen* considers the entire system of the business: Conduct improvement activities at all levels, with a systems view. The business philosophy of *kaizen* also calls for an unending effort for improvement that involves everyone in the organization — managers and workers alike.

The philosophy of *kaizen* in business concentrates on the processes that influence the outcomes — cause and effect. The *kaizen* philosophy also sees the business through two lenses: setting new standards and maintaining existing standards. More specifically:

- ✔ ***Kaizen* maintenance** establishes the policies and rules that help maintain the performance levels set by the present managerial and operating standards.

- ✔ ***Kaizen* improvement** focuses efforts on the continuous improvement of existing standards and processes or the innovation of new ones.

In both cases, the philosophy of *kaizen* calls on you to apply all appropriate training, materials, tools, and supervision to both improve as well as maintain your standards and processes on a continual basis.

Kaizen has been attributed as the basis for the many successes of the Japanese in global automotive, electronics, and other business and consumer markets. In Japan, *kaizen* is the overarching strategy for business. Everyone is encouraged to make regular suggestions for improvements. In companies like Toyota and Canon, hundreds of suggestions are defined, written, shared, and implemented by employees every year. And these suggestions aren't limited to anyone's specific work area. *Kaizen* is based on making changes anywhere that they might lead to real business improvement.

Kaizen in action

Kaizen requires everyone be involved — from the CEO to the last office or factory worker. But of course everyone's role is not the same. At each level of management, the roles and responsibilities of *kaizen* are different:

- ✔ **Senior managers are responsible for defining the vision and direction of *kaizen* for the organization, setting goals, and creating the culture in which *kaizen* can thrive.** Wherever *kaizen* requires investment and innovation, senior managers provide the resources required for implementation. Senior managers also ensure that the direction of improvement continues to improve customer value and improves the business in the direction of the ideal state.

 ✔ **Middle managers are required to ensure that the employees have the skills, materials, and tools to perform *kaizen*.** They ensure that *kaizen* is occurring across functions in the organization and achieving the goals. They guide and teach the organization through questions and problem solving. They also implement *kaizen*.

 ✔ **Supervisors make sure that *kaizen* is occurring on both an individual and a workgroup level.** Supervisors also ensure that the people follow standard operating procedures and practices. Supervisors train and coach employees and foster morale. They provide their own *kaizen* suggestions.

In addition, all managers must practice *kaizen* themselves. They show leadership by doing.

In the following sections, we present the Lean definition of waste, introduce the Plan-Do-Check-Act (PDCA) cycle used in *kaizen* and review the foundations of *kaizen* implementation.

Eliminating waste

You eliminate waste in the value stream by doing *kaizen:* continuous improvement activities. When you examine the value stream in small increments, you see waste that you may not have seen before. Through the lens of *kaizen* glasses, you suddenly see the extra movement, the work that can be done more effectively, or the effort that doesn't truly transform the product or service.

This waste may be the result of people and systems that are not performing to the established standards and practices, or you may need to define improved standards and practices. In either case, when you eliminate this waste, you improve not only the value stream, but also the conditions for the people who work in it.

Examine your value stream for waste, or *muda,* according to the seven forms of waste:

 ✔ **Transportation:** Is there unnecessary (non-value-added) movement of parts, materials, or information between processes?

 ✔ **Waiting:** Are people, parts, systems, or facilities idly waiting for a work cycle to be completed?

 ✔ **Overproduction:** Are you producing sooner, faster, or in greater quantities than the customer is demanding?

 ✔ **Defects:** Does the process result in anything that the customer would deem unacceptable?

✔ **Inventory:** Do you have any raw materials, work-in-progress (WIP), or finished goods that are not having value added to them?

✔ **Movement:** How much do you move materials, people, equipment, and goods within a processing step?

✔ **Extra Processing:** How much extra work is performed beyond the standard required by the customer?

In addition to these seven "classic" areas of waste, Lean Master Shigeo Shingo defined an *eighth form of waste: the underutilization of people*. While waiting is part of the underutilization, the eighth waste is more about not allowing your people to contribute fully their talents, ideas and energy to their work environment. When you don't fully engage on your people, you are missing out on a lot of opportunities for improvement and satisfaction. How can you entice your people to continuously improve?

Examine each of these eight forms of *muda* from the basis of existing operating standards and practices. Are the standards defined? Are they followed? If not, *kaizen* compels you to implement training and support in order to perform to established standards. If waste is occurring in these areas, despite performance to standards, *kaizen* requires you to define and implement improvements.

In addition to *muda,* explore your value stream for waste due to variation — *mura* — and also waste due to overburdening or overstressing the people or system — *muri.*

Using the Plan-Do-Check-Act cycle

The Plan-Do-Check-Act (PDCA) cycle is the Lean operating framework — the methodology for implementing *kaizen*. PDCA is a short-cycle iterative improvement scheme. It fits perfectly into the continuous-improvement philosophy of *kaizen*.

The PDCA cycle was first developed in the 1930s by Walter Shewhart, the Bell Telephone physicist often call the father of statistical quality control. PDCA was brought to Japan in the 1950s by W. Edwards Deming; in Japan, it's known as the Deming cycle. Alternatively, it is referred to as Plan-Do-*Study*-Act (PDSA).

Here's what the four parts of the PDCA (or PDSA) acronym mean:

✔ **Plan: Define the issue you are addressing.** Create a plan for change, identifying specifically what you want to change. Define the steps you need to make the change, understand risk and predict the results of the change.

✔ **Do:** Carry out the plan in a trial or test environment, on a small scale, under controlled conditions. Measure the results of the trial.

✔ **Check or study:** Examine the results of your trial. Verify with data that you've improved the process. If you have, consider implementing it on a broader scale; if you haven't, go back and try again.

✔ **Act or Adjust:** Implement the changes you've verified on a broader scale. Update the standard operating procedures and ensure everyone is performing to the new standard.

Many organizations who have adopted a Lean Six Sigma framework alternately use the DMAIC (define, measure, analyze, improve, control) approach from Six Sigma rather than the Lean PDCA cycle. DMAIC can work in a Lean initiative, but it's different. DMAIC calls for the application of great statistical rigor and analysis in order to tackle complex problems. You involve specialists (black belts) who may take months finding root cause and devising the improvement plans. PDCA is *kaizen*: improvement methodology, practiced by everyone, with a trial-and-check step supported by data.

Standardizing work

Kaizen requires you to have standards — standard specifications, standard processes, standard systems, standard procedures, standard work instructions, and so on. Measure and perform all work to standard. After you implement any improvement, you must standardize to perform consistently to this improved state. (See Chapter 12.)

Innovating with Kaikaku

Kaizen is generally considered to be steady, incremental change. But what if there is a need for fundamental change, dramatic improvements, or a new system? When radical change or innovation is required, *kaizen* takes a different form, called *kaikaku,* which means reform or innovation (*kaikaku* is also sometimes known as *breakthrough kaizen, flow kaizen,* or *system kaizen*).

Kaikaku still uses the PDCA methodology, but to solve bigger problems. *Kaikaku* changes are usually capital intensive. When true innovation happens, you change the game. Seek inspiration from other applications, environments, or industries, and use new technologies or apply the results of new discoveries. *Kaikaku* can happen in a workshop environment. If you do a workshop, you will want to do some preplanning before the event because the changes are usually significant. For instance, you may have a manufacturing facility that you completely change to improve material and product flow. Or a discount store that eliminates the garden center and replaces it with a grocery department. Both are radical changes that require pre-planning to minimize operational disruption.

Here's another example: *Milk runs* for inbound product pickup are commonplace today; the materials are picked up on a regular schedule and routed from multiple suppliers by a single truck. When milk runs were first introduced, though, they were a radical departure from the commonplace method of receiving product shipments. The inspiration for milk runs came from the food industry; the manufacturing industry innovated it. In this case, the change was not implemented overnight; small-scale implementations were expanded to form a new business standard.

Use 3P — the production preparation process (see Chapter 10) — as part of your *kaikaku* planning. This will help you avoid waste and maximize your resources and investment.

Improving the Value Stream with Kaizen

As you use the Plan-Do-Check-Act (PDCA) cycle to improve the value stream in *kaizen* projects, you'll find improvement opportunities across the entire value stream. *Be sure to prioritize and select projects based on their impact to customer value.* Your goal is to make regular, steady, incremental improvements, as opposed to large, breakthrough changes. Use your current-state and future-state VSMs to guide project selection.

A common problem in *kaizen* is oversized projects. Either you've selected too large a project, or you've allowed the project scope to creep up to an unmanageable size. To avoid oversized projects, focus on eliminating a single form of waste at a time, rather than multiple forms or all eight forms (see "Eliminating waste," earlier in this chapter) at the same time. Don't try to fix the entire value stream in a few projects.

Selecting projects

You can perform *kaizen* projects at three different levels: the individual level, the team level, and the management level. A Lean project can be part of routine daily business, part of an improvement initiative, or part of a formal workshop. Scope the project depending on the size and type of waste you're targeting for reduction.

Select your projects based on a combination of several factors. Begin by analyzing the VSM and selecting the biggest contributing problem areas — those that directly affect customer value. Then, employ both qualitative and quantitative measures to seek out the data that highlights the key issues, particularly through direct customer feedback. Finally, use your experience to target the waste areas for improvement. Initial projects should be ones that will be highly visible to the customer and will make a significant impact on the business; these characteristics will create momentum for a Lean transformation.

Many Lean companies also have a suggestion program for identifying projects. In Japanese companies, these have proven to be prolific sources of project ideas. The ideas can come from anywhere, but usually they begin from within local areas or workgroups.

Take before and after photos and videos of the physical aspects of the problem you're addressing. The images will give you an objective visual record of the improvement, facilitate knowledge transfer to other parts of the organization, and help you to realize how far you've come.

Project methodology

Lean projects follow the simple but specific framework of the PDCA cycle. The level of depth, as well as measurements, analyses, and controls may vary, but the foundational methodology is the same. After you've defined the project scope, begin the project cycle.

Within the *kaizen* methodology, one critical rule is that you must go to *gemba* — the Japanese word that means "where all activities are taking place." As described by *kaizen* Master Masaaki Imai, *gemba* is where customer value is added in the value stream. *Gemba* is the most important place for management. Imai urges all managers to go to *gemba*.

The Plan Phase

During the Plan phase, objectively describe the change you want to make, in order to address the problem identified by the selection process and as represented in the current-state VSM. Include the following:

- ✔ Identify the processes you intend to change.
- ✔ Describe the steps needed to make the change in both the prototype/test and production operation environments to achieve the future-state VSM.
- ✔ Ensure you protect your customer during the trials; they are always your first priority.
- ✔ Predict the results and risks of the change.

At this point, consider performing a Process Failure Mode and Effects Analysis (PFMEA) to evaluate potential failures in the process. Consider what could go wrong, the impacts, and identify and prioritize risk-abating actions.

Use the same quality data and analysis tools as you develop the implementation plan.

What to expect: The project individual or group evaluates the situation using the data, as well as personal — and sometimes, physical — evaluations. They determine the changes that they intend to make, the steps needed to make those changes, and the measurements they'll take to confirm the proper effects of the change. They predict performance targets and create an action plan that includes the definition of who makes the change, what is to be done, and when it will occur. They identify the required resources. Normally, the individual or project group will make the changes themselves, but sometimes outside resources are required. If a physical layout or a work area will be changed, the team will construct before and after layouts during the Plan phase. The team plans to make sure that the customer is protected during the time they are making trial improvements.

Before you move to the Do phase, make sure you have clearly identified the fundamental issue or problem you are going to improve — not just a symptom. Clear problem definition is vital, so you do not waste time or resources chasing the wrong problem.

The Do Phase

In the Do phase, you implement the plan in a trial or prototype environment — on a small scale and under controlled conditions.

What to expect: The team will demonstrate the improvements — and they will also reveal issues that may be associated with the full-scale implementation. Having selected a proper test or prototype environment, the test will be small enough to be conducted quickly, but large enough that the outcomes are valid and representative. The team will identify the differences between the test and target environments so that you can properly extrapolate the results. They will also capture data to support the decision to proceed.

The Check (or Study) Phase

In this phase, you're examining the results of your trial or prototype implementation. Quantify the degree to which the changes you made improved the trial process, and predict the extrapolation of these results to the greater process.

What to expect: The project individual or group will review the trial data and determine whether the change is a valid improvement — using statistical methods, if necessary. If the trial objectives were met, then the project proceeds to the Act phase. However, if the improvement was not sufficient, the team might rerun the trial, or return to the Plan phase. If the trial did not solve the issue, the project returns to the beginning for failure analysis and new planning.

It is OK to "fail" as long as you take the time to learn from it. The best lessons come from experiments with unexpected results.

The Act Phase

In this last phase, you implement the changes on the full scale of the process. Update the VSM, the standards and specifications, and verify performance. Report the results.

What to expect: The project individual or group implements changes to all affected process people, systems, and technologies. They update all standard documents and procedures, including work instructions and visual controls, to reflect the change. Monitor the changes to ensure that the expected outcome is real and as expected. Update the current-state VSM to reflect the changes. Finally, communicate outcomes to affected stakeholders and management.

Communicate and involve management, stakeholders, and customers throughout the process. By the time the Act phase happens, they should not be surprised by the changes.

Individual projects

Kaizen philosophy empowers every employee to improve her work area, as well as suggest improvements in any other work area. With such grand empowerment comes the rightful expectation that every employee will also participate in the improvement of those work areas. In a *kaizen* environment, employees implement the ideas, not specialists.

Kaizen calls for small, incremental improvements to the value stream. *Kaizen* at the individual level is often related to improvements in an individual's work area, or in how the individual performs her work. These changes are normally low-investment enough that the individual implements herself on a regular basis.

Even at the individual level, the project follows the same PDCA cycle, using the same measurement and analysis tools. Focus individual projects on the direct work area and responsibilities of the individual. They should go faster than the group projects; individual projects are often completed in a matter of hours or days. If the job being studied does not occur on a daily basis or is highly complex, then the duration may be longer.

Although Lean is a disciplined system, it's also a creative system. *Kaizen* sets the stage for creativity to shine through. *Kaizen* enhancements can be as simple as creating a fixture from a piece of wood to perform an operation, outlining the shape of your tools on a tool board so you can see that all of the tools are present, or adding a guide to more quickly align and staple a stack of papers.

Remember _MacGyver?_ He was that character on a U.S. TV program by the same name in the 1980s. With little more than a piece of dental floss, a chunk of wood and a wad of gum, he could always create something to escape from the tight spot he managed to find himself in on every episode. At the individual _kaizen_ level, use what is available to create quick, simple, creative solutions.

Group projects

Kaizen projects performed at the self-directed group level follow the PDCA cycle, but the scope is typically much larger than the scope of projects performed at the individual level. Group projects may last weeks or even months. Observing the process, collecting the data, identifying the form of waste, defining and implementing the improvements, measuring the results, and standardizing the new work — it all takes time.

A risk to group success is that the team loses focus and interest, because the project takes too long or is not well defined. Before you leave the Plan phase, make sure you have a well-defined project. It is best to move singular or simple solutions quickly through the PDCA cycle so you show progress and maintain people's interest.

Management projects

Management projects usually address strategic issues, administrative processes, cross-functional problems, or support systems. They tend to be technical and complex in nature. Their aims are to:

- ✔ Reduce bureaucracy within the organization and its systems.
- ✔ Ensure that the measurement and business systems support a Lean enterprise.
- ✔ Ensure that requisite facility improvements are in place.

Use task forces and cross-functional teams to conduct management projects. These projects follow the PDCA cycle but may use statistical methods and simulations that are more advanced. Be sure to include the right people, those who have the best functional knowledge of their area and the overall process understanding.

Work team projects

A work team that dedicates part of its normal working time to *kaizen* can tackle a Lean project. A work team project involves and affects the whole team, not just an individual. Work team projects are usually self-directed, with the manager or supervisor advising team, instead of leading the project.

Work-team project meetings follow the principle of standardized work:

- ✔ They have a timed agenda.
- ✔ The team uses tracking documents.
- ✔ Before and after pictures and charts track the team's progress.
- ✔ The team meets in an assigned area near the work space, *not* in a conference room!
- ✔ In the assigned meeting area, the team displays key data that it uses for its problem-solving and improvement efforts.

Although the work-team projects are usually larger and more involved, they still follow the small, incremental, low-investment model that the individual projects follow. They also follow the PDCA methodology.

One of the challenges to work-team projects is that they can lose momentum and the team can become demotivated over time. The supervisor's job is to set goals for improvement, keep the team on track, and celebrate the wins. Management's role is to keep the supervisors on track and ensure that the improvements are aligned with the organization's ideal state vision.

Kaizen: The Workshop

One of the ways to quickly improve the value stream is through the use of the *kaizen* workshop. Also known as a *kaizen event* or a *kaizen blitz,* the *kaizen workshop* is a fast and furious run through the PDCA cycle, typically in five days or less. During the *kaizen* workshop, the project team directly targets a specific area to find *muda, mura,* and *muri,* and remove it from the value stream. The source of waste may be anything — quality, communications, changeover time, organization, and so on — but regardless of the source, the workshop process you follow and your end goals are the same.

To focus properly on the workshop, the project team halts its normal work completely and does not produce its normal product or service. Advanced planning is required to ensure that you do not adversely affect your customers or other areas of the business while the improvements are happening. *Kaizen*-workshop solutions are famous for requiring minimal investment and yielding great benefits to the value stream.

Most people think of a production or manufacturing area when they think of a *kaizen* workshop, but remember that *kaizen* is for everyone in every area of the business. One Lean company understood that every area benefits from *kaizen*. They event held a *kaizen* event on the trunks of their salespeople's cars!

Planning the kaizen workshop

For your *kaizen* workshop to be successful, you need the right project scope and the right team working full-time together, usually for three to five consecutive days. To pull this off requires planning. In this section, we will tell you how to scope a *kaizen* project, select the right team, and follow the workshop agenda.

Kaizen workshops interrupt operations for a few days. With proper planning this doesn't have to be a problem. Coordinate within the organization to ensure you create enough inventory to protect customer deliveries.

Workshop scope

In most cases the team has the current-state VSM in hand. The workshop team should also have baseline metrics established before they begin. These, along with customer satisfaction, quality, and operational data, help decide where to focus the *kaizen* efforts. If the area has never experienced a *kaizen* workshop, focus first on 5S.

Conduct the initial *kaizen* workshops in or near where the work occurs and scope them to have a significant impact for the organization. The best *kaizen* workshops are those that solve a nagging issue (preferably an issue directly related to the customer); otherwise have them seek to accomplish something believed to be impossible (such as reducing machine setup time from days to minutes).

Take before photos or videos of the work area or current-state conditions, including office areas. These will later show how far the *kaizen* journey has taken you — like vacation photos!

Workshop project team

The *kaizen*-workshop project team should be cross-functional and include senior managers, the value-stream owner, people who work in the area, representatives from support functions, resources with special technical or business skills, and usually even a few people from elsewhere in the company who are unrelated to the area.

You may wonder why a *kaizen* workgroup contains people from unrelated areas. Isn't it a waste of their time? The answer is a resounding "no!" The role of the unrelated team member is to ask the innocent and objective questions that make the team think in new ways. Outsiders also provide valuable experience and perspective on other areas of the business.

You can directly involve your customer in the workshop, if the scope of the project is appropriate. They can provide unique Voice of the Customer (VOC) perspective in the moment.

Successful Lean organizations have members of the leadership team, if not the CEOs themselves, participate or even conduct the initial *kaizen* workshops. Leaders must always take a very active role in the *kaizen* process, demonstrating the support and commitment for the transformation, as well as creating relationships with employees whom they might not otherwise meet. At the same time, the leaders must "authorize" change, not dictate change. Leaders do not have all the answers; their role is to "lead." The people who make the product or provide the service are those closest to knowing what has to be done to eliminate waste. The leader's job is to create a long-term vision, empower the employees, ask questions, and enable the change.

The *kaizen* workshop usually lasts from three to five days, depending on the experience level of the team and the number of hours per day that the workshop lasts. If you have multiple shifts, the *kaizen* should not only include representation from all shifts, but also occur during part of each shift. Although you may have standards in place, depending on how disciplined the organization is, you usually find that different shifts do different things.

A typical agenda

The agenda for the *kaizen* workshop is prescriptive and deliberate. Table 9-1 shows a sample agenda, indicating the major activities that occur during the workshop.

Table 9-1   The *Kaizen* Workshop: A Typical Agenda

Day	Theme of the Day	Topics and Activities Addressed during the Day
1	Training	Train on Lean concepts and principles
		Create team connection and interaction. (team building)
		Train more on *muda, mura,* and *muri*
		Review the current-state VSM
		Train on data-gathering tools and continuous-improvement tools
		Complete pre-*kaizen* metrics.
		Plan for Day 2.
2	Current-state analysis	Analyze current process.
		Brainstorm improvements.
		Design new work methods.
		Plan for Day 3.
3	Process implementation	Implement 5S+ safety
		Streamline flow
		Implement process changes — participants do the hands-on work
		Instruction of changes
		Identify additional improvements
		Pilot changes in work area
		Plan for Day 4
4	Observe and refine	Validate Day 3 improvements
		Verify full-rate production
		Refine improvements
		Establish standard work
		Plan for Day 5

(continued)

Table 9-1 *(continued)*

Day	Theme of the Day	Topics and Activities Addressed during the Day
5	Sustain and celebrate	Establish visual controls
		Complete all changes to standards
		Establish follow-up plan
		Complete post-*kaizen* metrics
		Present the results and celebrate

Conducting the kaizen workshop

After you have your plan in place, it's time to rock and roll. The team members work hard during the workshop, doing work that is not normally in their job descriptions and making a lot of improvements to the value stream in a short amount of time. In this section we tell you what to activities to expect and remind you to celebrate your successes.

Workshop activities

Have you ever watched one of those home-improvement makeover shows, where the homeowners, with the help of a design team, remodel a room in a house over a weekend? Or an organization show, where they take a few junk-laden rooms in a house and make the owners get rid of 90 percent of the contents? Whether they realize it or not, these shows are doing *kaizen* events in these peoples' homes. They're implementing 5S (sort, straighten, scrub, systematize, and standardize). They work long hours in a short time and, at the end of the show, there is a complete and amazing transformation.

Usually, the designer or show host asks the homeowner, "What is not working with this space?" Then they create a plan to address these issues. In this case, the homeowner is the customer. In the case of a work scenario, you have customer data that answers the "What's not working in this space?" question. It could be related to poor performance or, better yet, it could be related to new business. No matter what the focus, you as a team member will roll up your sleeves, get your hands dirty, work long hours, and do work that is dramatically different from you daily activities!

If the aim of the workshop is to free up floor space, then you'll be cleaning out the unnecessary items, like inventory, tools, boxes, and things that just don't have a real home in the area. The team creates a new process flow and rearranges the equipment as needed. When the space is free, cordon it off to protect it.

Oftentimes multiple *kaizen* workshops will create pockets of space, but not necessarily *usable* space. You need an overall plan for the facility to coordinate floor-space-clearing *kaizen* workshops.

An automotive facility received new work into an already full plant. Through the implementation of multiple, coordinated workshops, it was able to create usable space. Over a six-week period, the customer was not impacted at all, yet 39 work areas were transformed over six weeks to create 60,000 square feet of usable space. All the teams participating in the *kaizen* knew that free space needed for the new business — what need to happen and why it needed to occur. The coordination among the teams working toward a common goal was the key to the success.

If the workshop goal is to increase equipment uptime, then the team will usually clean the equipment. If appropriate, the team may paint the equipment a light color. If, for example, the team is working on a stamping press; the new paint provides a clean surface for all to see leaks or other issues. They use maintenance data and history to investigate the issues. They may examine spare parts availability and inventory. They establish a new preventive-maintenance standard. By the end of the workshop, a real transformation will occur.

Celebrate the win!

By the end of the workshop, you may not recognize your area! The team will be highly motivated. During the span of a few days, they will have incorporated many changes, and usually a few items will remain open. The follow-up plan will enable the team to ensure they close all the items. Seek to close all open items within 30 days of the workshop.

If the *kaizen* is part of a coordinated effort, like in the automotive example, then not only celebrate the success of each step taken, but also celebrate with everyone when they reach the collective goal.

Sustaining the kaizen-workshop gains

After the workshop is complete, one of the most important steps must occur: changing the standards to include the changes. Frequently, teams omit this vital step, causing the gains to be short lived and many of the benefits to be lost. The supervisor is responsible for ensuring that the employees are following the standards. Each employee is responsible for executing to the new standards. Develop this shared responsibility during the workshop.

If clearing out floor space was your goal, then consider constructing a barrier around the new space. Put a sign in the area communicating why the space was cleared out. Monitor the area to make sure that "mysterious" items don't suddenly appear to fill the space again. If you aren't diligent, the space will fill up again.

Establish regular weekly and monthly (7-day, 30-day, 60-day, and 90-day) verification points so everyone can ensure the changes are functioning in a regular daily environment as designed. Schedule reviews with managers (preferably conducted in the improved work area!), particularly if you need them to provide resources. When all of the items are complete, conduct a final review session of what results were achieved and what lessons were learned that could be leveraged to other areas of the business. Did you achieve the goals and objectives laid out at the start of the *kaizen*? This communication is vital to securing management support for sustaining the improvements, and garnering their commitment to do more *kaizen* workshops.

Kaizen workshops are powerful — so powerful that some organizations have found themselves using them as their only approach to *kaizen*. Be careful not to limit yourself this way: It will relegate Lean as a "special program" and limit success. To sustain Lean practice, use *kaizen* as the way you do business.

Part IV
The Lean Toolbox

The 5th Wave   By Rich Tennant

Frankly, I liked it better when we ran around barking like heck and scaring them into the pen.

In this part . . .

You develop the Lean lifestyle for your business with tools that facilitate customer understanding, value, flow, pull, perfection, and leadership. In this part, we tell you about the tools in the Lean toolbox and how best to apply them on your Lean journey.

Chapter 10

Customer and Value-Stream Tools

. . . .

In This Chapter

▶ Looking at customer focused tools

▶ Using value-stream tools

▶ Working with basic process tools

. . . .

*N*o matter where you work or play, having the right tools for the job is important. Imagine trying to play a round of golf with a hockey stick, or scaling a mountain in flip-flops. You wouldn't. To maximize your performance and results, you would get the right "tools" for the job, whether that job is a round of golf, a mountain trek, or a Lean transformation.

In this chapter, we introduce you to the Lean tools used to understand the customer and the value stream. With these tools, you can capture the customer's wants and needs, evaluate the value stream, and work with basic data. Along with the flow and pull tools described in Chapter 11, the perfection tools in Chapter 12, and the management tools in Chapter 13, these tools are part of the overall Lean toolbox. You need all these tools to support Lean practices.

Communing with the Customer

In any business, really understanding who your customer is and what your customer is all about is vital — but this is particularly true for anyone embarking on a Lean journey because Lean is all about delivering what the customer values. The tools in this section help you capture the voice of the customer, understand the customer's wants versus needs, and evaluate the competitive marketplace.

Capturing the voice of the customer

You not only need to know what the customer wants; you have to translate that information into language that the various parts of your organization can understand — and use. The *house of quality,* one of the main tools of Quality Function Deployment (QFD), is the most popular and effective tool for making this translation. The house of quality is essentially a sophisticated product planning matrix.

The house of quality is really more like a *neighborhood* of quality, by the time you're finished with it! Each matrix defines the relationship between what you're trying to accomplish and how you'll accomplish it. Figure 10-1 shows the interrelationship of the houses of quality, outlined here:

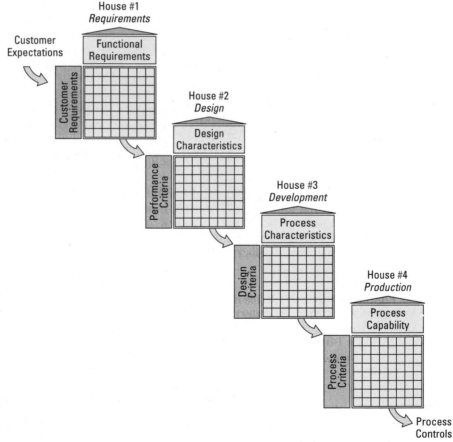

Figure 10-1:
The relationships among the four houses of quality.

✔ The first house translates the voice of the customer (VOC) into functional requirements.

✔ The second house translates the functional requirements into product-design requirements. In a service environment, it translates functional into service-design requirements.

✔ The third house translates product-design requirements into process-design requirements; in a service environment, service-design requirements into process-design requirements.

✔ The fourth house translates the process-design requirements into process-control requirements.

You gather the VOC through any and all means, including customer surveys, focus groups, personal interviews, product clinics, customer service and warranty data, or third-party industry reports. Multifunctional teams work together to construct the various houses. Having marketing involved in the fourth house is just as important as having manufacturing involved in the first house — they complete the picture. It's marketing's job to make sure the customer's voice is properly translated into tech-speak, but it's everyone's job to understand the customer and how everyone impacts customer satisfaction.

Inside the interior of the house of quality are a series of matrices. Figure 10-2 shows the interior floor plan of the house of quality. You construct from left to right. The filled circles indicate a strong relationship; the open circles, a moderate relationship; and the triangles, a weak relationship.

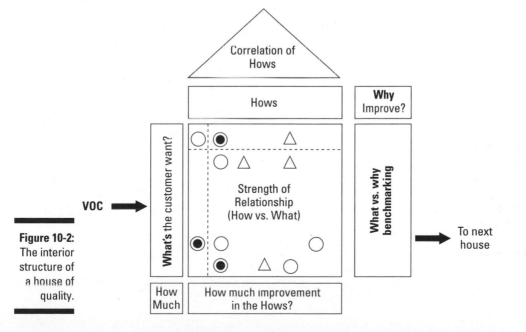

Figure 10-2:
The interior structure of a house of quality.

Understanding customer satisfaction

Kano modeling is a way to differentiate the customer's requirements into needs, wants, and delighters. When you're capturing the VOC, the customer may not explicitly state all of their requirements — or your opportunities for customer value. Kano modeling provides you with another way of understanding your customer (see Chapter 6 for more on Kano modeling). Table 10-1 shows you an example of data for a Kano model.

Table 10-1		Example of Kano Modeling	
Item	*Needs (expected requirements)*	*Wants (one-dimensional requirements)*	*Delighters (unexpected requirements*
Hotel room	Bed	Nonsmoking	Free in-room wi-fi
	Television	King-size bed	Coffeemaker
	Cleanliness	Specific room location	Bottled water
	Safety	Fresh linens on-demand	Free full breakfast

Sizing up the competition

Benchmarking is the process you use to compare your products, processes, or services usually against your direct competitors. You should benchmark yourself against the best in the world in a given segment or activity: you may not be a retail store, but you can compare your customer service against the highly touted Apple Store or Nordstrom's — and you should!

Benchmarking steps

Individuals or teams, depending on the scope of the study, do benchmarking. It is important that the people involved in the study have practical and technical skills to be able to understand the information thoroughly and use the data properly.

The first step in benchmarking is to identify what you're evaluating (that is, the key characteristics of the activity, product, or service). Then you make your comparisons against your direct competitors and the best in the world for that particular characteristic. Based on those comparisons, you evaluate how you perform, identify gaps, and then brainstorm ways to close the gaps. You might try to directly copy and incorporate your findings into your process. You could create new ways to adapt their ideas to your system. Or your team could innovate to try to surpass the market standard.

Benchmarking is not a one-time process. The market is always changing, and your competitors are always on a quest to unseat the market leader. Think about sports teams — they're always jockeying for the number-one position, overall as well as in key performance areas. By analyzing these areas of performance and then making adjustments to their training process, player rosters, and strategies, coaches around the world strive to be the best in their realm.

Benchmarking in action

Nowhere is benchmarking more apparent than in the World Cup. Once every four years, the world stops to watch the top countries vie for the title of best of the best. Traditionally, Brazil has always been one to beat; this soccer behemoth has dominated the game for decades. Although they may not always win, Brazil is always at the top of the list of the ones to watch.

In the two years prior to the finals, qualifying matches are played to narrow the field. During that time, all the coaches — from small Caribbean islands to the traditional powerhouses of Brazil, the Netherlands, Spain, Germany, and Italy — are benchmarking their play and adjusting their strategies in hopes of qualifying their country's team for the finals. Table 10-2 shows average key metrics, from a sampling of five matches, used to evaluate team performance.

Table 10-2	Example Benchmarking Analysis					
Metric	*Benchmark*	*Your Team*				
	Brazil	Spain	Netherlands	Germany	Uruguay	Team Dummies
Average % time of possession per match (in minutes)	56%	58%	52%	51%	46%	42%
Average goals per match	1.80	1.14	1.71	2.29	1.57	0.67
Average goals made by opponents per match	0.8	0.29	0.86	0.571	1.14	1.67
Total shots	89	121	93	102	102	69

(continued)

Table 10-2 *(continued)*

Metric	Benchmark	Your Team				
Average fouls committed per match	1.8	1.14	3.28	1.57	1.57	3.86
Total yellow cards over match play	8	8	22	12	10	25
Total red cards over match play	1	0	0	0	1	2

The benchmarking process does not end here. The coach and staff must do something with the data to create change, improve skills, and modify strategy. For Team Dummies, these are the general steps you would follow and repeat continuously:

1. **Establish target performance goals for your team.**

2. **Study the competition (match films, player positioning, or training regimes).**

3. **Brainstorm ideas for improvement.**

4. **Create and implement a game plan.**

5. **Evaluate performance over a set period of time.**

Your overall strategy would address the fundamentals of running and passing, how and where the bodies are positioned on the field, the array of players used, and which players occupy which positions. The detailed game plan might include drills to improve free kicks, training sessions at higher altitudes or humidity levels to build up resistance for real game conditions, or experimenting with different players in different roles. The benchmarking process provides a foundation and direction for improvement.

When benchmarking the competition, you evaluate not only overall performance, but also the performance of the parts. The automotive industry for years has used *teardown rooms*. Within the room are a collection of the manufacturers' vehicles alongside vehicles from the competition. Typically, an entire vehicle is parked in front of tables full of disassembled components of the same model. Representatives from various functional areas spend hours evaluating the parts and the parts in context of the overall vehicle, in order to plan their next iteration of product or gain ideas to solve ongoing product issues. Teardown rooms are an effective strategy if your company is product based.

Working with the Value Stream

The customer-related tools help you understand what your customer wants. The value stream is how you provide goods and services to meet those needs. Chapters 7 and 8 help you understand how to analyze the value stream — through value-stream mapping. The tools presented here are supplementary to the value-stream map.

Quantifying the value stream

When you're quantifying the value stream, three measurement tools are beneficial: takt time, box scores, and lead time.

Takt time

Takt time sets the pace for the value stream based on the rate of customer demand. Takt time is the total net daily operating time divided by the total daily customer demand. (You can find out more about takt time in Chapter 7.)

Box scores

Lean box scores — like the box scores of professional baseball — summarize and track performance to key metrics. Table 10-3 is an example of a box score. (We discuss box scores in greater detail in Chapter 7.)

Table 10-3	An Example of a Box Score	
Metric	*Current State*	*Ideal State*
Total average value-added time	40.4 minutes	37.2 *minutes*
Total average non-value-added time	746.6 minutes	0 minutes
Total average lead time	787 minutes	37.2 minutes
Changeover time, between types	10 minutes	1 minute
Actual cycle time	113 seconds	54 seconds
Takt time, seconds	54 seconds	54 seconds

Lead time

Lead time is the elapsed time for one item to make it through the system from the initial step to customer shipment (for example, when you make an online purchase, lead time is from receipt of your order to the shipment of that order). Understanding the lead time and percentage of value-added time of a process are critical in Lean. Although this information is displayed on the value-stream map, teams often use a lead-time reduction chart to consider just the lead time.

The lead-time reduction chart is a simple Ladder diagram. The chart is constructed top to bottom on a sheet of paper. The beginning of the process starts at the top of the page. The steps are listed in sequence, with non-value-added activities on the left side and value-added activities on the right side. *Draw the boxes in proportion to time*, visually depicting the percentage of value-added and non-value-added time. Figure 10-3 shows an example lead-time reduction chart.

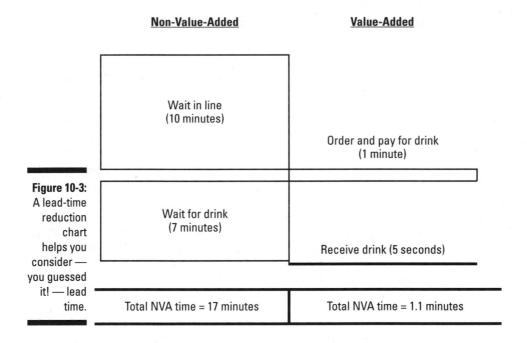

Figure 10-3: A lead-time reduction chart helps you consider — you guessed it! — lead time.

After you make the lead-time reduction chart, you work to eliminate the non-value-added activities and minimize the time required for the value-added ones.

On the case like Sherlock: Investigating your value stream like a detective

Detectives learn early-on the importance of asking the right questions. You start by covering all the basics and then dive deeper to uncover the truth. When you analyze your value stream, be the ace detective. In the following sections, we show you how.

The 5 Ws — and 1 H

What, when, why, where, who — and how. Sounds simple enough. Yet time after time, teams don't have the patience to dig up the true answers to these questions when analyzing the value stream. Half of the equation is asking these key questions; the other half is really listening to the answer. After you've listened, ask clarifying questions to ensure that you truly understand what's happening in the value stream and why it's happening.

This tool is useful in many scenarios within Lean, whether you're proactively improving a situation or reactively solving issues.

Lean is a people-focused methodology. "Who?" is one of the questions, but it is not the first question asked nor is it the only question asked. Point and blame is *not* the name of the Lean game.

Spending three, four, or even five days observing one process is not unusual. Let the process "talk" to you. You're looking for waste — *muda, mura, and muri* (see Chapter 2). You may not spot examples of each right away, but given enough time, chances are you will.

Spaghetti diagrams

Spaghetti diagrams, also known as *Layout diagrams,* are really helpful when you're analyzing the flow of traffic or movement of people and product. Think about the last time you misplaced something in your house. If you created a spaghetti diagram of that mad search to find that important paper or set of keys, it would look something like Figure 10-4.

You think this example is far-fetched? Most spaghetti diagrams look worse. People don't realize how much wasted travel or movement occurs. Every day, people look for tools, information, and parts — particularly at the beginning of Lean, before standards are implemented and enforced. In the beginning, just mapping the movement is enough to show you one place to start. As you progress, you can add more details, like the distance traveled or the effort involved.

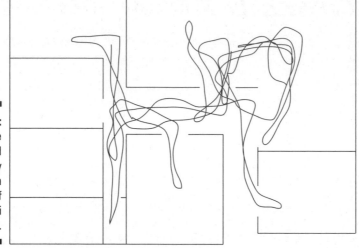

Figure 10-4:
Where the
!@#$ did
I put my
keys? An
example of
a spaghetti
diagram.

Spaghetti diagrams are simple to make and very eye-opening. In Chapter 16, you find a case study where the team used spaghetti diagrams when analyzing the layout of a lab in their hospital. Here's how to make and use one:

1. **Get a layout or blueprint of the area.**

2. **Pick the subject to follow.**

    This subject can be materials, information or people.

3. **Record every movement of the target until it's finished.**

4. **When the diagram is finished, brainstorm ways to eliminate the excessive travel.**

5. **Improve the process or job design to eliminate the excess movement.**

    You may want to do this during a *kaizen* event.

Spaghetti diagrams are important tools for information technologists. Data and network diagrams can reveal waste in the flow of information processing — both at the logical level and at the physical implementation level.

Using color can give you additional insight from your spaghetti diagrams. If you're tracking components and assemblies, you can use certain colors for components and others for assemblies. If you're mapping a work team, you can use one color for each team member or job function. You can see things like where how parts can end up in the wrong place or where people are crashing into or tripping over each other. This additional information will enable you to create better solutions and a safer work environment.

Ahead of the Curve – Using 3P

The impact you can make on the value-stream before you implement your initial process is far greater than what you can do tweaking an existing process. The 3P methodology (Production Preparation Process) enables you to prevent waste in the process before you purchase the first piece of equipment or locate the workstation. In the early stages of product or process design, you bring together a multi-disciplined team to design the most effective process to meet the voice of the customer requirements. You can also apply 3P to relocation projects or product redesigns.

Here are the basic steps of the 3P:

1. **Identify the product or process needs.** Use the data from QFD, product prototypes, marketing information, or any other data that's fundamental in helping you understanding the customer requirements.

2. **Diagram the requirements.** Use a fishbone diagram (see Chapter 12) or another graphic tool so you can understand the requirements in basic terms or keywords.

   Breaking down the functional requirements into the most basic description possible will open up creativity. For example, think about the difference between "contain liquid" (basic) versus "fill water bottle" (specific).

3. **Find and evaluate nature for inspiration.** Have your team identify where in nature your functions occur. After you have identified examples and understand the essence of what occurs in the natural world, you can translate how the natural examples apply to your situation. Look for simplicity. For example, if you need to move a large group of people, you may look how ants, flocks of birds, or herds of cattle move as large groups for inspiration.

4. **Identify design alternatives.** Your team will subdivide into smaller teams to design process/product alternatives based on the ideas found in Step 3. Your goal is to find the simple, flexible, smallest solution to meet your customer's needs.

   Seven is your magic number. Create seven design alternatives before you select one to move forward. Six is too few to tap into your team's collective creativity, and eight is too many.

5. **Build prototypes and mock-ups.** Cardboard, Styrofoam, duct tape, and Velcro are your friends during this phase of the process. Create, revise, and refine the prototypes until you have a process that meets all the customer requirements. Identify a lead solution to carry forward in the process. You may also use simulation and virtual reality tools.

6. **Conduct a design review with the key stakeholders, including the original design team.** Review the lead design solution with the multidisciplinary team to ensure that you are meeting all of the customer requirements with the solution.

7. **Implement the design solution.** After your team has selected the solution to move forward, create the implementation plan. Include the project leader, resources, timing, budget, responsibility allocation, and process in your plan.

3P is applied commonly in product manufacturing. If you search the web for examples of 3P, you will find a wide variety of applications. In healthcare, you will find applications in places like hospital pharmacies and intensive care unit designs. The common thread is in bringing together the people who have to interact and live with the environment, process, and products every day, so they can provide input in the design phase — before the first machine, desk, computer, or counter is installed. This process leads to increased customer satisfaction, reduced costs, engaged people and improved processes from the beginning.

Figure 10-5 shows you a graphical overview of the 3P methodology.

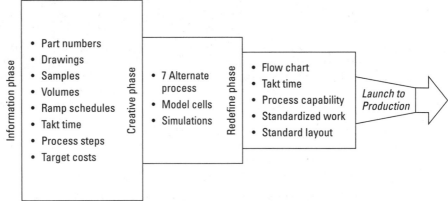

Production Preparation Process (3P) Goals:

* Design products for Lean production
* Incorporate error-proofing and Just-In-Time
* Guarantee process capability and cycle time
* Build quality into the system

Information phase
* Part numbers
* Drawings
* Samples
* Volumes
* Ramp schedules
* Takt time
* Process steps
* Target costs

Creative phase
* 7 Alternate process
* Model cells
* Simulations

Redefine phase
* Flow chart
* Takt time
* Process capability
* Standardized work
* Standard layout

Launch to Production

Figure 10-5: Overview of the 3P methodology.

Working with Software Tools

Lean practitioners regularly debate whether the best way to gather data and create initial charts in a team environment is manual versus computer-generated. When working in a local team setting to establish initial value streams and analysis, many teams find it easier to engage everyone by using simple manual methods: whiteboards, paper drawings, and even yellow-stickies. At the enterprise level or in an information systems-enabled environment, most teams now maintain data and analyses with software tools after the initial creation. Several software platforms exist to aid in the creation of value-stream maps, houses of quality, and data analysis charts.

Lean practitioners use both specialized and general-use programs. Programs like Visio enable you to quickly draw spaghetti, arrow, and affinity diagrams. Tools like Lean View have value-stream mapping capability while enterprise-class architecture software like ARIS allows you to produce VSMs and connect them to process flows, organizational charts, systems, metrics, applications, and data. QFD/Capture is one of the better known house-of-quality construction packages. On the Internet, you can also find templates that function in Excel for everything from house of quality to spaghetti diagrams. (See Chapter 19 for other places to go for assistance.) See Chapter 12 for additional information about software tools used for supporting Lean methods.

Chapter 11

Flow and Pull Tools

In This Chapter

▶ Preventing interruptions to flow

▶ Organizing the process for flow

▶ Orchestrating the material flow

*L*ean fundamentals include the concepts of flow in the value stream and pull from each customer through the value stream; Lean tools help you implement these flow and pull techniques. Use these tools to set the pace of your system and eliminate restrictions or blockages to flow. Start with the flow tools. Applying the flow tools first clears out the obstructions and gives you a solid foundation upon which to use the pull tools to create a *kanban*-based pull system

Along with the customer and value-stream tools in Chapter 10, the perfection tools in Chapter 12, and the management tools in Chapter 13, these tools make up the overall Lean toolbox. You need all these tools to support Lean practices. To maintain balance in your overall system, you must use the full complement of tools in the Lean toolbox.

Attempting to implement Lean can fail if your organization tries to implement a tool in isolation or at the wrong time (this has been particularly true with pull tools). You can't use just one Lean tool like *kanban* and expect to be wildly successful; it would be like trying to build an entire house with just a hammer. You have to look at your system as a whole. For example, a system plagued with defects or equipment outages will never be able to produce to a pull signal at a given takt. For this reason, success requires you to use all the tools, follow the principles, and apply the philosophies of Lean. No cherry-picking!

Flow

You can see the power of flow all around you. Traffic flows — unless it is rush hour, when the demand exceeds the capacity of the road system, or someone has made a mistake and caused an accident. Music flows — as the musicians play together to a defined tempo. If one musician got out ahead or fell behind, the flow would be disrupted, and that disruption is the difference between beauty and cacophony. In our bodies, blood flows as a life force; and we know that obstructions can be debilitating — even fatal.

In each of these examples, you can see how perfect flow achieves the goal, but also what happens when flow is interrupted. In Lean, eliminating waste is eliminating obstructions to flow — of people, products, services, information, or materials. It's easy to realize that flow is dependent upon all the elements of a system working in concert. When one part of the system is not functioning properly, you won't have flow. When all parts are working together, flow happens.

Smoothing the waters — 5S (plus one)

To establish orderly flow, start with *5S* — the practice of eliminating waste by organizing the workplace; sort, straighten, scrub, systematize, and standardize. Note that many organizations have recently added an additional *S* to the original *5*: it is for *safety*, so sometimes you'll now hear it called 6S, although 5S is the historically used term.

5S is simple, practical, and an effective way to clean up your act. You implement 5S in two phases. Phase 1: Get rid of all the junk! Stop working around it. Phase 2: Create a system so there is a place for everything and everything stays in its place. Fundamental to these two phases is ensuring the safety of the people through effective layout and design.

Unless you have a very small facility, don't try to address the entire facility at once. You'll overwhelm everyone, and you risk not really eliminating items, but just shuffling them around. Before you start the 5S process, determine the bounds of the area you're addressing.

The five steps of the 5S process are:

1. **Sort.**

   Divide all the items in the workplace into three R categories:

   - **Retain:** Retain items that are essential to the functioning of the work area. These items fall into two main groups: regular use and occasional use.

   - **Return:** Return any items that belong to another department, location, supplier, customer or neighbor.

   - **Rid:** Rid the area of all other items. Physically move them straight to the recycle bin or dumpster for disposal, or a staging area for immediate disposition. Note that any item located in the staging area must be tagged with clear information about its disposition.

   Isolate the *rid* items from the others. Red tags are particularly useful for items that the team wants to throw out, but that need some type of authorization for disposal. The tag should include the date it was moved to the area, the contact person and her contact information, the desired disposition, and the functions that need to sign off on the disposal. As a general rule, no item marked for disposal should remain in a staging area more than 48 hours.

   Apply the 3R technique to your digital information as well. It is easy to create multiple files in multiple locations; these excess inventories can potentially lead to errors and misinformation. Delete any obsolete or duplicate files or email messages. Of course, backups are a good practice, but they are still type-1 *muda* (see Chapter 2).

2. **Straighten.**

   Find a place for everything and put everything in its place. Move the items that are always needed to where they're needed. Establish and delineate the standard location for every item. Label everything. Make it visual. Better yet, make it sensory. Move those items that you don't use frequently to a standard place, near the area — but not a place that could disrupt flow. Create a standard for the colors you use in your facility. For example, you may choose yellow to indicate aisles, green safety stations, red hazards, and so on.

3. Scrub.

Clean the entire area. Whether you're in an office, a kitchen, or a factory, this means deep-clean *everything!* If the area or equipment needs a fresh coat of paint, get out the brushes and the rollers. And cleaning is everyone's job — not just the janitor's or painter's. This step is important for several reasons:

- People working in a clean area tend to have a more positive attitude and be more productive.

- When everyone cleans, everyone has a clean mindset.

- Clean equipment helps you to detect leaks and problems with equipment faster.

- Clean and clear areas make safer work environments.

4. Systematize.

Now that you've gone to the work of cleaning the area once, establish the schedules and systems to maintain the area regularly, just the way it is on the first day after you've cleaned it.

5. Standardize.

Turn a one-time event into the way you conduct business. This step is the most difficult one because you're creating new habits and levels of performance expectations. Forming new habits requires constant reinforcement and time, before the new habits become the standard.

6. Safety: *the 6ᵗʰ S.*

Safety is fundamental in building respect for people; having a safe environment also makes good business sense because millions of dollars are lost every year due to working-condition-related accidents, injury, and medical restrictions. Many large organizations have zero-accident objectives as part of their business plan. When evaluating a work area, regardless of whether it's a manufacturing shop, an office or a supermarket, ensure the safety of all people — it's good business. Evaluate areas for trip hazards, unguarded equipment, spill risks, cords on the floor, sharp objects, electrical issues, and any other risks that could cause accidents or harm the people interacting with the space. Find ways to eliminate or minimize these situations as quickly — and regularly.

Evaluating your workplace for ergonomic issues is part of safety. Eliminate conditions causing *muri* — repetitive tasks, physically harmful conditions, awkward biomechanics, and so on. Evaluate your accident and injury data for issues and eliminate the root cause.

Housekeeping tours are a good way for managers to accomplish several goals:

- ✔ Stress the importance of a safe and orderly environment.
- ✔ Practice a form of standardized work.
- ✔ Connect with the organization.

Management tours should cover entire facilities, inside and out. Tours should not be ad hoc — they should follow a set process, with an established checklist of items to review, including an agenda and facility route, restroom visits, and safety equipment. Non-conformances should be recorded and addressed — in the case of safety issues, contain them immediately. On the next tour, follow up on these items. Refer to Chapter 13 for more information on *gemba* walks.

You'll encounter resistance to the long-term maintenance of the 5S/6S results. Engineers who need to work with parts and highly creative people who need a little chaos to feed their creativity are some of the biggest resisters. You have to establish the standards for your organization. Some organizations require that desks are cleaned off every night; others have deemed this cleaning up at the end of the day as non-value-added. Both sides have merit. Determine what's right for your organization.

Take one, make one

The ideal state of Lean is continuous flow production, calibrated perfectly to customer demand. When you can organize your work area and perfectly balance your operational times so that your document or widget is always in a state of value-added transformation, you've reached Lean nirvana. You may never actually get to this point, but you should never stop trying to get there. To do so, you have to think constantly about how you organize the value stream. The tools in the following sections will help you to move closer to the zenith of continuous flow.

Don't get hung up on the language of *continuous-flow production* or *single-piece flow*. The terms may have originated in a manufacturing environment, but they apply whether you're making products or providing services. You "flow people and information through a service process" just as you "flow material and information through a manufacturing process." In both cases, the goal is to keep things moving effectively — no stops for queues or inventory or unnecessary movement or transport.

Finding common ground through Group Technology

You will often see all accountants located in the same physical office, even though their customer may be in another floor or building. Or you might see all the molding machines placed in one area, far from the subsequent processes. This functional grouping usually leads to a lot of unnecessary waiting, transport, and inventory.

Group Technology (GT) helps you work toward continuous value-added flow. With GT, you identify commonality in process through the analysis of all the products. Your aim is to identify product (or service) families. You use this information to reorganize how you do business. So instead of organizing by function, you organize everything you need to produce a complete product or service for the customer.

The term *product* is used here generically, to refer to physical products as well as nonphysical items like software, transactions, and service processes (such as hospitality and healthcare). Refer to Chapter 15 for more on how services are like products.

To perform a GT analysis, review all your products and the operational steps they require. A product family contains the same or highly similar operational steps. Table 11-1 shows a group technology analysis example. The shaded parts represent a product family because they pass through the majority of the same types of operations.

Table 11-1   All in the Family: A Group Technology Analysis

Process Operation Types

	Type 1	Type 2	Type 3	Type 4	Type 5	Type 6	Type 7
Part Number 16958439			X	X		X	X
Part Number 16980437	X		X	X		X	X
Part Number 17389433		X	X				X
Part Number 14967210		X	X		X	X	
Part Number 997325	X			X		X	
Part Number 26390548		X		X	X		X
Part Number 340955	X		X	X		X	X
Part Number 7304-4659-32	X		X	X		X	X

After you've identified all your product families, you can start to organize the areas that produce them by family rather than by operation function.

The power of organizing the production area by group technology rather than type or function is that you begin to eliminate excess waiting, inventory, or transport.

Organizations that have a low-volume, high-mix custom environment often struggle to see how group technology applies to them. Even if your product details are unique every time, recognize that at a macro level, your products pass through similar processing steps. You can use a sampling of past products to identify generic product families. Then when you spec out a new product, you can slate its production for a specific area.

Creating work modules

Traditional organizations are set up as functional departments, whether it's an office or a manufacturing facility. The results of group technology analysis and reorganization will naturally reduce inventory, improve quality and communication, and save space. This is particularly beneficial for office workers, who often cluster in modules. Ensure each work module, sometimes called *work cell*, contains all the functions required to make the product or complete the service.

The extended value chains of global business are increasingly creating situations where the people working on products or services are not in the same location — or even the same continent. This means physical clustering becomes virtual clustering, but all the same needs exist. Use information and collaboration technologies to create virtual clusters.

Managing the monuments

A Lean work module contains all the operations that can be moved together into a continuous-flow arrangement. Sometimes you have fixed *monuments* (equipment or processes that are difficult to move, or large-capacity equipment that services multiple product families). Examples of monuments are the shipping dock, plating and painting operations, operating rooms, or glass furnaces. When this undesirable situation occurs, the flow is interrupted.

Some options for managing monuments include the following:

- ✔ Arrange affected work modules around the monument.
- ✔ Establish supermarkets (an in-process, controlled storage area) to create controlled storage and flow to the monument operation.
- ✔ Create continuous-flow work modules before and after the monument.
- ✔ Consider purchasing smaller, more flexible technology to achieve the same function, and then incorporate it into work modules.

Challenge your belief that there is nothing you can do about a monument. Use the 5 Whys and then ask yourself, "How can we do this operation differently?" For instance, one company thought its paint facility was a monument. After persistent questioning, it found a way to incorporate a lower-technology miniature paint booth into its work module. Through persistence and a new perspective, it lowered inventory, eliminated a paint line that required lots of maintenances and frequently broke, and improved quality defects related to inventory and in-facility transit.

Many manufacturing operations use conveyors to move parts in the process, from monuments or other operations. Be careful about installing conveyors, because they are form of type-1 *muda* both work-in-process and transportation. Use conveyors sparingly. They are best used in environments where other methods could cause harm to the people because of weight or exposure.

Balancing the operations

Base the capacity of a module on the collective demand of the customer for the product family as well as the capability of the team members. Figure 11-1 is an example of a product family operations graph (also known as a line balance chart). This graphs the operation times compared to takt time (see Chapter 7) for a product family. In this case, independent of the part being made, operation times are falling below a benchmark takt time of 60 seconds, indicating excess capacity. If operations exceeded takt time, you would consider additional capacity, which usually means adding people, for the module.

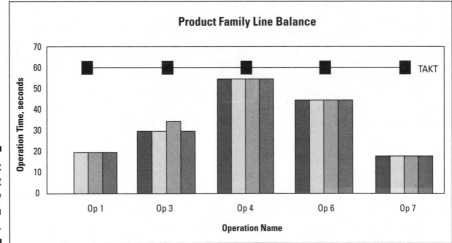

Figure 11-1:
A product family operation graph.

Now take the part number with the longest operation time and evaluate it for line balancing. You then can seek to combine operations — such as 1 with 3 and 6 with 7 — and still meet the takt time. Figure 11-2 shows the results. As you can see, the combination of operations 6 and 7 cause the cycle time to exceed the takt time, so you can't combine them yet. Figure 11-3 shows the final line balance. The work cell requires four operators to run five operations. Going forward, the team would then seek to reduce the time required to complete operations 6 and 7, by at least 3 seconds — the time to balance to the takt time — and enable the cell to run with three operators.

One way to make the extra time of operator 7 visible is to have the person stand idle rather than finding non-value-added busy-work for them to do. Having them stand idle emphasizes the unused time, or waste.

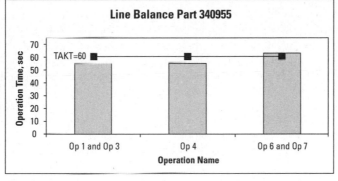

Figure 11-2: Operational line balance — a first look.

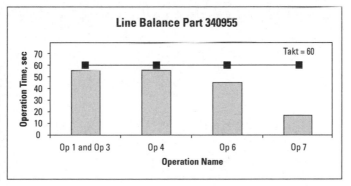

Figure 11-3: Operational line balance — implementation.

When evaluating *each* workstation or work area within a work module, apply industrial engineering techniques like left-hand/right-hand analysis or Therblig analysis (see Chapter 19 for more information). Evaluating and standardizing the movements at a micro level will increase flow, eliminate waste, and improve the effectiveness of the operations. Improvement at a micro level will enable the team to shave off the three seconds needed to eliminate that fourth operator.

Identifying bottleneck operations

Within any module, you'll have a bottleneck operation — the one that limits throughput and runs at or near to the takt time. This operation becomes the critical operation to flow because there is no slack time or no option to add more people, if there is a machine issue. To identify the bottleneck, create an operations graph showing all the operations in the value stream.

Storing at the point of use

Point of use storage (POUS) means you store what you need, in the quantity you need it, at or near where you use it. This storage should be incorporated into the 5S standards. You have to identify the bill of materials, quantity used, and size of each component in order to establish where you'll store each item, what type of container you'll use for storage, and where best to locate the items. Document this information in the Plan for Every Part (PFEP), discussed later in this chapter.

POUS storage can be applied to the office environment. You may use tape and paper clips many times during the day, but shipping envelops only once a week. Organize the storage where you need the item according to when you need it.

When establishing POUS storage and work module arrangement, remember to evaluate the ergonomic impact on the operators. Considerations like shelf heights, reach distances, standup versus seated operations, and maximum heights are among some of the critical characteristics to evaluate. Investigate current industry standards and governmental regulations for more information.

Understand bottlenecks, output, work balance, staffing, and storage requirements before you arrange furniture. You can quickly gather, and analyze flow within your modules. Failure to understand these foundational elements of a work cell will lead to ineffective modules — full of *muda!*

Arranging the work module – the U shape

The recommended shape for a work module is a U shape, flowing *counter-clockwise*. U shapes don't work in every application, but they're a solid place to start. (The reasons for counterclockwise flow are numerous, but fundamentally, the right hemisphere of our brains process spatial relationships, so humans flow better to the left.) The U shape also provides a safer environment, where maintenance and material replenishment occurs on the outside of the U, and the people making the products are the only ones inside the U.

Create a layout before you start moving to ensure everything fits in the space allotted. Depending on how difficult it is to move equipment, you can use a layout tool like Visio or AutoCAD, scaled "paper-doll" cutouts of the equipment, or even full-size mockups of the module to establish the plan. If you've never created a work cell or work module before, and you have large pieces of equipment like presses or molding machines, you'll want to use full-scale, three-dimensional replicas. This enables the team to ensure that the plan will work.

Use the 3P (Production, Preparation, Process; see Chapter 10) before purchasing new equipment. Creating simulations or physical mockups gives the people an opportunity to interact with the environment before a large investment has been made.

When you understand the foundational requirements, you're ready to set up the module. Figure 11-4 is an example of a work module layout.

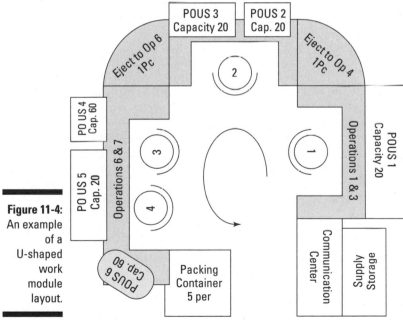

Figure 11-4:
An example
of a
U-shaped
work
module
layout.

If this is your first module, start with a pilot or test module. This will help you learn, work out the bugs, and introduce the organization to the concept before you physically tear up the entire facility.

The use of *autonomation* (automation with a human touch), or *jidoka,* in a workstation has two benefits:

- ✔ Automatically unloading equipment enables an operator to do other tasks, instead of having to stand around until the machine has finished.

- ✔ Automation that stops equipment when defects or nonstandard conditions are detected prevents bad products from progressing through the value stream.

People in the process

The work in modules is run by teams, sometimes referred to as *employee involvement teams.* These teams are usually autonomous, self-directed work teams. Often a team leader emerges or is named based on experience. The team leader is responsible for the implementation and performance of the cell:

- ✔ Production output, quality, delivery, and controllable cost performance

- ✔ Line balancing

- ✔ Cross training and team behavior

- ✔ Performing *kaizen* (everyday improvements)

- ✔ Maintaining the work area (cleaning and daily equipment maintenance)

- ✔ Problem solving

Supervisors build capability, guide problem solving, coach, and mentor the team. They may have more work teams reporting to them. The daily task load is shifted to the team.

When moving to a Lean work cell environment, the teams and the supervisors will need training in new skills such as problem solving — and particularly the interpersonal skills of conflict resolution, teaming, coaching, and communication.

Preventing blockages to flow

After you've created your work modules, you have to make sure that they run continually as designed. In other words, you have to eliminate any and all causes that prevent flow — flow of quality, material, or equipment.

Ensuring quality at the source

In addition to the use of autonomation, you can establish quality at the source by using source inspection, progressive inspection, and *poka-yoke* (error-proofing).

Source inspection

Source inspection means you review your work before you pass it on to the next person or station. What you review, how you review it, and how much time it should take to review the work is identified as part of the standardized work for the operation. The benefit to source inspection is to identify, correct, and contain a problem before it enters into the value stream via the next processing operation.

Progressive inspection

Progressive inspection means that the operator reviews key characteristics of the product or service from the previous step before beginning a new transformational step. Once again, these inspection steps should be designed into the standardized work plan. Investing in critical inspection before any further work is performed protects the customer and minimizes the risk to the value chain.

Poka-yoke

Because inspection is a form of *muda*, a more certain and proactive type of quality at the source is error-proofing, known as *poka-yoke* or *mistake-proofing*. A *poka-yoke* is something in a product, process, or procedure that physically or procedurally prevents you from making a mistake.

Examples of *poka-yoke* are everywhere. Whenever you fill up your car at a gas pump with both diesel and regular gas, you're using a *poka-yoke* device. The size of the diesel spout is larger than the gasoline spout, so the diesel spout can't fit in the regular gas tank opening — which prevents you from doing serious damage to your engine! Another example: many electronic devices only allow you to plug in a specific way. In addition, online surveys have logic to check that you've answered all the questions or filled in the right numbers before you can proceed to the next step.

In performing *poka-yoke,* begin by evaluating each operational step for common quality problems. Identify guides, gauges, fixtures or code that will ensure the operation is done correctly every time. Follow the Plan-Do-Check-Act (PDCA) methodology to evaluate the effectiveness of your *poke-yoke*. Installing stops or prevention devices on equipment, or incorporating checklists into standardized work will help the situation. But the best way to error-proof is through the design of features in the product, or in the upfront design of the process or equipment via the 3P methodology (see Chapter 10).

Design for Assembly and Manufacturability (DFA/DFM) is a methodology to identify ways to design-in error-proofing and improve the ease of assembly. Performing Failure Mode Effects Analysis (FEMA) on the design and process (DFMEA/PFMEA) will help you to identify the risk and frequency of potential failures. With this information, you can prioritize your error-proofing efforts to mitigate risk.

Part of the foundation of Lean is "Respect for People." Never use terms like *dummy-proofing, fool-proofing,* or *idiot-proofing!* The proper terms are *poka-yoke, mistake-proofing,* or *error-proofing.*

Although error-proofing may seem like detailed, picky analysis, it can mean the difference between life and death. Consider this situation: A restaurant served a small child margarita mix with alcohol instead of lemonade because the container was mislabeled. Or in a hospital, two medications — one designed for adults the other for infants — have similar names, and they're placed in almost identical packaging. If the manufacturer changed the `container shape, size, or color so that the two medications were obviously different, the people in the hospital would be less likely to make the fatal mistake of delivering the wrong medicine to the wrong patient. It would also help the manufacturer to ensure they were providing the right medication in the right container every time.

Figure 11-5 is an example of a *poke-yoke* worksheet — a reference tool that can help you prevent mistakes.

Devising flexible and reliable equipment

When you no longer can hide behind inventory and waste, the role of your equipment becomes more important. It must be ready and functioning properly when you need it. You'll also need to change how you design and purchase equipment for modular manufacturing: you want to find the smallest, simplest, most flexible equipment that fits the job and meets your customer's requirements.

Remember that your goal is to be able to make the full complement of product mix every day, so your equipment has to be able to be changed-over very quickly.

Maintaining the equipment

Total Productive Maintenance (TPM) is a method for ensuring you maximize productivity while ensuring equipment and tooling is fully maintained. TPM is divided into three areas:

✔ **Autonomous maintenance:** *Autonomous maintenance* means that as part of the operations within a work module, the work team performs their own routine maintenance tasks. This frees up the more skilled maintenance trades to focus on more specialized planned and predictive maintenance activities. Use standardized work descriptions for the maintenance tasks so the operators can safely perform regular maintenance at the proper time.

✔ **Planned maintenance:** Because major, high-risk, or high-wear components must be serviced and even occasionally replaced, you proactively schedule equipment, tooling and fixtures to be taken out of service. This *planned maintenance* is vital in a Lean environment. As you replace components, collect data to develop potential predictive failure scenarios. You can use the data tools in Chapter 12 to understand the performance of the components from a statistical perspective. You then can use this information to create predictive maintenance routines.

✔ **Predictive maintenance:** If you can anticipate failures, you can better manage people and control costs by performing maintenance activities at just the right time — not just the scheduled time. This is *predictive maintenance*. You can also identify which parts and what quantity to keep in inventory for routine maintenance, planned maintenance, and emergency response.

Inspection Method		Setting Function		Regulative Function		Company Name
Source Inspection	●	Contact Method	●	Control Method	●	ACME, Inc.
Information Inspection (self)		Constant-Value Method		Warning Method		
Information Inspection (successive)		Motion-Step Method				Proposed by: Zelda
Theme		Misaligned material causing wrinkles				

Before Improvement

Insert descriptions and pictures of issue before *poka-yoke*.

After Improvement

Insert descriptions and pictures of issue after *poka-yoke*.

Effects	Eliminated misalignments	Cost	$150

Figure 11-5: A *poka-yoke* tracking sheet.

The aim of TPM is to maximize the Overall Equipment Efficiency (OEE) and minimize production losses due to equipment failure or malfunction. OEE is a performance metric tracked on the Balanced Scorecard, especially for manufacturing organizations. It is calculated like this:

$$OEE\% = Availability \times Performance\ Rate \times Quality$$

Even with the best TPM plan in the world, unexpected downtime will still happen. Create emergency response teams who respond at the flash of an andon light. These teams should have standardized work descriptions and diagnostic checklists to follow.

Mastering the quick change

What do an actor between entrances, a Formula 1 team in the pits, and a stamping press in a factory all have in common? All of them must use quick-change techniques to be successful. In Lean, quick changeover is known as *SMED,* which is short for *single-minute exchange of die.* In this case, the *die* refers to a tool that cuts or forms material in some type of press or a forging device. The die has to be reconfigured in order to make a new product, and the goal is to complete the changeover in just one minute. From this original use, the term SMED has come to mean any quick setup process or other reduction of setup time. The aim is to minimize downtime or lost time between the end of one activity or product and the beginning of the next. In Chapter 16 you find an example of how SMED is used to reduce the changeover time in operating rooms of a hospital.

When evaluating your changeovers, use video to record what is happening. It will help you to identify what actions you can eliminate or move off-line. You can also share your videos with other teams who have similar processes.

Here's how to organize a quick change:

1. **List all the steps, required tools, and materials to change from one thing to the next.**

2. **Identify which activities can be done before or after the change (offline, or external, activities) and which must be done in the moment (online, or internal, activities).**

3. **Create standardized work for all offline activities. Organize tools and material offline to support the online ones.**

4. **Refine and standardize the online activities to minimize lost time.**

5. **Constantly evaluate the performance of the overall changeover process to improve the performance time and eliminate waste.**

For the Formula 1 pit crew, fractions of seconds in the pit can mean the difference between victory and defeat. For the theater actor, fractions of seconds can be the difference between a missed entrance and a stellar performance. For the factory, implementing quick setup enables production of the full complement of products every day — ultimately the difference between the product or service availability that means a satisfied or dissatisfied customer.

Pull

We tell you about flow tools and pull tools in the same chapter because they work in harmony with one other to keep the entire value stream moving toward the customer at the rate the customer consumes. You can't have flow linked to customer demand without pull and vice versa. All the tools in this section make the system work better, with minimal waste.

Smoothing out the bumps

To provide the customer with what they want, when they want it, while keeping the value stream flowing at a steady pace, you need to smooth out the production schedules. This concept is known as _heijunka,_ which means "production smoothing, leveling, or level scheduling." The concept is this: Instead of making large batches of one product and then storing them in a warehouse until the customer orders them, ideally you make an amount of all the products, every day, as the customer consumes them.

The faster the changeover times (SMED — see "Mastering the quick change," earlier in this chapter), the easier it will be to smooth out production.

Figure 11-6 contrasts traditional lot production with level production. The same amount and type of product is made in each scenario. Notice that in level production, the various products are interspersed, throughout the sequence.

The calculation of the optimal sequence is a complex algorithm. It is based on cycle times, available work hours, setup times, and demand. You can use software to help you with production optimization; some ERP systems as well as specialized software will help you determine your optimal mix.

Production smoothing protects the suppliers in the value stream from the bull-whip effect, where small fluctuations from the customer end can translate into radical volume swings in the supplier community.

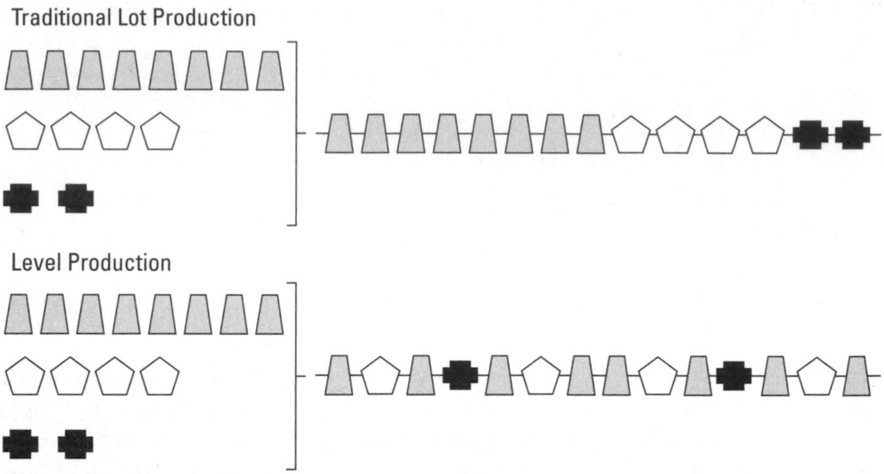

Traditional Lot Production

Level Production

Figure 11-6:
Lot versus
level pro-
duction.

Signaling replenishment

In a Lean environment, you don't use forecasted demand schedules — these represent *pushing* production. Forecast schedules are typically only broad indicators; they don't usually correlate well with actual customer demand. In Lean, the value stream is signaled to action through a real demand indicator known as a *kanban*.

Creating kanban

A *kanban* signal can come in many forms — a card, a buzzer, a light, a computer-generated signal, or even an empty space or container that needs filling. You determine the most effective *kanban* for each specific application. In a work module that is relatively balanced, the empty space may be the best solution. With the supply base, the electronic *kanban* card may be the most effective method. Whatever method you use, the *kanban* must signal how much, and of what part, needs to be delivered to what location.

Using the philosophy of "take one, make one," as inventory is consumed, the signal (*kanban*) is sent upstream to call for replenishment activities. One common way to think about *kanban* is the two-bin system: It's like batters in baseball — one at the plate and one on deck.

The number of *kanbans* you need is a function of the average demand per unit of time — usually daily — total time and container capacity. The calculation is as follows:

Number of *Kanbans* = ([Average Demand $_{(Time)}$] × [OC + PT + TT] × [1 + BT]) ÷ CC where:

- ✔ OC = Order Cycle
- ✔ PT = Processing Time
- ✔ TT = Transit Time
- ✔ BT = Buffer Time (not over 10 percent)
- ✔ CC = Container Capacity (not more than 10 percent of Average Demand)
- ✔ Average Demand is a function of Time (daily, weekly, monthly, quarterly, and so on)

In manual processing, a *heijunka* box is designed to house the *kanban* cards related to the production sequence. Slots that represent a specific part number and increment of time during the day contain the *kanban* for the parts to be made during that time. In automated processing, this function is performed with queues in a workflow.

Controlling inventory with supermarkets

Sometimes, because of monuments or other process constraints, you cannot have a continuous-flow system. When this happens, you create what's called a *supermarket*. A supermarket is like your corner grocery, in that every item has a designated location and amount. The inventory is tightly controlled and *kanban* signals are used when a "customer" makes a "purchase" from the store. The supplying operation is the owner of the supermarket. The *kanban* signals the replenishment upstream.

Supermarkets should be located to minimize the "transportation" waste of excess travel. It's better if you don't have to use them, but sometimes you can't avoid it. If you implement supermarkets, you must control them; if not, you may find you've given away the store!

Planning for Every Part — PFEP

Plan for Every Part (PFEP) is a master planning document (usually in the form of a database or spreadsheet) used to plan where raw material, supplies, parts, and/or products are to be stored within the facility. The PFEP is also used to create the overall logistics plan. The planning information includes the stock number, part name, inventory levels (minimum and maximum), method of transportation and the storage locations (supermarket, central warehouse, point of use, and so on).

Connecting ERP and kanban

Kanban is considered to be somewhat the opposite of Material Requirements Planning/Enterprise Resource Planning (MRP/ERP) planning systems. *Kanban* is a *pull* system, and ERP/MRP is a *push* system. Each has its advantages.

For example, when you use *kanban*, you don't need system-generated demand forecasting. But you still must maintain accurate business records. ERP uses a records management technique to relieve inventory called *backflushing,* where the stock of a part or component is presumed to be reduced by one each time a part is made or a work order is booked. It's easy, but prone to error. Not all experts agree that backflushing is the best way to maintain the inventory records. You have to decide the best method of data management for your organization. Whatever method you use, approach it with the mindset of eliminating waste to find the most effective solution for the organization.

Moving to pull scheduling will require changes to your current scheduling processes — remember that you're working to eliminate waste, and some of what you have historically viewed as value added scheduling was really type-1 *muda* (see Chapter 2).

Be sure to coordinate your ERP/MRP order parameters with your demand timing. Failure to do this could result in excess orders to the supply community.

If you are using an MRP system, you must coordinate with your suppliers to make sure that they understand your discrete order requirements. For example, if you need your supplier to ship 1,000 parts every week on Tuesday, they must comply with that requirement. If they do not understand the requirements and ship to a different rhythm, it could invalidate your logistical plan, create inaccuracies in the system, and ultimately cost you money.

Changing logistics

When you're operating in a Lean system, you have to rethink the way you approach logistics. Traditionally, a supplier might send a truckload of stuff "whenever." Instead, set up your organization for success by implementing creative logistical solutions, aimed at supplying you with what you need, when you need it, in the quantity you need it.

Collecting from multiple suppliers: The milk run

Sending a truck on a fixed route at pre-determined times to collect product from a several suppliers is known as a *milk run.* Instead of having to deal with many partially loaded trucks at your facility, you can attend to fewer shipments, which contain a predictable load and arrival time. The milk run is generally used for suppliers near your facility — within four hours is a good guideline to use.

Shipping less than truckload (LTL)

LTL shipments, if done correctly, can be cheaper than waiting to cube out full trucks. (*Cube out* is the process of maximizing shipping density of a load in a semi-trailer.). LTL shipments are used when the suppliers are not located in a place that you can feasibly construct milk runs.

Delivery windows

Delivery windows enhance the both the predictability and stability of incoming materials. To establish a delivery window, you schedule suppliers to deliver a specified amount of product, to a specified location or dock, within a specific window of time. In many industries, these are governed by service-level agreements (SLAs), and failure to comply with the delivery windows may result in hefty fines to the supplier or even loss of the business.

Delivery routes

Delivery routes dictate the timing, location, and amount of material moved within the value stream. Delivery routes help to regulate the pace of the material flow. Think of a city bus route — it's like a delivery route. People are moved through a city by a bus that picks up and drops off passengers at set locations according to an established time schedule as signaled by passengers at the bus stop (a *kanban*). In a product manufacturing environment, material is moved by a specific type of equipment, according to a set schedule, to established locations as signaled by *kanban*.

Using the Plan for Every Part (PFEP) tool and a facility layout will help you to establish your delivery routes.

Global considerations

In today's world, you need to look beyond your own city, region, country, or even hemisphere when planning logistics. It is best if parts are made near your facility, within a one-day drive, but this may not be practical in today's global environment. Parts may come from anywhere in the world. By performing a total cost analysis on your components, including the evaluation of various shipping methods, you can arrive at the best option. If you decide that your parts coming on a slow boat from China is the best solution, then you can consider the material in transit as buffer stock. Although not a traditional application of pure Lean, this solution enables the system to still flow.

Assuming that the overseas supplier is the cheapest option is not always the case. Evaluate the total cost picture to make the best selection.

Supply chain visibility and management software can help you mitigate your risk to disruptions. Increasingly, manufacturers and logistics companies are developing "control towers" that enable them to see worldwide demand and flow and make adjustments instantly. This requires information to be gathered from sources worldwide, as well as access to global order management systems.

Chapter 12

Perfection Tools

● ●

● ●

*I*n a Lean environment, you compare everything to a standard and then work to improve it. You don't change anything indiscriminately or "just do it" to improve performance. You use information, analysis, and visual tools to help you deliberately identify where waste and defects are cropping up.

Along with the customer and value-stream tools in Chapter 10, the flow and pull tools described in Chapter 11, and the management tools in Chapter 13, the perfection tools in this chapter make up the overall Lean toolbox. You need all of these tools to support Lean practices.

In this chapter, you discover first how to create standardized work — the foundation upon which activities and processes are built and the basis upon which improvements are made. Then, you organize *kaizen* events for continuous improvement. And finally, by using visual-management tools, you understand how to create a world where it's possible to "manage by eye." This includes the everyday statistical tools that help monitor and analyze the performance of the system. This is the part of the toolkit that enables you to strive for perfection.

Beginning with Standardized Work

Your pursuit of perfection begins with establishing *standardized work,* sometimes referred to as *standard work* or *standard operations.* Standardized work is the definition of consistent, predictable methods of doing things. Think of the checklist that a pilot performs before each flight as one example of standardized work. Standardized work provides the foundation for the implementation of many other Lean techniques and is also the launch point for improvement. It is not rigid, stagnant, unchanging policies and procedures that no one follows. Quite the opposite: It's the work everyone follows.

Begin with the routine work tasks that most directly affect your ability to deliver to customer demand. Describe the work simply, yet in such a way that you can measure both the variability and waste in its operation. Your description should also enable you to apply methods and tools to continually improve performance over time. Repeat this process until you have standardized work for all activities.

The best people to define standardized work are the people who actually do the work. Some requirements may be non-negotiable, like the use of safety equipment. Define what those requirements are and why they are not negotiable and then let the people go from there.

Standardized work sets the foundation for improvement. To apply analysis and improvement tools, you must first characterize what you're doing now — the current processes. You have to standardize processes to have a basis for measurement. You must establish a culture and mindset around defining, measuring, and following standardized work.

Do you think that following something as simple as a checklist isn't all that important? According to the World Health Organization, 234 million medical operations are performed globally each year, and at least *half a million deaths* per year would be preventable with effective implementation of the WHO Surgical Safety Checklist worldwide. Standardized work matters!

Guiding rules for standardized work

Five rules govern your approach to implementing standardized work. Follow these rules as you develop your standardized work practices:

- **Adjust to human ease and effectiveness, not machine efficiency**. The goal of standardized work is to help people be more safe and effective at what they do. Define work processes and procedures to optimize people — not machines. Machines are tools that assist people, *not the other way around!* By design, it is OK for a machine to wait on people. The limitations on machine capabilities should not control your implementation of standardized work.

  When people are waiting for machines, it is a visual signal that you have waste in that operation and can improve.

- **Standardize all repetitive work.** Standardize any and all work that's performed repeatedly. Standardize both the easy stuff and the more difficult processes. You'll receive the benefits from standardizing all processes.

  The more you can repeat a process, the better you can standardize it and reap the benefits. Strive to look for what's repetitive so that you can standardize it.

Do not standardize for standardizations sake. The goal is not the standard but operations that are safer, of high quality, more effective, and engage the minds of the people doing the operations.

✔ **Keep equipment and systems in condition.** Materials, computers, machines, and other systems support your work processes. Keep these in standard condition to ensure you're producing both a high quality of output and an even flow of work. Breakdowns and lack of quality materials will disrupt your flow and impact product and service quality. Repair or upgrade substandard systems. See Chapter 11 for more on maintenance.

✔ **Make standardized worksheets visible and accessible.** People stray from performing to work standards. Everyone needs constant references and reminders. Keep standardized worksheets visible and readily accessible. Capture key metrics — and report deviations. Be certain that you're making it easy to know when variations occur.

✔ **Revise regularly.** Update and improve standardized work whenever you can. Jump on every chance to reduce variation, minimize inventory, improve workflow, and keep individual cycle times balanced with the overall takt time. Change the standard as often as necessary.

How will you respond when you see someone deviating from the standard? Your response will either build trust and collaboration, or create division. To build a culture of continuous improvement, the best way to address someone who is varying from the standard is to ask questions. Questions like "How have you improved the process with your method?" "What is your understanding of the standardized work for this process?" are better than, "Why aren't you following standard operations?"

People will routinely find better ways than the standard. Don't treat standardized work as the end in itself. Standardized work is the routine, but when you have an improvement to the standard, make the adjustments regularly through *kaizen*.

Implementing standardized work

Wherever possible, perform standardized work — tasks, activities, processes, and procedures — that you can conduct in a standard manner. It's specific, documented, measurable, and repeatable. Standardized work can apply to a person working by herself, or a group of people working collaboratively. It can also include equipment and systems as well as human-to-machine interfaces. This standardization of work occurs not only in production or operations areas, but across the enterprise — in all functions and throughout all value streams.

To implement standardized work, follow this six-step process:

Step 1: Check equipment

Analyze your facilities, systems, and equipment to ensure that they're in proper and sufficient condition to meet the needs of the process activities. Adjust and tune systems to maximize ease of use and effectiveness. This includes information systems and programs.

Step 2: Check time

Determine the initial cycle time for the work — how long it takes you or your team to complete a unit of work. Then, compare that cycle time to the takt time requirement — how long you should be taking, based on customer demand. When you have these two values, determine the difference. Are you high or low? Chances are that the work time is longer than the takt time. You must make adjustments to equalize them. Usually, this means adjusting the time it takes to complete a unit of work, rather than attempting to adjust the takt time. To reconcile work time-takt time discrepancies, perform the following analysis and improvement efforts:

- ✔ Analyze the workflow, sequencing, and organization of your internal process, and identify where you can gain speed and efficiencies.

- ✔ Restructure your internal process as necessary so that your cycle time is in concert with the takt time.

- ✔ Institutionalize the new production times as part of the standardized work instructions.

Step 3: Check work-in-process

Your next step is to minimize work-in-process (WIP), which is waste (*muda*) due to inventory. Examine your work module or area for ways to reduce the amount of inventory or WIP required. You want to define standardized work for all processes in such a way as to require minimal amounts of WIP. Be sure to establish the acceptable range for inventory levels.

Step 4: Post it

After you've verified your support systems, balanced your productivity rate with the takt time, and established the inventory range, baseline your process and issue standard instructions. Standardized work instructions can take nearly any form — as long as they're precise, understandable, and measurable — and as long as they can be followed by the individuals performing the work.

Standard instructions can be printed on paper, read on a computer screen, printed on signs, or transmitted by any manner of communication — as long as it works. Examples of standard instructions include the following:

✔ **Instruction sheets:** Describe the procedures, including the organization, flow, and timing of the activities; the WIP range to maintain; and supporting equipment and environmental conditions, where applicable. Instruction sheets should be brief, easy to read, visible, and referenced.

✔ **Operating manuals:** Describe equipment, facilities, software programs, and other systems in terms of how they're used in the process activity. Operating manuals should be developed as training and reference documents that are kept handy in the workplace.

Poka-yoke (error-proof) your work instructions. Wherever possible, implement methods that help ensure people *will* follow the instructions properly; these methods should ensure that people will be prevented from *not* following the instructions, too.

Step 5: Monitor, measure, and manage

Congratulations — you've crossed the starting line! You've implemented a unit of standardized work and can now observe it in action. Actively monitor the activities and continuously measure performance of the work module. Regularly compare performance to standards, and strive to maintain performance to standard:

✔ For any variances you observe, where the work activity is not conforming to the standard instructions, identify and understand the cause and intervene to correct the deviations — and restore the activity to comply with the standard (or update the standard through *kaizen*).

✔ Seek to identify waste, and identify the cause of the nonconformance.

Step 6: Adjust and update

When a change is warranted, make it — and make it quickly. Making rapid and detailed revisions to standard should be a normal, routine process; make sure you can implement formal changes swiftly and easily, and introduce them into your environment smoothly. The rapid adjustment process is critical to continuous improvement. Condition your team to absorb regular updates.

Because you want everyone working to standard, the standards must always be right and proper — and this means your update process must be routine and smooth. If your standards are out of date, everyone will quickly conclude that it's no longer necessary to work to standard, and you've lost the battle.

Updating standardized work is an integral part of *kaizen*! If you're doing *kaizen*, you'd better be updating standards.

In a continuous improvement environment like Lean, standards aren't written in stone — they're made to be changed. This may not be the way you've worked in the past, so it may be a challenge to create this mindset. Develop a process for regularly modifying work standards. Be sure everyone in your organization understands and supports the modification process. Budget the time and effort for crafting and absorbing modifications into your operations planning. Make change routine!

Standardizing operations is one of the most important tools of a Lean enterprise. Standardizing work processes helps you to achieve a consistently high quality of product and services, performed by proud and productive workers, received by satisfied customers, within a safe environment and strong cost performance. Reducing variation in work processes (*mura*) leads to remarkable productivity improvements.

Improving with Kaizen

Kaizen is the act — and art — of continuous, incremental change and improvement. *Kaizen* tells you that even if something isn't broken, it can and *must* be improved: Do it better and make it better. The continual, incremental changes of *kaizen* occur in all areas and at all levels — large and small, internal and external — in ways that improve the whole organization. Lean *kaizen* maintains the focus on customer value and the reduction of waste in the value stream. (Refer to Chapter 9 for an in-depth discussion and explanation of *kaizen*.)

Kaizen sees the enterprise through two lenses — setting new standards and maintaining existing standards. *Kaizen* maintenance is the act of establishing the policies and rules that help maintain the performance levels set by the present managerial and operating work standards. *Kaizen* improvement focuses you on the continuous improvement of existing standards and processes, as well as the innovation of new ones.

In all cases, *kaizen* requires you to apply training, materials, tools, and observation to improve and maintain standards on a continual basis.

The Lean culture is one of continuous improvement. This comes in the form of everyday improvements or special *kaizen events* — you need to incorporate both.

The kaizen event

The *kaizen event* — also known as a *kaizen workshop* or *kaizen blitz* — is your most powerful and effective tool for engaging everyone within a work module or process area to perform a focused improvement activity. A *kaizen* event is a complete run-through of the plan-do-check-act (PDCA) cycle, typically lasting three to five days. During the *kaizen* event, the team focuses on a specific area to find waste or other hindrances to value creation and remove them from the value stream. The improvement may be in safety, quality, changeover time, communications, organization — almost anything. *Kaizen* events are famous for requiring minimal investment and yielding great benefits.

One place to start is on the "bottleneck" operations — those that run at or near takt. When you improve your bottleneck operations, you improve your ability to deliver to your customer.

The *kaizen* project team halts its normal work completely and will not produce its regular product or perform its services while it's participating in the *kaizen* event. You must perform the necessary advanced planning to ensure the customers and other business areas, are not unduly impacted while the improvements are discovered and implemented.

Organizing the improvement team

Everyone from the affected work group or process area is on the *kaizen* improvement team. Leave no one out — no one. In addition, involve members from support organizations, suppliers, and, of course, customers. To ensure maximum participation and contribution be sure to let everyone know why they are involved.

If you are conducting a *kaizen* event in a manufacturing area, you may want to include someone from design and development engineering. They will gain perspective from the environment and contribute insight to the team. If you are doing *a kaizen* event in the operating area of a hospital, include orderlies and maintenance personnel; they are integral to the changeover and can provide a unique perspective. It's OK to involve someone not directly related to the focus of the event; they usually ask the best questions and provide an outsider's perspective.

Have a Lean expert, or *sensei*, lead the *kaizen* event (See Chapter 5 for more information.) The *sensei* not only understands the tools, but can explain how to apply them for maximum value. This expert leader also manages the event, monitors progress, and keeps everyone on track. The *sensei*, who has the Lean perspective, can answer questions and solve problems using Lean concepts.

Selecting the project

Begin a *kaizen* event by validating and analyzing the value-stream map and identifying the most significant problem areas. Employ both qualitative and quantitative measures to ferret out the data that highlights the key issues — being particularly responsive to direct customer feedback. Use the team's experience to target waste areas for improvement. Select projects whose results will be highly visible to the customer and will make a significant impact on the value stream.

Random continuous improvement is a waste. Having a *kaizen* event so you can check a box is a waste of resources, and you risk demotivating people. Have a focus, like solving a customer issue, improving flow, increasing quality, reducing scrap, eliminating losses, or improving safety.

Many Lean companies have a suggestion program for identifying candidate projects. These are a prolific source for project ideas. The ideas can come from anywhere in the organization, but they usually come from within work groups.

Conducting the event

Focus the *kaizen* team on one area. If necessary, segment the group into several teams to attack different areas. Structure the workshop to follow the PDCA structure:

- ✔ **During the *plan* phase, objectively describe the change you intend to make.** Identify the processes you intend to change, and brainstorm improvement ideas. Define the steps needed to make the change, and form a prediction of the results of the change. Use data quality and analysis tools to support the plan development.

- ✔ **Use the *do* phase to implement the plan in a trial or prototype environment — on a small scale and under controlled conditions.** Keep it small enough to conduct the test quickly, but large enough for the results to be statistically valid.

Lean is a visual process. Be sure to make drawings, take pictures and video, draw charts, and graph activities throughout the process. Because visuals are so communicative, they speed the *kaizen* event process and document the changes made.

✔ **In the *check* or *study* phase, examine the results of your trial or prototype.** Quantify the extent to which the changes you made improved the trial process, and extrapolate the results to predict the effects on the larger process.

✔ **In the *act* phase, implement the changes on the full scale of the process.** Update the value stream map, standardized work and specifications, and verify process performance. Report out the results.

Because the *kaizen* event is conducted within a week's time, you will need to perform follow-up work to complete the change process. Track the completion of change items, and don't hesitate to perform additional changes and updates as required. Follow-up items should be completed within 30 days of the event.

The *kaizen event* is one form of *kaizen*. Ideally, you also have everyday *kaizen* projects also occurring in your organization. (See Chapter 9 for more about *kaizen*.)

Seeing with Visual-Management Tools

If a picture is worth a thousand words, visual-management tools in action are worth a thousand minutes, a thousand steps, and many thousands of dollars! When you use visual management, you don't waste time, energy, or effort looking for things, people, or defects. You can better see what's happening and whether things are running according to plan or not.

Keep the visual management tools simple and standard. Make them sensory — color, lights, sound, visual cues, or space. The more senses you appeal to, the more quickly you can gain status information.

Use cartoon drawings. Whether creating visual aides, writing up an issue, or conveying safety information, simple cartoon drawings bridge any language or literacy gap. Lean companies frequently use simple cartoon drawings throughout documents, meetings, facilities, and operations.

Andon

An *andon* is an electronic information or signaling device that may include graphics, colored text, and maybe even audio. *Andons* are used throughout public and private environments to communicate important status and failure messages to employees and customers. *Andon* is focused in particular on informing when a process or product is in jeopardy of failure, or has failed. You know that little light that comes on your dashboard, warning you that you're low on gas? That's an *andon.*

In manufacturing environments, an *andon* can be as simple as a three-color signal board that indicates in-spec, near-limits, and out-of-limits conditions for a running process. In service environments, *andon* displays can indicate queues and customer wait times. Transaction *andons* can be computer programs that warn operators of imminent failure conditions in data processing systems or at interface points.

Consumer *andons* are increasing in popularity. Displays in airports indicate departure and boarding status. Freeway signs indicate accidents and backups. And then, of course, there's that little dashboard light when you're low on fuel.

Display boards

Display boards, or dashboards, communicate vital information about the customer, process performance, standardized work, *kaizen* improvements, or team status. Display boards serve as effective and useful communication centers.

Not to be confused with marketing devices for impressing customers, display boards don't need to be too fancy — they just need to communicate. Display boards are operational nerve centers for the the organization, located where the action is. They can even be handmade and include data charts, photos of customer contacts or team members, and process data before and after *kaizen* improvements. Figure 12-1 shows an example display board.

Cross-training charts

Ideally, everyone is trained to do every job according to the standardized work design. Cross-training charts track the team's progress to this objective and identify people and their skills. In a cross-training chart like the one shown in Figure 12-2, all operations within a work module are listed across the top and each of the team members is listed by name along the left side.

When a team member is trained in a standard operation, a circle is placed at the intersection of his name and the operation. When she can competently perform the function according to the standardized work, the circle is filled in. Figure 12-2 is an example of a two-crew operation. On each team, at least one person can perform all the operations to the standard.

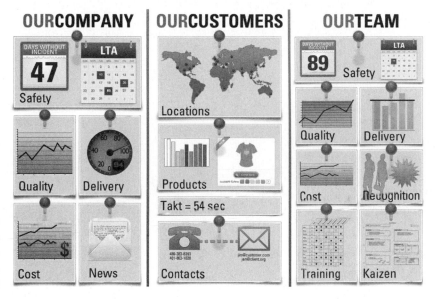

Figure 12-1:
A display
board.

Cross-training charts are a powerful visual tool. At a glance you know:

- ✔ Who can fill in when others are absent, without risking performance
- ✔ Who is the most expert member of the team
- ✔ When untrained employees are performing operations
- ✔ Where the team is weak

Additionally, cross-training charts provide valuable information when creating training and development plans. Post your cross-training charts on your area display board.

	Team	Operation 1	Operation 2	Operation 3	Operation 4	Operation 5	Operation 6
Ariel	A	●	●	●	●	●	●
Daisy	A	●	●		○		
Donald	A			○	○		●
Huey	A	○		●		●	
Mickey	A	●	○	○	●	○	●
Ursula	A		●		○	●	
Belle	B	●	●			●	○
Dewey	B		○		○	●	
Eric	B	●	○	●	○		○
Louie	B	●	●	●	●	●	●
Peter	B	○			●		○
Wendy	B	●	○	●	●	○	●

Figure 12-2:
A cross-training chart.

Resolving issues using A3

A3 is a single sheet issue resolution and planning document; it gets its name from the international A3 paper size (11" x 17" in the US system). The idea is that on one single sheet of paper, you have all of the information you really need about a situation. You design your A3 to fit your needs; however, a typical A3 include the following sections:

✔ Title

✔ Owner of the issue and date of the document

✔ "What is the problem?" — Background information

✔ "What are the current situations related to this issue?" — Current conditions

✔ "What do we want it to be?" — Target condition/Goals

✔ "What is the true cause of the issue?" — Root cause analysis

✔ "What are the actions to resolve this issue?" — Countermeasures to close gap or reach goal

✔ "What is our plan?" — Plan defining who, what, when, where, and how to measure and verify the implementation of the countermeasures

✔ "How will we track progress, share learnings, and handle issues during plan implementation?" — Follow-up actions to ensure the issue is resolved and doesn't reoccur

Develop your A3 sheets from *gemba* (see Chapter 13); it's the only way you can truly understand the real issue. Figure 12-3 shows one example of an A3 template.

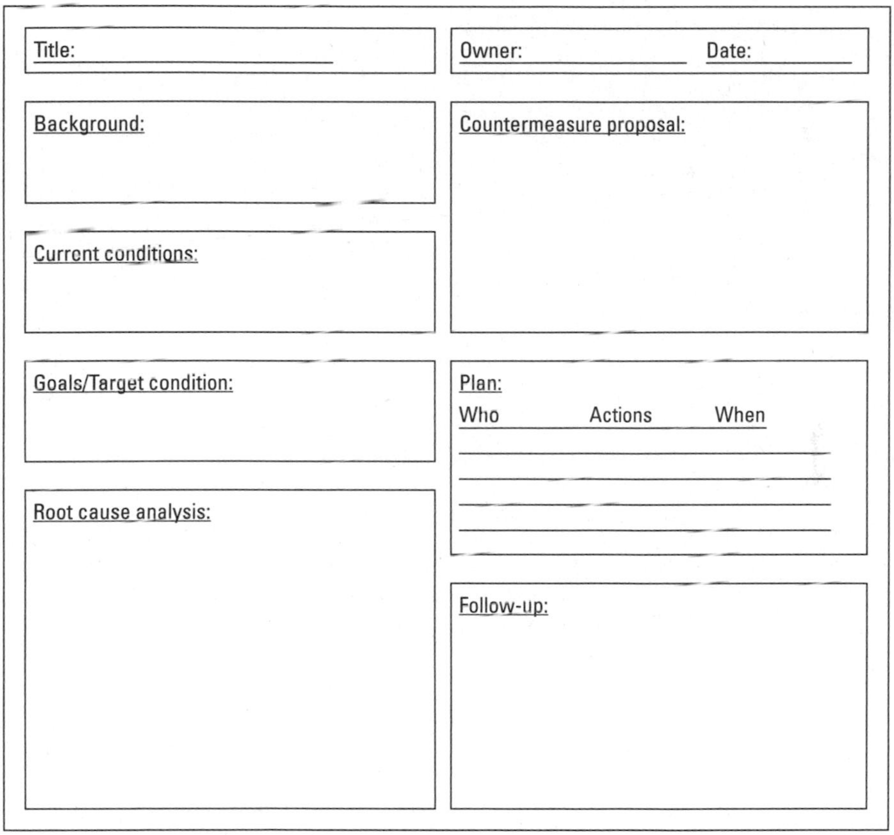

Figure 12-3:
Visual issue management using A3 reports.

Everyday Improvement Tools

The Lean toolkit contains yet another set of tools: tools for analyzing the data from processes, reducing variation (*mura*) and improving their internal performance. These quality tools are well-established and have been used in quality circles for decades. Systems like Total Quality Management (TQM) and Six Sigma also use these tools.

The beauty of the Lean everyday improvement tools is in how simple they are to use. They're visual; they show you what you need to see. They don't require advanced math or statistics to use and understand. They can be done by hand, on a calculator, or a computer. These tools can be used by everyone within the philosophy of *kaizen* for regular, continuous improvement. They support opinion with facts and data.

The 5 Whys

To seek out the cause of an issue or problem, you ask why it happened. But probing just one layer gets you to just the first cause of the problem. The root cause is usually much deeper. You have to keep probing. Noriaki Kano, creator of the Kano model, likens this to drilling down, "going an inch wide and a mile deep" to gain real understanding, rather than the superficial understanding gained from the converse — a mile wide and an inch deep.

The 5 Whys is a simple probing tool that helps you get to the root cause of a problem. At each level of explanation, keep asking "Why?" until you get to the true underlying reasons. You often have to ask at least five times.

Why five times? The number five is arbitrary. The point is not the number — it's the probing. You may get to the bottom in 2, or it may take 10 or 20 or 50 times, depending on the complexity of your situation.

Never take the first answer as the true reason. Keep asking "Why?" until you're satisfied that you've found the real root cause.

Consider this humorous example: The marble surface of the Washington Monument in the United States was disintegrating. That's terrible! Let's ask why:

- Why is the surface of the monument disintegrating?

    Answer: Extensive use of harsh cleaning chemicals have eroded the marble veneer.

- Why are we using such harsh chemicals?

    Answer: An inordinate number of pigeons collect around the monument, and they deposit high levels of pigeon poop on the marble surface.

✔ Why are there so many pigeons?

Answer: Pigeons eat spiders, and there are an unusually high numbers of spiders on the monument.

✔ Why are there so many spiders on the monument?

Answer: Spiders eat gnats, and there's a high gnat population at the monument.

✔ Why are there so many gnats?

Answer: Gnats are most active at dusk and are attracted by bright lights. The National Park Service illuminates the monument at dusk, attracting the gnats, which increases the spider and, therefore, the pigeon population.

The solution? Adjust the timing and characteristics of the lighting.

At each level of this example, you could have stopped asking and begun treating the symptoms, never reaching the bottom and discovering the true cause. This example also illustrates that the fix to the real problem is often simpler and more straightforward than attacking the symptoms!

Probe deeply, but carefully. You'll likely need to go to the next "Who?" in order to find someone with the expertise to answer the next "Why?" Also, examine the problem from different angles, because you may get different answers, depending on whom you ask.

The seven basic tools of quality

The quality toolbox contains many, many tools for analyzing and improving the quality of products and processes. Some of the more involved tools, such as analysis of variance (ANOVA) and process capability analysis, are powerful and important. However, you don't use those advanced tools every day.

The basic everyday quality toolset consist of seven simple tools that anyone can use. These are long-standing tools that first appeared in the 1968 book by Dr. Kaoru Ishikawa (yes the same guy who created the Fishbone diagram) and have been used in quality circles for decades. If you apply these basic tools regularly, you'll conquer the majority of your quality challenges.

In keeping with the philosophy of visual management, these tools are primarily graphical in nature. Graphical representations communicate more information than raw data and present the data in a form that often enables the problem to be obvious.

Tool #1: Fishbone diagrams : Cause and Effect

As you probe the nature of a problem and ask the 5 Whys, you'll begin to paint a mental picture of which causes are affecting what outcomes. You represent this graphically in what's known as a Cause-and-Effect (C&E) diagram — sometimes called a Fishbone diagram, after its graphical appearance.

This diagram is sometimes known as an Ishikawa diagram, named after Kaoru Ishikawa, who first applied it in the shipyards of Kobe, Japan, in the 1940s.

The Fishbone diagram enables you to represent the influences and connections on a particular outcome. Figure 12-4 is a generalized Fishbone diagram that exemplifies the categories and subcategories that can make up the chain of causation.

A Fishbone diagram is simple to create and apply. You can draw one on a whiteboard or the back of a napkin. You simply identify the major categories of influence on an outcome. Within those categories, you indicate the causes and how they connect. You can immediately present a picture of all the causes and contributions to an outcome, and suggest the next level of probing and analysis.

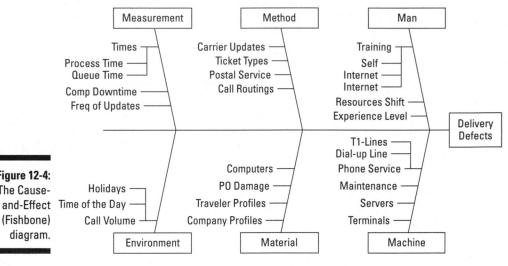

Figure 12-4:
The Cause-and-Effect (Fishbone) diagram.

Tool #2: Pareto charts: Finding the significant few

A *Pareto chart* is a special type of bar chart where the values are arranged in descending order, with the largest contribution first. It is named after the Italian economist Vilfredo Pareto, who discovered the "80-20 rule," now also known as the *Pareto Principle* (the principle that 20 percent of the causes are responsible for 80 percent of the outcomes). The Pareto chart is a fast and effective way to identify the significant few influences — and separate them from the many insignificant ones.

To make a Pareto chart, you simply stack up observations with the greatest values or impacts on the left, and observations with decreasing values onward to the right. Figure 12-5 is an example that shows categories of cost in an expenditure profile. From this chart, you can easily see the significance of each cost element to the total — and that salaries are the largest contributor, with equipment second, and everything else minor by comparison.

As shown in Figure 12-5, a Pareto chart shows both the absolute number as well as the percentage of contribution. The right vertical axis indicates percentage, and a line is plotted that depicts the cumulative percentage total, up to 100 percent with the last rightmost item. From the figure, you can quickly see that salaries and equipment combine to represent over 80 percent of the cost.

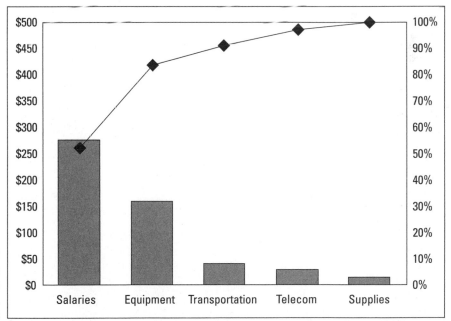

Figure 12-5:
A Pareto
chart.

Tool #3: Check sheets: Capture and see

A *check sheet* is basically any standard way you can gather data and view an activity as it's happening. The name comes from the historical use of a piece of paper or chart on which someone would indicate activity and check it as it was occurring. Figure 12-6 shows an example of a check sheet.

Police use "murder maps," a form of a check sheet, to track where the murders or other crimes happen. Armed with this information, they can properly staff neighborhoods, create relationships with the neighbors and work to solve and prevent crime. This same idea can be used in any situation to visually identify defect patterns so that corrective and preventative actions can be taken.

You can set up check sheets for a variety of uses:

- **Tallying:** Simply count up the occurrences of an event, such as runners crossing the finish line.

- **Defective items:** Mark the occurrence of defects by category.

- **Process distribution:** Indicate the occurrence of an event by value. This will build a histogram.

- **Location plot:** Mark the location of an event on a graphical depiction.

- **Defective location plot:** Mark the location of a defect.

- **Causation:** Indicate the likely cause of events as they occur.

- **Work sampling:** Indicate how time is spent by category.

Steering Wheel Assembly Check Sheet

Wheel station number: ___A 35___   Check Sheet number: ___112___

Wheel batch number: ___6-4494___   Date: ___2011/11/11___

Station operator: ___Ray William___

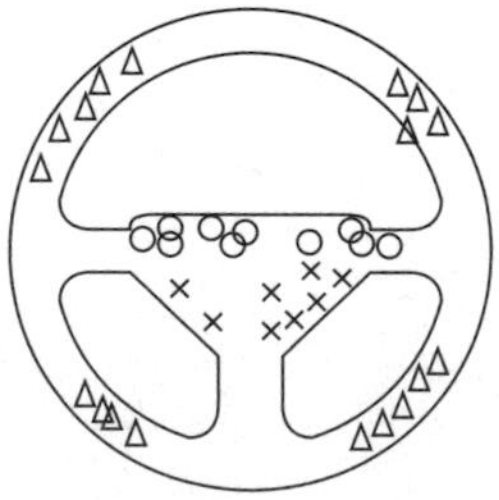

Wheels Checked: ‖‖ ‖‖ ‖‖ ‖‖ ‖‖ ‖‖

Defect	Symbol	Count
Cut	×	‖‖ |||
Bubble	○	‖‖ ‖‖
Scuff	Δ	‖‖ ‖‖ ‖‖ ||

Figure 12-6:
A check sheet.

Tool #4: Scatter plots: Relationships at a glance

A scatter plot is the simplest of all plots — and yet, it's also sometimes the most revealing. In a scatter plot, you graphically depict the relationship between two items or variables (see Figure 12-7).

Making a scatter plot is easy. Just draw and label a couple of axes and plot the data. Then sit back and look at it. What do you see? Is there a trend (known as *correlation*), or is it just random? Based on what you're seeing, you can draw conclusions about what's likely to occur next.

The scatter plot shows at a glance whether a relationship exists between the two variables, and what the nature of that relationship might be. The number of dots on the plot indicates how much data you've collected — the more data, the more valid the observations.

In this example, there's an obvious correlation between year and local index. Further analyses would indicate the nature of that correlation.

Tool #5: Graphs: Depicting the data

Using graphs is a great way to see the differences among items In a small set of related data. One popular type of graphs is the bar chart because they are easy to make and easy to read. Figure 12-8 shows an example of a bar chart.

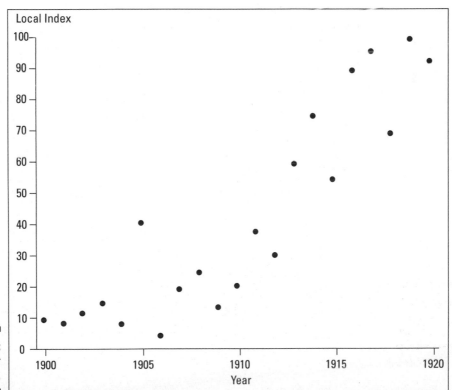

Figure 12-7: A scatter plot.

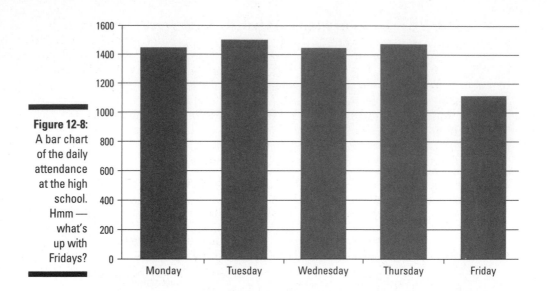

Figure 12-8:
A bar chart of the daily attendance at the high school. Hmm — what's up with Fridays?

Each entry is a count of the data for that category, and is displayed in a vertical column as a rectangular solid bar that is proportional to its value. A common variation on the bar chart is called a *stacked bar chart,* where two or more items that make up the value are displayed independently. Figure 12-9 contains a stacked bar chart.

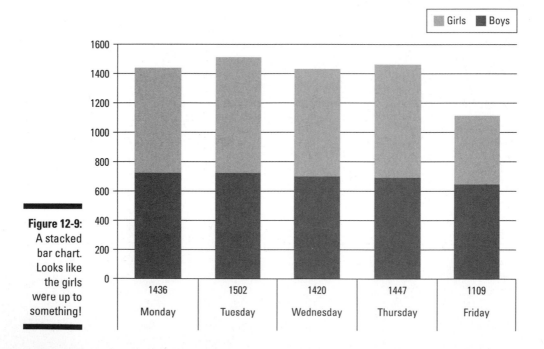

Figure 12-9:
A stacked bar chart. Looks like the girls were up to something!

In a bar chart, you look at the tallest and shortest, to understand the range, and get a sense for the mean and the deviations. You look at the bars relative to one another, to get a sense of trends, correlations, or other relationships. From the bar chart, you'll have a sense of what to examine or look for next. It turns out that that new vampire movie was released last Friday!

In addition to bar charts, other useful graphs include line graphs, circle graphs or pie charts, and pictorial graphs.

Tool #6: Histograms: Frequency of occurrence

A *histogram* is a type of bar chart that is organized to show counts of how frequently something occurs. In a histogram, each bar is of equal width and represents a fixed range of measurement. Over a period of time, you can easily see how the data is distributed (see Figure 12-10).

Histograms are enormously powerful ways to see how processes function and the degree of variation and other factors influencing performance.

Tool #7: Control charts: "Make it so"

The control chart (see Figure 12-11) is considered the single most important tool of statistical quality control. The control chart was developed not by Jean-Luc Picard, but by Dr. Walter Shewhart of Bell Labs in the 1920s as a statistical means for understanding manufacturing processes and improving their effectiveness. It serves as the basis for determining whether a process is in or out of statistical control.

Figure 12-10: The histogram on the left shows a "normal" distribution of data, whereas the histogram on the right depicts a non-normal two-peaked "bimodal" distribution.

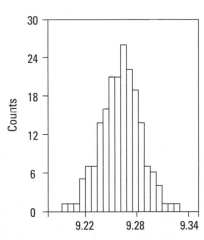
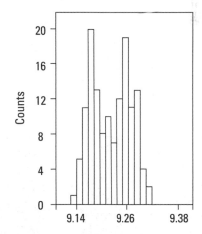

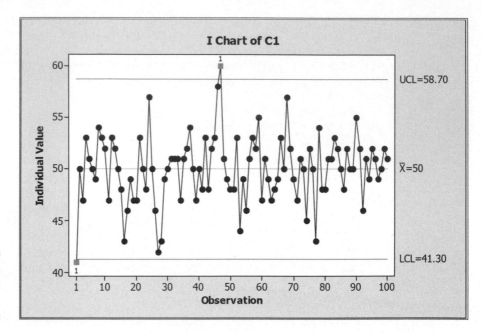

Figure 12-11:
A control
chart.

The control chart is a graphical display of the value of some process or quality characteristic over time. It displays the running value of the item, and usually includes the centerline target value as well as the upper and lower control limits.

Typically, as long as the sample values fall between the upper and lower control limits, the process is "in control." However, if the distribution of values is systematic and non-random, this is an indication of a special cause of variation, indicating that the process is not in statistical control and should be examined further.

A collection of the sample values in the control chart over time will form a histogram, as well as permit statistical analysis of the variation in the performance of the quality characteristic.

Sometimes you'll see *stratification* or even *flowcharts* or *run charts* substituted in place of the graphs listed as tool #5 of the seven basic tools of quality. Stratification is a technique for seeing patterns within data, such as data by shift, population or environment; seeing patterns can help you identify correlation and causation. Flowcharts (see Figures 2-1 and 2-2) are a graphical model of a process in sequential order, beginning with the first step in a process and charting the tasks and steps through to the end. Run charts are time-based plots of a process characteristic over time; they look similar to control charts, but without the control limits; it's the resulting value of the variable over time. These alternative quality tools might be just as applicable to your Lean project or initiative as the graph tools. Use the tools that are most appropriate to your situation for removing waste and adding customer value.

Using Qualitative Tools

After establishing the seven formal statistical tools of quality control (see previous section), the Japanese Union of Scientists and Engineers (JUSE) established the *new seven tools* — a set of qualitative tools. The new seven tools are just as important as the original seven tools. You likely use several of these tools already.

- **Relations diagram** – Use a Relations diagram when the interrelationships of a situation are complex. Draw and label boxes for every element of a problem, then draw arrows where one element influences another. Elements with the most outgoing arrows are root causes; the most incoming are outcomes.

- **Affinity diagram** – Collect ideas (usually on cards or Post-It stickies), identify natural relationships, and sort into groups for further review and analysis. Affinities are great inputs to Fishbone and C&E matrices.

- **Tree diagram** – Divide a problem or idea into progressively smaller parts, until you have tasks that the team can execute to address the problem or issue. A tree diagram is similar to a work breakdown structure.

- **Matrix diagram** – Compare alternatives in a matrix based on the relationships of criteria. Identify relationships with symbols and see what the resulting patterns imply.

- **Prioritization matrix** – Establish a list of criteria in order of priority and compare a set of options according to the criteria.

- **Process Decision Program chart** (PDPC) – Using a tree diagram, identify potential risks for each activity and then identify one or more viable countermeasures for each risk.

- **Activity network (arrow diagram)** – Similar to a PERT chart, map project or process tasks in required order with durations and resources, and connect them with arrows indicating the proper flow, indicating the project or process "critical path" and related dependencies.

These tools are especially good for qualitative analysis. The names may sound complicated, but they are easy to use. To see more examples, go to www.syque.com/quality_tools/toolbook/toolbook.htm.

Chapter 13

Management Tools

*L*ean is a strategic initiative. You undertake Lean because it makes good business and financial sense as a long-term direction for your organization. Yet, Lean requires not just a strategic vision, but a deep, personal daily commitment to improvement; you are changing your culture (see Part II). You need to have the right measurement system. You need to closely watch the short-term and long-term metrics. You need to learn from your experiences — both the successes and the failures. And you need to help everyone be actively involved on a daily basis.

Without the attention of managers and the participation of executives, the changes developed in a Lean implementation are not sustainable. In this chapter, we introduce you to tools that support the development and tracking of the business strategy, tactical initiatives, and the overall performance of the business.

Like other aspects of Lean, managerial tools are visual. Along with the customer and value-stream tools in Chapter 10, the flow and pull tools described in Chapter 11, and the perfection tools in Chapter 12, these tools make up the overall Lean toolbox. You need all these tools to support Lean implementation.

The chapter concludes with a general discussion of software tools to support Lean in the global extended enterprise. Although Lean is about simplicity and the elimination of waste, it is also about the appropriate implementation of technology. Follow a philosophy of: simplify and eliminate, then automate and integrate. This will help guide the management team to the appropriate level of technology implementation.

Managing Strategy

A successful management team manages both the long-term strategy of the organization and the tactical, day-to-day activities of the business. It's the same in a successful Lean organization: creating the master plan and measuring everyday progress to that plan. And in keeping with Lean fundamentals, the process of strategy development, deployment, and measurement should be simple and visual.

Strategy and measurement tools are plentiful in the marketplace, and the ones included in this section align with the tenets of Lean. The Plan-Do-Check-Act (PDCA) cycle central to *kaizen* also provides a great foundation for strategy development and implementation. Collectively, these tools help the management team effectively lead their organization through the Lean transformation.

In all that you do, your mantra should be "Simplify, eliminate, automate, then integrate." Lean is all about simplifying, eliminating waste, and then helping people use tools and technology to integrate functions and processes. Management teams can easily fall prey to consultants or IT vendors offering the latest and greatest whiz-bang solutions to all their problems. Automating bad business practices will not fix your problems. Magic wands do not exist. Whether developing strategy, performing *kaizen* activities, or evaluating technology, don't stray from the essence of Lean: Eliminate waste in everything you do.

Hoshin: balanced planning

The term *hoshin kanri* means "direction setting." The Lean planning system built around it is known as *hoshin* planning or policy deployment. The *hoshin* planning process is a proven, effective strategic planning process that follows the PDCA improvement cycle. In *hoshin,* the organization makes plans and then conducts a regular standardized self-analysis. The results provide inputs for updating the plan.

Hoshin planning is a two-pronged approach of (a) strategic planning and alignment, and (b) everyday operations fundamentals. The goal of *hoshin* planning is to ensure that the organization is developing its longer-term (two-to five-year) objectives and strategies, as well as managing short-term everyday business execution. It is also fundamentally based on the principle that you achieve the best results when everyone in the organization fully understands the goals and is involved in the planning processes to achieve them.

Using the seven qualitative tools (see Chapter 12) helps you create your *hoshin* plans.

Hoshin planning, to be truly effective, must also be cross-functional, promoting cooperation along the value stream, within and between business functions. The different departments of an organization must collaborate and support each other to achieve the remarkable results only possible through synergy and cooperation.

Understanding the hoshin planning process

Hoshin planning systematizes strategic planning. The format of the plans is unified via standards and measured through tables. This standardization provides you a structured approach for developing and producing the organization's strategic plan. The structure and standards also enable you to have an efficient way to link the strategic plan through the organization. This ultimately leads everyone to an organization-wide understanding of not just the plan but also the planning process.

Hoshin planning is a seven-step process, in which you perform the following management tasks:

- Identify the key business issues facing the organization and relate them to how you provide value to the customer/consumer.
- Establish balanced measurable business objectives that address these issues.
- Define the overall vision and goals.
- Develop supporting strategies for pursuing the goals, including how you apply Lean to achieve these goals.
- Determine the tactics and objectives that facilitate each strategy.
- Implement performance measures for each business process.
- Measure business fundamentals.

Be sure you identify measurable objectives, goals, and supporting strategies with process and functional owners to address critical business issues.

Setting the hoshin tables

Hoshin plans aren't the result of academic exercises; they don't collect dust on a shelf. You check them regularly against actual performance. In the *hoshin* process you employ a standardized set of reports, known as *tables,* in the review process. Managers and work teams use these reports to assess performance. Each table includes:

- ✔ A header, showing the author and scope of the plan
- ✔ The situation, to give meaning to the planned items
- ✔ The objective (what is to be achieved)
- ✔ Milestones that will show when the objective is achieved
- ✔ Strategies for how the objectives are achieved
- ✔ Measures to check that the strategies are being achieved

The different *hoshin* tables are:

- ✔ *Hoshin* **review table:** During reviews, present plans in the form of standardized *hoshin* review tables. In each table, show a single objective and its supporting strategies. A group or the individual responsible for several objectives should generate several review tables in order to cover all objectives.

- ✔ **Strategy implementation table:** Use strategy implementation tables to identify the tactics or action plans you need to accomplish each strategy. With implementation tables, present the following information:

  - The tactics needed to implement the strategy
  - The people involved in each tactic and their exact responsibilities
  - The timeline of each tactic, usually presented as a *Gantt chart* (a time-phased graphical representation of project activities and tasks)
  - Performance measures
  - How and when you will review the implementation

- ✔ **Business fundamentals table (BFT):** A business fundamentals table depicts the elements that define the success of a business process. In the table, you show how these elements are monitored through their corresponding metrics. Examples of business fundamentals are safety, people, quality, responsiveness, and cost. You must have the BFT figures in control before attending to the long-term strategies.

- ✔ **Annual planning table (APT):** Record the organization's objectives and strategies in the annual planning table. Then pass the APT down to the next organizational structure. Flow this pass-down process throughout the entire organization. Each level of your organization develops its plan to support the overall top-level organizational plan.

You can find software packages to help you create these tables.

The real change occurs when you're clear and specific about where you are going and who is responsible for each item in the implementation plans.

Making and proliferating the annual plan

Senior managers are ultimately responsible for establishing the strategies, goals, and balanced performance measures used to address the organization's issues for the coming year. Some organizations find it helpful to use issue teams. These teams consist of the functional, process managers and senior leaders most involved with a given issue. Together, they formulate the objectives and strategies, which best address the critical business issues at hand and maintain or improve customer satisfaction. Ultimately, the senior leadership must be convinced that the selected strategies will make it possible to achieve the objectives and resolve critical business issues.

Record the organization's objectives and strategies in the annual planning table. Pass the APT down to the next organizational structure. As the plans cascade through the organization, the strategies of one level become the objectives of the next level down in the organization. This provides direction and hierarchical linkage to the plan's highest level. At each succeeding level, strategies are owned, expanded, and turned into implementation plans that contribute to reaching the objective and the overall goal.

As each succeeding level accepts its portion of the plan, it has been involved in the plan's development by adding detail where it can best contribute and add value. This is also how the organization buys into the plan; it now has some ownership of the plan itself. The *hoshin* methodology is a strategic planning process with the built-in ability to empower the organization.

Implementing hoshin

The implementation *Do* process includes the execution of the *hoshin* activities, along with the timelines and checkpoints for specific events. Use the implementation plan as an ongoing decision-making tool. Plot or note the actual performance to plan along the planned events and checkpoints.

The implementation plan usually requires you to coordinate both within and between functional departments and process owners. Implementation plans are not just the responsibility of an individual completing the lowest-level annual plan. Each level and process in the organization must articulate and own detailed responsibilities to ensure support for and successful completion of the organization's plans. This is how you make the *Do* step of PDCA happen.

The annual hoshin review

Because *hoshin* is a cyclic process, the review of the previous year's performance is the basis for the next year's plan.

> ✔ **For the objectives that were completed successfully,** perform an analysis to determine what went right and to determine if the supporting strategies and performance measures initially established were truly appropriate. Also, note any exceptional results and how they were obtained. This step is critical to capturing knowledge of how to exceed goals, and then transferring that knowledge to the organization.

Recognizing major contributors to the success of the plan builds the team and reinforces the importance of plan achievement.

> ✔ **For each objective not attained,** determine the reasons for the shortfall. Analyze the detailed supporting data of all strategies associated with the objective. Ask the strategy owners to identify what their teams would have changed in the plan to have been more successful in the year just completed, as well as for the future. This process of both looking back and ahead improves organizational learning.

Conduct reviews at all levels of the organization. Starting at the lowest level that has plan ownership, complete the review and pass the information up and across the organizational structure (management levels). Have each level use the review tables from previous structures (management levels) to complete its own review. Foster discussions between the different structures of the organization to achieve consensus on the review table results.

In addition to listing objectives from the previous year's plan, use the review table to call attention to important issues for the coming year. When the review reaches the senior managers, the *hoshin* review tables highlight the areas in which the organization made significant progress and attained the identified goal, and where changes should be made or more work is needed.

Complete the review using information from:

> ✔ *Hoshin* review tables
>
> ✔ Corporate objectives
>
> ✔ Business plans
>
> ✔ Economic projections
>
> ✔ Customer inputs
>
> ✔ A quality assessment (if conducted)

The senior managers can determine whether the prior year's critical business issues and objectives are still appropriate for the coming year. This also is the time to make sure the organization is providing value to its customers as described in the plans. Also they ensure that the plans are consistent with moving the business in the direction of the long-term vision (ideal state).

Reviewing progress periodically

Although the planning cycle is annual, review business fundamental metrics monthly to ensure that performance is trending in the right direction. Review the annual plan quarterly to ensure that the plan is still the right plan. If the metrics aren't trending in the right direction, identify countermeasures to get the plan back on track. The actions may comprise as many as three phases:

- ✔ Alleviating the immediate problem with an emergency countermeasure.

- ✔ Preventing the problem from recurring with a short-term fix.

- ✔ Determining and removing the problem's root cause. This is the permanent solution that will prevent the problem from recurring.

The final annual review is essentially a compilation and summary of the *hoshin* review tables accumulated during the year. This final review returns you to the *Study* step described earlier. The *Study* step plays a crucial role in improving organizational learning ability. When actual performance and results are compared and a deviation-from-plan analysis is completed, those closest to the strategy make visible to the organization's leaders a great deal of information.

Reflection — thoroughly analyzing what went right or what went wrong in each strategy — is an important aspect of management reviews. Determining objectively which strategies and actions worked — and which strategies actions need improvement because they failed to hit their targets — is required in the organization's learning process. This is not a blame session! Focus on the strategies and actions; don't point fingers.

The Balanced Scorecard

The health and effectiveness of an organization is reflected only in part by its financial performance. Corporations report revenues, costs, and earnings; nonprofits measure fundraising; government organizations track budgets. Although the numbers are important, everyone knows that numbers are only one of several indicators of its true condition. To create a more balanced picture, Harvard researchers Dr. Robert Kaplan and Dr. David Norton developed a concept in the early 1990s called the Balanced Scorecard.

Kaplan and Norton recognized that a retrospective on financial performance alone is a wholly insufficient way to measure and guide organizations in the emerging postindustrial information age. It is both impractical and inappropriate to use financials as the sole basis for evaluating and managing the broad spectrum of customers, employees, suppliers, and distributors, as well as the processes and technologies that enable a modern enterprise. You need something more holistic.

As Kaplan and Norton formalized it, the Balanced Scorecard is a framework for both evaluating and managing an organization along the lines of four distinct perspectives: financial (of course), but also customer, process, and learning. Figure 13-1 shows the conceptual framework. In the Balanced Scorecard approach, the organization creates measurable indicators in each of the four areas, which are used both to track progress as well as manage achievement toward its vision. Simple and easy to understand, the Balanced Scorecard has been applied in some form as a standardized system of measurement in a majority of the world's companies.

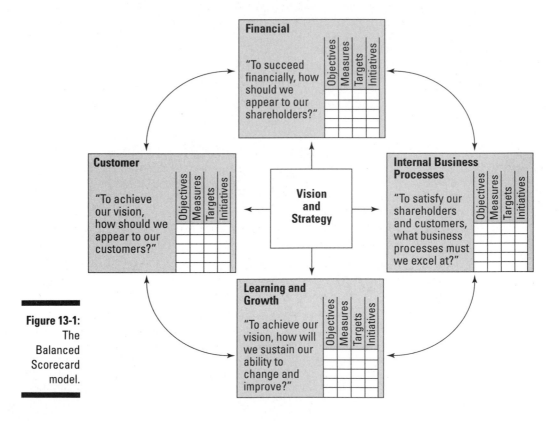

Figure 13-1:
The
Balanced
Scorecard
model.

Balanced Scorecard basics

The underlying framework for the Balanced Scorecard methodology is built on many of the same principles as Lean, including the following:

- ✔ Focus on the customer and, in particular, on the fact that the customer defines value
- ✔ Structured application of measurements and controls
- ✔ Quality at the source
- ✔ Continuous improvement, through measurement and feedback
- ✔ Engagement, empowerment, and development of employees

Consistent with *hoshin,* the balanced scorecard incorporates the outputs from internal business processes as well as from vision and strategy planning. It requires the organization to develop metrics based on strategic planning priorities, as well as the operational business fundamentals. This enables everyone to observe the outcomes of the measured processes and strategies and track the results to guide the organization and provide feedback.

Scorecard sections

The standard Balanced Scorecard contains four cards — one each for customer, financials, processes, and learning. They are purposely interdependent, forming a holistic view of the enterprise:

- ✔ **Customer:** The customer card focuses on the measures that demonstrate the ability of the organization to provide quality goods and services, effective delivery, and overall customer satisfaction. This includes both internal and external customers.
- ✔ **Financial:** The financials card mirrors that of most top-level financial reports, consistent with the nature of the enterprise (public, private, nonprofit, governmental).
- ✔ **Process:** The internal process card reports on the status and performance of the key business processes that constitute the core business functions (that is, what generates value for the customer).
- ✔ **Learning:** The final card is a report on the learning, development, and growth elements of the people, systems, and culture of the organization. This includes skills, communications, motivation, and agility.

You can easily see how the standard Balanced Scorecard would reflect the status and performance of a Lean organization. For this reason, the Balanced Scorecard is an acceptable tool of measure and works synergistically in a Lean enterprise.

You can use the Balanced Scorecard as more than a measurement system — you can also use it as the basis for a management system as well. This is true, to the extent that you get what you measure. If you're embarking on a Lean journey, however, be careful about mixing your management systems. In the Lean world, Balanced Scorecard is a framework for reporting.

Create your scorecard to fit your organization. Although the standard Balanced Scorecard is prescriptive, you may find it more beneficial to track a different mix of categories — such as safety, people, quality, responsiveness, or cost. Find the right fundamental business metrics for your organization and review them on a frequent basis — at least monthly.

Go and Observe

Lean managers know that they cannot effectively lead their organizations from their office. They need to be where the action is, where customer value is created — to build relationships, to understand the real issues, and to set performance expectations. You can create the most eloquent annual plan, but without involvement in the day-to-day activities, those plans are pipe dreams.

But it's more than just getting out of the office. The tools of this section create a framework for these managerial activities. *Gemba* walks, for example, aren't random strolls through an operation — they're focused on Lean implementation, safety, quality, or some other perspective. Whether conducted by an individual or team of people, the intention of a *gemba* review is clear.

At any level, the best way to know what is going on in the business is to "go, observe, and get the facts."

The power of 3 Gen

The principle of 3 *Gen* — *genchi* (like *gemba*), *genbutsu*, *genjitsu* — compels us to go to the actual place, observe the actual product or service and gather actual facts. In other words, get up off your butt and go find out for yourself — for real! Recognize that the electronic channels — the telephone, video conferencing, and the Internet — aren't enough to transmit the whole story. Yes, the overhead of travel (whether it's next door, on another floor, in another building, or across the ocean) is, strictly speaking, non-value-added, but it far overcomes the loss of detail, context, texture, and personal interaction.

Reality is the *only* way you will truly solve problems and know what is really happening is to go to the actual place (*gemba*) where your products or services are produced.

In the modern, technology-enabled, hierarchical and geographically-dispersed work environment, people seldom feel compelled to wander much beyond the space between the conference room, the break room, and their office or cubicle (or, for the tele-commuter, the space between the kitchen, back porch, and home office!). Communications happen via e-mail, conference calls, net-meetings, and on-line presentations. The risk is that you never really get the true information; this is why it is vital to practice 3 *Gen*. Here are some examples of 3 *Gen* in action:

✓ Interacting with customers to better understand their needs and behaviors

✓ Visiting the manufacturing, distribution, and retail facilities prior to beginning design work

✓ Seeing the show-room floor before developing the marketing materials

✓ Experiencing the product in action before designing the next generation

✓ Spending time with customer service to better understand warranty issues and alternative customer product usage

✓ Visiting your suppliers — and *their* suppliers — to understand capabilities and constraints

Next time, before drawing premature conclusions based on hearsay, opinion, or even all that hard data, consider 3 *Gen* — go to the actual place, observe for yourself the actual product and gather actual facts. 3 *Gen* is sometimes translated at the *3 Actuals*.

Losing connection with you ultimate customer can lead to costly mistakes and erroneous decision-making. You must understand what your customer is experiencing to stay in step or ahead of them.

Sometime you will see words such as *genbutsu* written as *gembutsu* this is because when the Japanese characters are transliterated to English both *gem-* and *gen-* are correct.

Gemba walks

Gemba is where you go when you "go and observe." *Gemba* is where the action is — the actual place where value is created for the customer. It is the kitchen in a restaurant, the operating room in a hospital, or a retail floor in a store. *Gemba* is where the real business occurs. If you don't go to *gemba*, you'll never truly understand your business or its issues.

The *gemba walk* is an observation tour. This is not a "run through that area, wave hello, and get back to your office" tour. The key is to observe and ask questions about things you notice. During a *gemba walk*, you may focus on a single selected item from the *hoshin* plan, like safety, housekeeping, performance, or customer satisfaction. For example, if quick changeovers are a priority, find out when setups will happen and go watch them. You may even be able to suggest additional improvements.

Though *gemba* walks aren't scripted, you must have a main intention or a standardized framework. If the theme of the walk is safety, you'll observe everything about safety, from employee actions to metric performance to the condition and location of safety equipment.

You may be wondering, "What do I do on a *gemba* walk?" Here's a list:

✔ Build relationships with people in the organization, and break down barriers to change.

✔ Learn to observe your organization with "Lean" eyes. Initially, go on *gemba* walks with your Lean *sensei* (see Chapter 5) to learn what and how to observe.

✔ Train others to observe by conducting regular and frequent walks — as a staff and with individual staff members. Have individual staff members shadow you — it's a powerful way of educating them.

✔ Review performance metrics as tied to the *hoshin* plan.

✔ Review A3s, team performance charts, *andon* status, housekeeping, and display boards (see Chapter 12).

✔ Talk to people. Seek to understand what they do and what their issues are. They're the experts at their job function, so ask about what you're seeing. Most people love to talk about what they do.

✔ Whenever possible, help people make the connection between the global issues and strategy of the company with the issues of your *gemba*.

You can build rapport with your organization while you're on a *gemba* walk. Listen to their issues and take action to help them out. Over time, you'll earn their respect and build trust. Eventually, they'll look for you during the walks to recommend improvements and give you feedback.

Housekeeping tours are a special form of a *gemba walk*, and a good way for managers to accomplish several goals:

> ✔ Stress the importance of a safe and orderly environment. (If you find safety issues, correct and contain them immediately. Follow up in future tours to make sure a permanent solution is implemented.)
>
> ✔ Practice a form of standardized work.
>
> ✔ Connect with people across the organization.

Management tours should cover the entire facility, inside and out. They should also follow a set process, including an established checklist of items to review, an agenda, and facility route (including restrooms and safety equipment). Nonconformities should be recorded and addressed. These items should be followed up on the next tour.

Management Information Tools

More and more tools and software are available to facilitate all manner of business process improvement, analysis, management, and controls. These tools are increasingly broad ranging and capable. Software poses a bit of a conundrum to the Lean practitioner, however, because software is inherently complex, and complexity is an anathema to Lean. Furthermore, you risk becoming captive to the tool, which is also a Lean no-no. However, a well-designed software program can be an effective tool for enabling your staff to perform both tactical and strategic tasks faster and more accurately, thereby reducing several forms of waste.

 Per Lean doctrine, keep your computer and software application usage as standardized, streamlined and simple as possible. That may sound like an oxymoron, but you can contain the size, scope, and proliferation of your computer applications. Use them where they're needed.

Lean process facilitation software

You can apply software to the practice of value-stream mapping and related Lean activities. Leading tools include enterprise-class tools like ARIS from Software AG (www.softwareag.com), and practitioner tools like iGrafx Flowcharter (www.igrafx.com). These tools also offer additional features, including process mapping, simulation, and some analytical capabilities.

The seven basic tools of quality addressed in Chapter 12, as well as the larger universe of statistical and analytical tools, are aptly facilitated by well-established providers. If you look in the Start menu of your PC, you'll likely find one of them: Microsoft Excel (http://office.microsoft.com/

excel), which performs most all of the basic statistical analysis functions for you. For more high-powered statistics and analysis, Minitab (www.minitab.com) is the king of desktop data analysis and statistics software. If you need more than basic statistics, such as regression analysis, analysis of variance (ANOVA), statistical process control (SPC), measurement systems analysis (MSA), design of experiments (DoE), reliability analysis, multivariate analysis, and non-parametrics, Minitab is the tool for you! Minitab also comes with a Quality Companion tool that performs process mapping, Fishbone diagrams, Failure Modes Effects Analysis (FMEA), value-stream map comparisons, and more.

Spider charts

Spider charts, also known as *radar charts,* are popular Lean management tools. By plotting multiple performance measures radially, spider charts are effective at showing the performance of several performance characteristics in a single graph (see Figure 13-2).

Spider charts are popular Lean tools because they're graphical, they're visual, and they communicate information rapidly. With a spider chart, you can do things like:

✔ Graphically observe the performance of business metrics to a set goal.

✔ Observe the relative value of different suppliers.

✔ Make logical comparisons between competing strategies or approaches.

✔ Instantly see the strengths and weaknesses between alternatives.

Spider chart are easy. Follow this quick process:

1. **Identify the information you want to compare.**

2. **Generate a list of approximately five to ten evaluation criteria.**

3. **Score the alternatives for each of the criteria.**

4. **Draw the chart and identify as many axis arms (spokes) as there are criteria.**

5. **Label the spoke arms of the chart — one arm for each criterion, and put hash marks on each spoke that represent counts.**

6. **Score a given alternative on each axis arm — and connect the dots with a straight line.**

7. **Repeat for each alternative. When you finish, it looks like a spider web.**

When using a spider chart to track progress to a goal, fill in the space representing the actual performance. This will help you to visualize how far you have to go.

Now observe the results and analyze the chart. What do you see? Look at the balance, the extremes, and the total area within each score. Spider charts are a powerful and revealing graphical management tool.

Don't be surprised if you change your scoring over time. People often set high expectations or they learn that their initial evaluations were too generous. If your web is filling in, it is time to re-evaluate your criteria. Remember the goal is continuous improvement.

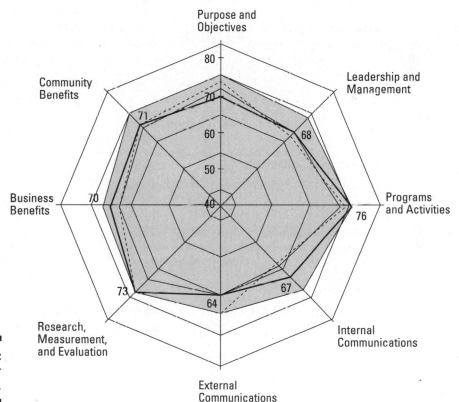

Figure 13-2:
A spider chart.

Visualizing Processes

Managers create displays and dashboards to monitor key processes and track performance at nearly any level or location, as it is occurring. You must have transparency into processes and operations to see what's happening and know what action is needed to maintain flow. Your management dashboards should be flexible and easily customized to provide anyone the view of what matters most to them — as well as what matters most to everyone else.

Management dashboards can be manually generated, but because the information is typically spread out over multiple locations and is available through information systems, dashboards are usually computer-generated. Automated dashboards can display everything from pie charts, maps, and histograms to run charts and control charts with upper and lower spec limits. Refer to Figure 13-3. Managers gain process intelligence through computerized visualization of key performance indicators, generated in real-time.

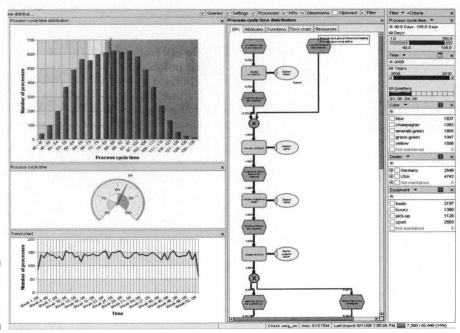

Figure 13-3:
Process
intelligence.

Courtesy of SoftwareAG.

In keeping with Lean, your dashboard should be simple to read and visual in presentation.

Management dashboards related performance-visualization tools are increasingly deployed broadly across all types of businesses and organizations, making objectives and metrics easier than ever to monitor, manage, and improve. This, in turn, enables *kaizen* and permits organizations to strive toward even higher performance goals. With these sophisticated visualization techniques, your business performance can become an upward spiral that enables your enterprise to strive for ever-higher performance goals.

Business Process Management software

One of the most powerful forces to emerge in the enterprise-level software world in the past decade is a suite of tools known as BPM — Business Process Management. BPM enables you to define processes that cross functional lines, integrating information from numerous systems like ERP, MRP, CRM, and others, and track processes through them as they perform.

BPM systems support process modeling, data capture, data analysis, visualization, and process control functions. They perform andon, enable the development and real-time display of management dashboards, and even build balanced scorecards. In short, BPM tools enhance the Lean enterprise.

Be sure you react properly to data. Single data points reflect instances; multiple points indicate trends. Improper point reaction can actually tamper with the system and cause waste. When you see data, go to *gemba,* see what is happening, gather facts, and determine appropriate reactions.

Part V
The Lean Enterprise

The 5th Wave   By Rich Tennant

"If we cut our dividend, reduce inventory and time travel to the 13th century, we should be able to last another year."

In this part . . .

The successful Lean transition is not only about the things you do, but also about how you overcome challenges. Some people will be resistant to change — as a group or as individuals. In this part, you discover how to address change, see how to implement Lean in different parts of the business, and understand how Lean organizations look across different industries.

Chapter 14

Lean within the Enterprise

· ·

In This Chapter

▶ Recognizing that Lean applies in all areas — not just manufacturing

▶ Understanding Lean at the enterprise level

▶ Identifying how Lean is practiced within different business activities and functions

· ·

L ean is an enterprise methodology. Some organizations have believed (mistakenly!) that it is only for the "production" part of their business, but it's applicable to all of the business. Take your supply chain, for example: if it takes you ten times longer to get your stuff from suppliers, you will not be able to supply your customer any faster. Also, by applying Lean across the enterprise, the multidisciplinary views and experiences help the core businesses better serve the customer. Because Lean principles apply to processes in general, *any process in any area of your organization can be improved using Lean.*

Practicing Lean anywhere benefits the practice of Lean everywhere. As we stress throughout this book, Lean is not a sideshow — it's not just something done by Lean experts or worker bees off in a corner of the organization. The more widely you practice Lean across the enterprise, and the greater understanding, acceptance, and support you achieve in each area, the better you will serve your customer and improve your business.

In this chapter, you see how to apply Lean from top to bottom and from wall to wall in an organization. From the support areas to the operational floor, and from the procurement office to the customer-service center, Lean practices reduce waste, time, and mistakes, and improve overall customer satisfaction and enterprise performance.

Lean Enterprise Management

Implement Lean across all functions and departments within the organization: Permeate the entire enterprise. Enable everyone across the organization to look for ways to eliminate waste. Encourage everyone to continuously and incrementally improve work processes — always doing it better, making it better, and bettering themselves and the whole organization to enable the core business.

In the Lean enterprise, people look at the whole business system. They conduct improvement activities at all levels with a complete view — seeing not just their own value stream and their own customers, but everyone's customers, the organization's customers, and the end consumers. Everyone examines the processes that influence outcomes — causes and effects — and sees the organization through the lenses of *kaizen*:

- ✔ *Kaizen* **maintenance:** Always maintaining performance levels by following standardized work
- ✔ *Kaizen* **improvement:** Continuously improving the existing standards and processes or innovating new ones

Across the Lean enterprise, people apply all their training and knowledge, utilize their materials and tools, and provide the support and supervision to both the improvement and the maintenance of standards. This business philosophy calls for never-ending efforts that involve everyone — executives, managers and workers alike.

It's a Lean, Lean, Lean, Lean world

Lean fuels a passionate emphasis on waste reduction and value creation anywhere and everywhere across the enterprise. It's in the excitement of enablement — the exuberance that comes from recognizing you have both the power and the ability to conquer obstacles that would otherwise frustrate you.

Lean above and beyond the floor

Don't look now, but most of what happens in many organizations isn't in hard-core physical manufacturing at all. While Lean was growing up in places like the automotive assembly arena, many organizations were evolving to deliver customer value in non-manufacturing realms. Nowadays, many enterprises conduct most of their business activities above and beyond what's known as the "ops floor." For operations to be successful, you must also improve all of the other activities. (In Chapters 15 and 16 you can find out more about how Lean is applied in non-manufacturing industries.)

Transactional Lean

Practice Lean in the *transaction processes* — business processes whose primary role is to transact information or process data. Just because you're not making something physical doesn't mean your processes are free of waste or you're effectively satisfying the customer. Transaction processes typically don't waste much material, but they can waste things that can be worth a lot more, including:

- ✔ **Time:** Poor transaction management wastes huge amounts of time. Apply the Lean practice of cycle-time reduction in these areas.

- ✔ **Facilities:** Transaction processes use facilities just like physical processes do — office buildings and data centers, mostly. Reduce excess square footage by managing transactions more effectively.

- ✔ **Energy:** When you're wasting space and churning more transactions, chances are you're wasting energy, too. Offices are big energy consumers, and data centers are even bigger energy consumers. Overtime, excess travel, rework — these all consume energy needlessly.

- ✔ **People:** Worst of all, by not engaging and utilizing people properly, organizations fall well short of their potential.

Waste is harder to see in transactional areas. You can easily see waste in the physical areas: parts, inventory, material, people who aren't working, and so on. But waste is harder to recognize in transactions. Is that person sitting in front of his computer adding value? Is the computer program he's running adding value? Is the process that's consuming the results of that program adding value? Are the data providing value? You have to look more closely — go to *gemba*!

The value-stream manager

The Lean enterprise has a unique role called the *value-stream manager*. The value-stream manager is responsible for end-to-end improvements and performance across one or more value streams. This role is important because it's focused on how to most effectively deliver overall value to the customer. It's a multifunctional role — integrating multiple disciplines and functional areas. A product-line manager, who owns the profit and loss (P&L) for a family of products or services, is a candidate to fill the value-stream manager role, because they oversee the many value streams for those products or services. A project or program manager with a focus on a single program or project could also fill the role. The value-stream manager might also be a uniquely assigned role within an operational area.

It's All about the Customer

Lean principles lead to organizational behavior changes in many ways. At the epicenter of this change is the customer. In Lean, the customer is the primary focus — it's not that the customer is always *right*; it's that the customer is *everything*. The customer defines value (see Chapter 6); the customer stimulates the demand for a product or service; the customer defines the requirements; the customer evaluates the results. Optimize all processes and activities within the enterprise to deliver customer value.

Within this philosophy, using the Lean toolkit enables you to flow information back from the customer to provide the products and services throughout the enterprise. Design information, customer usage information, demand information, operational information — it all flows to and from the customer.

But what about the direct relationship with the customer? How do you manage this in a Lean environment? Who touches the customer? What's different about Lean customer management?

Manage the customer following the same rules and protocol, and philosophy, as other Lean enterprise activities. Take the waste out of customer relationship activities; optimize the value stream of customer-facing functions; shorten the cycle-time of customer response; take a holistic systems view of the customer; and understand the customer's customer. Optimize the customer-facing functions just as you would for any function across the enterprise using *kaizen*.

Most organizations suffer from similar customer management challenges:

- Too many front-end processes and systems interacting with the customer
- Too many contacts, too many interfaces, and too many handoffs and delays in managing customer relationships
- Disconnected customer feedback from the rest of the organization
- Errors in selection, configurations, pricing, quoting, and fulfillment of customer orders
- Transactional customer relationships without intimacy or longevity

Lean organizations strive to create customers for life. The customer relationship is where their expectations meet your abilities, where you address their goals and desires by the outcomes of your enterprise and the capacity of your systems of development, production and support. Your Lean solutions will deliver high levels of satisfaction for both the customer and the enterprise.

Marketing the customer

Marketing is the dance — the arena where you and the customer develop mutual interest and excitement. It's what the dreams of future value are made of. Lean in marketing is the process of conceiving and refining the basis for exchange — what the customer might want, and what the enterprise might deliver. Tools like Quality Function Deployment (QFD) and Kano modeling are part of the transition between marketing and design.

When implementing Lean in marketing, the value stream is a flow of concepts and ideas; the products are emotions. Customer value is measured as demand. Waste is anything that doesn't stimulate this value stream. Companies that obtain market research faster and more accurately, and process it thoroughly, have an edge over their competition.

Integrate Lean marketing with the enterprise through systems and processes of capability, capacity, and profitability. Help your organization satisfy the customer interest you've generated by producing, producing timely, and producing profitably. The customer is telling you what they want, and your internal processes must effectively hear it — even if the customer's message is a message they don't necessarily want to hear.

Selling the customer

Sales processes are often transactional and systems-based, and they tend to be focused on the transaction process and revenue. Applying Lean to the sales process enables you to focus on customer value and ensure the right customers receive the right offer.

Selection and configuration

Customers need to quickly evaluate options in order to make selections and buy. Their ability to select and configure a solution quickly and easily is not simply a matter of efficiency; it's the enabler to a buying decision. Think about the experience of shopping for anything from shoes to computers. You need to find what you want quickly and easily, or you'll just become exasperated and go elsewhere. Sales managers ensure the customer has a fast, accurate, and focused path through the maze by applying Lean.

In the online world, tools like product configurators and guided selling tools enable customers to move quickly and easily through the buying process. These tools match supply and production capacity with customer buying preferences. Computer companies exemplify this process. If production of 600GB laptop hard drives is temporarily halted due to a typhoon in Malaysia, the Dell online tool will quickly entice buyers to select the 800GB drive through special pricing and incentives. The customers are getting a deal, while Dell turns a production problem into a marketing opportunity.

Quoting and pricing

In sales, apply Lean to remove waste and cycle time from the description, quoting and pricing processes. Use Lean practices to more effectively describe and demonstrate your products and services consistently; likewise with the quoting and pricing of products and services. Pricing sheets, price lists, complex bills of material, pricing changes based on options and configurations — these issues confuse both the customer and the sales team. Apply standardize work principle to product offerings. How can you best meet or delight the customer, while minimizing variation?

Lean organizations tend to have fewer, higher value product configurations. This enables reduced product variation and avoids end-of-season "fire sales" to get rid of unwanted inventory.

Ordering and fulfillment

Fulfillment processes are ideal candidates for Lean optimization because they are typically a combination of both physical and transactional processes that suffer from errors and delays. To avoid angry customers and high costs of rework and repair, apply Lean practices to the order processing and fulfillment operations at every level of the enterprise. Define the value-stream map, and optimize for cycle time, inventory levels, and defect prevention.

Servicing the customer

Service after the sale is the make-or-break function of the long-term customer relationship. It's likely the longest period of direct customer interaction — longer than the spikes of marketing or sales activity. It brings the customer back for more — or it drives the customer away, perhaps never to return. Because good service keeps customers coming — and poor service kills the customer relationship rapidly and permanently — you must apply significant energy and attention to optimizing the customer service function. Design your customer service process as part of the whole value stream and apply Lean techniques to ensure it's designed to best serve your direct customer, and is well-integrated with your marketing and sales processes.

The customer service process is markedly different in business-to-business (B2B) environments than it is in direct business-to-consumer (B2C) relationships. Design your customer service process to best serve the needs of you direct customers — whoever they may be.

The service process can provide valuable customer information — it's *gemba*. How the lessons learned in *gemba* are fed back into the organization will impact your ability to satisfy the customer and continue to improve your processes with the latest customer information.

Satisfying the Customer Through Products and Services

More than ever, the pressure is on businesses of all types and sizes to rapidly develop and bring innovative, high-quality products and services to market. New product development efforts are now characterized by ever-shortening product-development cycles, lower budgeted development costs, and required increases in product quality. More demanding customer requirements are constantly pushing the envelopes of features, customization, energy efficiency, environmental compatibility, reliability, maintainability, and life-cycle cost of ownership.

Lean development processes enable the enterprise to produce products and services faster, with fewer resources, and at higher levels of quality, while using less capital and making happier customers. Lean development practices help managers address a myriad of challenges that conspire against them, including uncertain requirements, chaotic work environments, non-reusable designs, increasing product complexity, prohibitively expensive prototyping and test regimes, last-minute design changes, and more.

Most of this section relates to a physical product, yet the fundamentals also apply to the service sector. Imagine your business is a call center or a retail floor. How will the customer interact with you? What tools and environments are you providing to your employees to best serve the customer? Imagine that you have a petite clothing department, but all of the clothing displays are at a "tall" person's height. Or a call center where the system does not allow the service representative to quickly and effectively respond to the specific customer situation. Design and development are just as important in the service world.

What happens during the design and development process affects what happens in the manufacturing, production, distribution and support processes. Development is near the headwaters of the enterprise value stream. When development is well-integrated in the value stream, greater efficiencies, reduced variation and higher quality outcomes occur throughout the life cycle.

Table 14-1 summarizes some of the techniques of Lean product development.

Table 14-1	Lean Development Techniques
Technique	*Description*
Kano modeling (must/should/could)	Understand customer requirements in terms of needs, wants, and delighters.
QFD – Quality Function Deployment	Capture and translate voice of the customer; value-based designs.
3P	Production Preparation Process starts at the design process to build Lean methods into the products/services and processes.
Design limits	Set high and low limits for performance, features, quality, or price.
Task linking	Use templates and checklists to manage the links and interrelationships among development tasks.
Delivery road map	Envision the schedule development deliverables.
Standard work	Produce recipes for performing tasks identically and consistently.
Reference standards	Follow established guidelines.
Short-cycle approvals	Manage by exception; provide value-added approvals and support.
Reuse	Identify where reuse of designs, production, and other life-cycle elements reduces time, complexity, or cost.
Meeting management tools	Hold standing briefings with defined outcomes; conduct waste-free meetings.
Complexity reduction	Optimize product quality, cost, and manufacturing by reducing complexity.
Visuals	Use status boards, Gantt charts, intranets; create visual pull systems for Engineering Change Notices (ECNs), Change Review Boards (CRBs), etc. Apply help sheets for exceptions to plan.
Formal freeze points	Enable parallel task execution.
Critical path management	Pull the development project through the critical path points on the development schedule.
Critical core management	Focus resources on core tasks that drive overall schedule, cost, and/or quality.
Brainstorming	Conduct events to address challenges and improve processes and outcomes. Refine the ideas to implement fewer, better solutions using PDCA.
Periodic process assessments	Continuously improve the effectiveness of the development process.

The systems approach

The first rule of development in Lean is to bring a complete, holistic view to the development process. Integrate the three major components of the development world — people, processes, and technology — and make sure they're mutually supportive. Keep them in alignment, not only with one another, but with the goals and strategies of the organization as a whole.

- ✔ **People** are the heart of the development environment. Lean dictates they are well trained in their disciplines and in Lean behaviors. They should also be highly skilled and intelligently organized.

- ✔ Development **processes** must be designed, standardized and followed. These processes must both minimize waste and maximize the capability of the people who use them.

- ✔ Supporting **technology** must be available, properly sized and configured, and focused on the solution. Technology should be selected to enhance and enable the performance of the people and the processes.

Hearing the voice of the customer

Every developer should hear that little birdie on his shoulder . . . *chirp-chirp!* That's the voice of the customer, singing in your ear, as you contemplate your next move. Are you listening? Can you hear the customer talking? What do you hear the customer saying? Can you say it? Can you explain it?

Use Lean tools to closely connect the development process with the customer. The customer's voice not only tells the developers what to design, but the customer's notion of value reveals much about the design process — and thereby helps the developers eliminate non-value-added steps and activities. Listen closely for details — any nuance that can further elucidate a requirement or specification that you can then translate into functional design for products and/or services. The Lean process hears the customer's voice first, foremost, and louder than any other voice.

The application of Lean to development comes from an intimate understanding of customer-defined value. Tune the people, process, and technologies to understand customer-defined value from the start. And to deliver on the value promise, product development must produce a product design that accomplishes the multiple goals of manufacture-ability and service-ability, as well as meeting and supporting the customer needs.

Front-loading the engineering process

Most of the cost of any final product or service is locked in long before the product is produced. Overly complex designs cannot be "leaned out" in the manufacturing process. Meanwhile, slow design efforts delay market readiness, and negatively impact sales and profitability. You cannot market and sell your way past products designed without the voice of the customer!

Suffice it to say that poor planning for design and development undermines Lean manufacturing. But short-changing the engineering cycle is just as counterproductive because rushing to production creates more problems than it solves. Designs arriving late to production cause poor yields, major manufacturing deficiencies and lingering engineering problems.

You can reduce the pressure on design and development time by applying Lean tools and practices like 3P (see Chapter 10) and DFM/A (later in this chapter) during the product-development process and by involving the manufacturing or service suppliers in the design process — this is called *concurrent engineering*. By taking the broader view of product (or service) development, you can also reduce manufacturing lead times, avoid assembly and service issues, maximize the life-cycle performance and product (or service) cost. As technology evolves, more teams are using simulation and virtual reality to improve the quality of the design process.

Concurrent engineering (also sometimes called *concurrent product development* or *simultaneous execution*) is the rational practice where all the enterprise functions are aware of the activities occurring beyond the borders of their own department. Concurrent engineering (see Figure 14-1) replaces a traditional serial product development process. In concurrent engineering (CE), everyone, including support areas, collaborates on each aspect of the product's life-cycle process, enabling more robust products and quicker reactions to changing conditions.

Apply product and service life-cycle rigor upfront, during the first design and development phases. This way, you maximize the effectiveness of the product development process and provide the most leverage through early problem solving, designed-in countermeasures, and cross-functional participation across the value stream. Furthermore, with this approach, you can reduce inherent uncertainty from the execution phase, reducing the downstream process variation that's critical to both speed and quality.

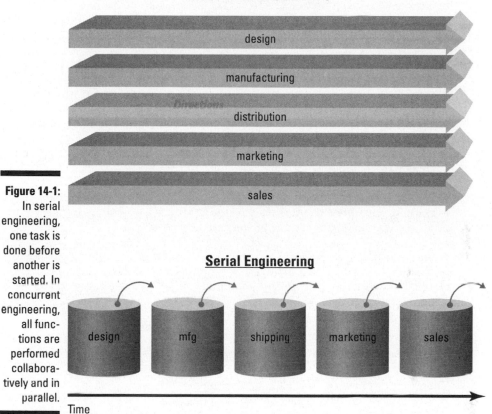

Concurrent Engineering

design

manufacturing

distribution

marketing

sales

Serial Engineering

design | mfg | shipping | marketing | sales

Time

Figure 14-1:
In serial
engineering,
one task is
done before
another is
started. In
concurrent
engineering,
all func-
tions are
performed
collabora-
tively and in
parallel.

Rigorous standardization — for maximum flexibility

A constant knock on rigorous methodologies like Lean is that they're suppos-
edly too rigid. Especially in the quirky, inventive culture of the design world,
people think that standards and processes do nothing more than take the art
out of the practice. After all, where's the creativity, if all you're doing is following someone else's best practice process, right? Nothing could be more
wrong.

Lean is not about becoming a robot, programming yourself to perform repetitive tasks with machine-like precision. Lean work standards, best practices, and waste-reduction initiatives in no way imply you're limiting creativity and flexibility. In fact, just the opposite is true.

The development processes in Lean organizations are far more predictable, effective, and value-added than is otherwise possible. This is because the development teams are supported by tools and resources (refer to Table 14-1). They eliminate the noise factor of unnecessary randomness and chaos in the support frameworks, enabling teams to focus more time and energy on the creative elements. Redeveloping infrastructure on every project or at every step is wasteful and distractive — it saps creative energy. Elements such as work protocols, reference designs, and standard processes enable designers and developers to spend more of their time being creative and applying their precious energies on the truly value-added tasks such as developing customer solutions. Such standards are also crucial to innovating new downstream Lean manufacturing capabilities.

People fear that systems like Lean are somehow confining or limiting. They're not — they're enabling and innovative! Without them, developing anything would take more time and effort — and time and effort are exactly what's in shortest supply.

Designing for manufacture

The practice of Design for Manufacturability (DFM) — or Design for Assembly (DFA) — is an important part of Lean practice. It isn't unique to Lean; DFM is part of concurrent engineering — it's recognizing that it doesn't matter how beautiful and elegant a design is if you can't actually build it. DFM is a collaboration between the design and manufacturing functions of an enterprise who ensure the product as-designed can be developed within reasonable manufacturing limitations.

Designing for Manufacturability helps you greatly improve product quality and reduce fabrication costs. You involve the manufacturing representatives early in the design process. After completing preliminary designs, you meet with the manufacturing team and review the product requirements and design intent. At that point the team can determine the manufacturing process requirements, and the manufacturing team can determine the process capabilities implied by the design in order to meet product quality, cost, and availability targets; they also share lessons learned based on past experiences, especially with similar products.

One of the most harrowing problem areas for physical products is *tolerancing* (the practice of defining tolerance limits on components, parts, and assemblies). Historically, designers define tolerance limits too casually — and in the process, inadvertently dictate the capital and process needs of production. Avoid tolerances that are beyond the natural capability of the manufacturing processes: too tight or too generous that they create stacking problems; both conditions can result in products that cannot be made or won't last. In addition, the manufacturing team should identify to the designers any manufacturing tolerance challenges and suggest design or requirements revisions. When new production process capabilities are needed, identify these needs early.

Simplify design and assembly so that the assembly process is unambiguous. Design components using *poka-yoke* so that they can only be assembled or utilized in one way.

Built-in learning

In the Lean enterprise, ensure learning and continuous improvement are fundamental parts of every job. Although certain work skills require special outside training, make acquiring and refining Lean process and improvement skills a regular and routine part of everyday work. Build in learning into your organization by including such practices as:

- ✔ During projects, reviews, and events, encourage everyone to learn and update their work standards and practices.

- ✔ Use reviews at project milestones and completion to provide additional opportunities for learning.

- ✔ Go to *gemba* (see Chapter 13) regularly to gain and validate knowledge.

- ✔ Make learning and continuous improvement a part of the problem-solving process. Focus multiple potential solutions on root cause, and design solutions to stop future reoccurrence.

When the product is software

Lean practices apply to the process of software development, just as they do to the development of physical goods and services. Developing so-called virtual products, like software, has its idiosyncrasies, but remember that *kaizen* is an all-encompassing philosophy, and that Lean improves *all* processes.

All the behaviors, practices, characteristics, and techniques of Lean that enable the continuous improvement of hard, physical goods also apply to software. These include the focus on the elimination of waste, customer value-added, engaged developers, reduced cycle time, and improved quality.

The most important Lean technique for software development is to simplify before you code — in other words, fix it in the design first.

Some of the other important Lean software development techniques include

- **Hearing the customer:** Particularly in corporate software environments, understand the customer. And understand what your customer is doing for *their* customer. Capabilities, timeframes, cost — understand your customer's issues and what's important to them. *Genchi genbutsu!*

- **Avoiding bloatware:** Pareto's Law applies to software utility: 80 percent of the value in most software is provided by 20 percent of the features. Don't waste time and energy designing and developing mainstream features that most users don't find useful.

- **Feeling the need for speed:** How quickly can you respond to a customer's need for new features or functionality? How much non-value-added activity churns while the clock is ticking? Software should be modular, flexible, and extendible; teams should be small, fast, and focused.

- **Maintaining "agile-ability":** Software development teams should be agile — modular design and system integration should enable work on any layer, feature, or capability. To do this, the team needs to be engaged, communicate, and collaborate constantly throughout the development process. The goal is just-in-time performing software, with information and control available on demand by any customer.

- **Simplifying the interfaces:** The key to modularity and extensibility is to keep the interfaces clean and simple. Examples include: interfaces between code modules; functional interfaces between applications and systems; usage interfaces between departments.

- **Working continuously, incrementally:** Add capabilities and new features regularly. Lean-agile software techniques call for continuously developing and deploying software in small feature sets.

- **Maintaining standards and standard practices:** Software shops really struggle with internal discipline, and yet it's an environment where discipline and control is as important as anywhere. Everything from filenames to coding standards, documentation practices, configuration management, change control, backups, upgrades and release management, and 5S (see Chapter 11) in the workplace.

- **Providing visual feedback:** The visual status, reporting, metrics, and controls are fully applicable in software environments. Use them liberally!

Lean Production Processes

The Lean movement began in the production arena, on the operational floor, in Japanese automotive manufacturing and assembly plants. This is where the Lean philosophy, Lean behaviors, and Lean techniques were first developed and later honed. There's a reason why so much of the language of Lean sounds like you're "making" a new Toyota!

This section is about production processes — that infamous "ops floor." This is the historical core of Lean.

Safety, often referred to as The 6th S (see Chapter 11), comes before everything else for all production activities. In the words of Taiichi Ohno at Toyota:

> *"Never forget that safety is the foundation of all our activities. There are times when improvement activities do not proceed in the name of safety. In such instances, return to the starting point and take another look at the purpose of that operation."*

Lean production techniques are much different from those used for 20th-century-style industrial mass manufacturing. The key principles are:

- ✔ The customer defines value, and all production people, systems, and processes are focused on adding to that value.

- ✔ Reduce and eliminate waste — wasted time, energy, space, people, materials, facilities, and equipment.

- ✔ Instead of focusing *only* on outcomes, focus on the processes that create value across the entire value chain that produce those outcomes. Use value-stream mapping, *kaizen*, and standardized work as key enabling tools.

- ✔ Safety is the foundation of all activities. People must be able to deliver value to the customer without being injured. Evaluate all processes to ensure the safety of all.

- ✔ Practice continuous flow — even if you have to rearrange facilities and systems and put in new control and measurement systems. Produce to a cadence, as measured by takt time.

- ✔ Through shortened equipment setup times, move to producing small lots, "every product every day," and ideally to single-piece flow.

- ✔ Reduce and eliminate inventory and storage. Move to a demand pull system that's initiated by customer action.

> ✔ Define standard work processes, and adhere diligently to them until you make a formal change.
>
> ✔ Create quality at the source.

Production is that place in the value stream where you create value for the customer via your product or service. It's where the action is — *gemba* — and where it's easiest to see the process in action. Apply visual tools for quickly seeing status and reference. Go there often to ensure you are delivering in the most effective way.

Lean in the production area has always been about doing more with less — improving quality and effectiveness while consuming less time, fewer resources, less energy, time, inventory, people, and capital. The classic title "Lean manufacturing" has been applied to the greater movement that eliminates waste *(muda, mura,* and *muri),* streamlines processes, and speeds up overall production, while enabling and respecting the people and delighting the customer.

The production arena is where most companies start their Lean efforts. Unfortunately, it's also where many stop them. Don't let this happen to you!

In the Lean enterprise, the quality function shifts from reactive to preventive; you develop quality "at the source." *Quality at the source* is a Lean principle where quality output is not measured just at the end of a process, but at every step along the way; and also, quality is the responsibility of everyone who contributes to the production or delivery of a product or service. The quality group analyzes cause and effect, works to predict failure modes, and prevents them from happening. This is a key role shift — from one of reaction to one of prevention. The focus shift to be active in *poka-yoke* (mistake-proofing) as well. As a result, the quality organization will move from inspection of product to a process/product auditing focus.

Leaning Up the Support Functions

In Lean terms, it's easy to see that overhead functions and departments typically add little or no value to the customer. Where's the customer value in a contract, an accounting procedure, expense report or database management system? Technically speaking, it's all non-value-added. As a result, enterprises tend to direct their improvement energies on core value-added processes and treat support functions as necessary evils, thinking of them as type-1 *muda.* Big mistake!

You have two reasons why your support functions are vitally important to the Lean enterprise:

1. Because indirect and overhead departments typically total over half of all costs, support areas should receive massive internal process-improvement attention. Like everyone else, they should Lean themselves.

2. Support functions must be in step with the core value creation operations. These functions provide people, parts, materials, and other resources to productive areas. If their processes impede delivery to the customer, then you are not delivering the most value to your customer.

You can introduce Lean in support areas by facilitating *kaizen* events, coupled with a modest amount of training. Support them with the following management behaviors:

✔ Facilitate a broad understanding of the function's contribution to the enterprise and how it delivers value to its customers.

✔ Define and measure the function's standardized work processes.

✔ Build VSMs that show how the processes align to the value stream and generation of customer value.

✔ Use performance measures to motivate Lean actions; reward Lean behaviors; incentivize the elimination of unnecessary overhead.

✔ Cross-train, enabling the shifting of work for rotations and peak load management.

✔ Define internal business measures in terms of customer value.

As a support function, declaring yourself type-1 *muda* does not excuse you from being part of the value stream. Applying Lean internally to your function is important, but you are not an island. Go to *gemba* and look for ways to contribute to the continuous improvement of customer value.

Lean in human resources

The Lean enterprise depends most of all on people; "respect for people" is one of the two pillars of Lean practice. We also know that Lean stimulates transformational and disruptive change in how people work, team, and communicate. This must be well-managed and supported through the short-term bumps and over the longer-term evolution. As a result, the human resources (HR) function has a critical enabling role in the Lean enterprise.

✔ **Talent acquisition and retention:** HR helps provide the right resources to teams and ensures they have proper skills and competencies, the necessary tools, and the ability to work in environments that reward improvement in a supportive atmosphere. HR uses hiring strategies to employ both permanent workers and temporary staff to handle fluctuations in business demand. And HR is even more critical in volatile market conditions, like emerging markets and high retiree rates, to hire and retain the workforce.

✔ **Culture facilitators to sustain Lean:** The HR function helps provide the tools and means by which employees at all levels create the culture that will sustain the Lean improvements. They facilitate communication across functional and hierarchical boundaries. This can include everything from role definitions, principles and values, issues and challenges, behavior expectations, cross-functional forums, celebration of successes, and more.

✔ **Compensation and reward systems:** HR implements the employee compensation systems and facilitates the reward mechanisms consistent with Lean principles and practices.

✔ **Training and development:** By closely aligning with the lines of business, understanding strategic directions, and supporting the staff, HR plays a key role in organizational readiness and performance through its training and development function. The goal is knowledge delivered in the most effective way, to the right people at the time when they need it.

By driving waste from its own internal processes, HR will also have more time to deliver value to its key customer: the employees. The greatest opportunities include recruiting, new-hire cycle time, training and development, benefits administration, satisfaction, and retention. In Chapter 16, you see how one company applied Lean to their on-boarding process in order to retain more of the people they hired.

Lean finance and administration

An enterprise Lean initiative requires you to transform the mindset of the finance and administrative professionals so they can better participate in delivering customer value. This goes beyond the practical insights and applications of applying Lean techniques to improve internal financial processes; your Lean journey requires a different type of accounting — an accounting that motivates the Lean practices throughout the enterprise.

Process teams need information that correctly measures customer value and waste. Managers need metrics for assessing the financial impact of *kaizen* events and Lean improvements. In addition, they need this information to be available simply and visually. Lean finance and administration delivers this.

- ✔ **Orientation to customer value:** Lean accounting is a transition from traditional budgeting and transactional-based financial management systems, which are oriented around process controls. Because these new systems presume that processes are in control, they measure costs and contribution margins from the value stream.

- ✔ **Metrics and measures:** Get the financial measures of performance in line with practices of creating customer value and the reduction of the seven forms of waste. It is best when you combine these in a balanced scorecard with the customer, process, and people measures.

- ✔ **Ease of understanding:** Use short, clear, visual reports and dashboards to convey status and results in value-stream terms that everyone can understand.

Lean IT

New programming tools and frameworks are enabling Information Technology (IT) to Lean itself and better fulfill its responsibility to provide the right technology and information systems to enable information flow within the value stream and the delivery of customer value. IT's role in the enterprise continues to evolve rapidly as technology evolves. Technology is now underpinning nearly every business function, enabling new business opportunities and facilitating closer interfaces with both the customer and consumer. The IT industry has developed platforms, tools, and capabilities that better enable Lean practices and is now better able to play a central role in the development and ongoing maturity of the Lean enterprise.

- ✔ **Lean across the extended enterprise:** Lean practices have been effective without technology in local environments and workgroups, but only IT can effectively integrate the full gamut of Lean practice across value chains that transcend multiple geographies and corporate boundaries. IT can enable processes, information, people, systems, and materials in the global domain.

- ✔ **Customer focus:** Chief information officers (CIOs) and IT practitioners have long recognized the need to improve their customer focus, but systems and applications have typically been designed to perform isolated functions. Newer technologies for business process management and service-oriented architectures can tie the signals of customer demand and other customer events and measures through the value stream, giving IT managers improved customer awareness as well as management controls over their applications and systems.

Many organizations attempt to fix broken business processes by patching them over with IT. But IT by itself will not fix a broken process. Fix the root cause of the problems. Simplify and/or eliminate waste before you automate and integrate processes.

As an example, a large manufacturing company had an understaffed purchasing department and was unable to provide manufacturing with the right parts at the right time. To keep supplying the customer, manufacturing continuously deviated from plan and substituted other components to build and ship the product. Manufacturing's solution was to have IT improve the deviation process so they could substitute parts faster. Instead of focusing improvement at the source of the problem (purchasing), the IT team was asked to improve a "work-around" process for manufacturing.

Internally, IT has a lot of house-cleaning to do and can improve itself considerably following Lean practice. A few examples:

- **Reduce non-value-added activity:** Streamline IT processes and eliminate outdated processes, paper reports, redundant processing, and multiple handling of information (internally in IT and externally in the business).

- **Customer pull:** Support customer and consumer needs on an individualized basis using IT tools which process and deliver information at the rate of customer demand. Avoid building software that tries to be all things to all users.

- **The end of batching:** Eliminate batch data runs by using systems that can support more real-time integrated and continuous-flow data processing.

Lean Supplier Management

The Lean journey within the enterprise is just that: It's *within* the enterprise. However, supplier performance — *outside* the enterprise — is of course a key part of the value stream, and it significantly and materially affects the performance of the enterprise. Working with suppliers within the Lean framework helps you optimize the value-stream across the complex interfaces between organizations.

Lean supplier management requires you involve multiple functions and departments within both organizations. It's the concurrent, cross-functional management operation — now extended through organizational boundaries. From a Lean perspective, your key suppliers are long-term partners. You form long-term relationships and recognize that their success is ultimately your success. Sometimes, it will require you to redefine the entire architecture around the supply process. It's worth it, though, because you can:

- ✔ **Add value:** Providing products and services effectively, with less waste, fewer defects, and undue costs

- ✔ **Flow information rapidly:** Smoothly, completely, bi-directionally, flowing both developmental and operational information

- ✔ **Administrate effectively:** Making contractual arrangements more easily, and performing effective change management

- ✔ **Continuous material flow:** Connecting and delivering goods and services without interruptions in support of your facilities and processes

- ✔ **Manage inventory:** Striking a balance of inventory across the supply chain co-create global inventory strategies and contingency plans

Behaving as one: The architecture of supply

Supply chains tend to tier according to volume and commoditization. The automotive industry, for example, has a first tier of suppliers who provide major components and assemblies to the vehicle brands. In turn, those suppliers have a second tier that provides sub-assemblies and smaller components. A third tier provides piece-parts. The computer industry is similarly tiered — as are most large, mature and global industries.

The number of tiers in an industry, and the number of providers in each tier, is based on the degree of product complexity and extent of both the commoditization of the product and the volume of product in the market. Consequently, there are many players in each tier of industries like automotive or computers, fewer in the oil and gas industry, and very few in an industry like running shoes.

Supply architectures tend to balance themselves naturally based on a variety of pressures and constraints, including:

- ✔ **Drive for simplicity** towards the fewest number of suppliers to manage, as well as the fewest number of parts to design, assemble, and support.

- ✔ **Leverage strategic competencies** around what you choose as your core versus what you bring in from outside providers.

> ✔ **Take advantage of price** either when you can make something for less than what the supplier can, or when the supplier can provide it for less than it costs you to make it.
>
> ✔ **Use readily available** commodities or near-commodity parts and supplies when they are easily available in the marketplace.

Binding the links

Because organizations connect on many levels, be sure you connect with your suppliers technically, contractually, and methodologically. Don't just leave it to your procurement staff to work the best deal as they see it.

Contractual ties

Lean organizations view suppliers as long-term partners, critical to their own success, and their contracts reflect this view. Try to bind supplier relationships with the longest possible contractual instruments. Short, re-competed contracts went out of vogue in the 1990s. Supply chains are most effective when everyone is part of a stable consortium. With this collaborative approach, the supply players can lower fixed costs and focus on continuously lowering variable costs. That, in turn, enables everyone to base performance measures on quality and delivery. Longer-term contracts and trusted relationships also facilitate improved demand management and production smoothing.

The purchase price is seldom the true cost of a product or service. The true cost contains logistics, quality defects, rework, product returns, warranty, legal and administrative costs – and profit. The more your procurement staff understands the true costs of their actions the leaner the supply chain can be.

Shared methods and models

Be sure to align your methods and approaches with your suppliers. As a Lean organization, you want your suppliers to practice Lean also. You want them to speak the same language, use the same tools, and measure value and waste the same way. If you've modeled your supply chain according to a reference model like the SCOR® model (Supply Chain Operations Reference model) from the Supply Chain Council, you can take mutual advantage of the process definitions, best practices and metrics to accelerate changes and improve performance.

Conduct *kaizen* activities together with your key suppliers. As they become better, you are contributing to your success through products that are more consistent and to their success and longevity as your supplier.

Technologies

You will need to exchange extensive information with your suppliers regarding products, orders, ship notices, invoicing, billing, and more. Integration technologies, exchanges and hubs, and protocols like RosettaNet enable enterprises to interface with their suppliers more effectively.

Let it flow

Flow information freely with your suppliers to build and optimize your value-stream map. Development and demand information are both part of the customer-supplier relationship. The more free-flowing the information, the more effective these relationships can be.

Development information includes design data, manufacturing information, expertise, consumer data, and other background information that assists the players in the supply chain in developing effective products and services. Often, this information is proprietary, and sharing requires trust — trust that you won't share it with one another's competitor or use it maliciously. However, sharing of information is one of the key leverage points of supplier management in a Lean organization.

Demand information is critical to the ordering and delivery of materials and services. For many years, electronic data interchange (EDI) facilitated the flow of demand information. More recently, online exchanges and other electronic systems have facilitated the nearly real-time flow of demand data. This includes long-term forecasting and replenishment data, as well as order and delivery data.

Logistics

In Lean, you manage the flow of supplies to minimize stocking, inventory, and cycle time — anything that wastes your resources. Lean logistics include the following:

- **Top-up systems:** Have commodity items delivered and managed at the customer's site — right at the point of use. Have the customer manage stock-outs.

- **Third-party kitting:** Subcontract the kitting process, usually to one of the commodity suppliers. This requires effective traceability management. Third-party kitting is popular in the aerospace and automotive industries.

- ✔ **Milk runs:** Instead of having multiple a supplier deliveries to your facility, you send one truck to collect from several suppliers according to a set schedule and route. You control the flow of materials to your facility.

- ✔ **Strategic global agreements:** Work strategically with your suppliers to create agreements about shipping methods and inventory levels in the global pipeline.

- ✔ **Distribution centers:** Have suppliers deliver to a central facility where the redistribution can occur in a way that best suits the customer. This provides a type of buffering against shortages, but it also enables assemblers to kit more effectively.

Don't just move the *muda*! Apply Lean techniques as you implement these strategies. Using third-party kitting? Work with the supplier to maximize effectiveness and eliminate waste through Lean.

Positioning stock strategically in the chain

When taken to its extreme, Lean has no stock, no inventory! But if there were a hiccup anywhere in the system, the entire supply chain would fall apart. You head off this doomsday scenario by positioning minimal stock strategically along the supply chain, according to risk scenarios.

In Lean, you prefer to hold stock toward the customer end of the chain — so that it's available immediately on demand. But keep in mind that this limits your flexibility because the stock tends to be committed to that customer. You can hold it earlier in the supply chain and increase flexibility, but it will have less added value.

Work with your suppliers to have a global strategy for your supply chain. Jointly plan contingencies for natural, economic, and accidental disruptions.

Chapter 15

Lean across Industries

. . . .

. . . .

*Y*ou will find Lean in every industry — from manufacturing to healthcare, pharmaceuticals, logistics, banking, retail, high-tech, construction, education and even government. Companies large and small, public and private, commercial and non-profits. It's clear now that enterprises in every industry are benefitting from applying Lean.

In this chapter, you discover more about Lean across industries, including, possibly, your own industry. You will also see that Lean is Lean — meaning that Lean is so fundamental that it's basically the same in any industry. You adjust the language to reflect the industry, but the same philosophy and principles apply; the same methods and techniques apply; all the same tools apply.

Starting with What's Common

Every business in every industry has issues — for-profit or nonprofit, public or private. In one form or another, all ventures have customers. They all have processes, whether formally documented or not. All employers have employees who generally want to do a good job, use their knowledge and skills, improve their quality of life, and feel good about what they do. Every endeavor has a place where it conducts its business — an office, a factory, a car, a computer, or even a table at Starbucks.

The commonalities are important because they help you to translate Lean from its manufacturing roots to "Wow, this all applies to me!" Follow this common framework to begin your path to Lean implementation, regardless of your industry:

✔ **Understand your customers.** What do they *really* want and need? What's their rate of demand? What constitutes satisfaction?

✔ **Characterize your most pressing issues.** What's going wrong? What are the priorities? Where are the mistakes and challenges coming from?

✔ **Map your value streams.** What are your work processes? Which are routine? How do material and transactions flow through them?

✔ **Calculate takt time.** What is the rate of customer demand? How frequently do they use your services or buy your product?

✔ **Clearly identify your goals and objectives.** Be specific; what are you trying to accomplish this year; in three years; in ten years?

✔ **Engage your people.** The people in your organization have great ideas for solving issues and satisfying customers. Leverage their wisdom. What are you already doing that engages them? What else can you do?

✔ **Identify wastes, and reduce them.** Look at your processes to find waste, contributing to *muda*, *mura*, and *muri*.

✔ **Implement *kaizen*.** Enable everyone to practice PDCA and participate in everyday improvement.

✔ **5S your work environment.** Clean up your act; then keep it clean and safe. (See Chapter 11.)

✔ **Apply the Lean toolbox.** Using a broad interpretation, pick the right tool for what you're trying to improve.

Lean Manufacturers

The manufacturing industry is Lean's heritage. The Toyota Production System (TPS) is the automotive manufacturing incubator where all the principles and practices of Lean were hatched and have matured over the past 50 years. If you're in manufacturing, it doesn't matter what your product is, how many you make, or how sophisticated your processes are (high tech, low tech, or even no tech): Lean is the world's most effective manufacturing operations strategy. Manufacturers may choose to implement Lean in response to any of the following strategies and challenges:

✔ Customer-driven initiatives

✔ Competitive pressures

✔ Quality issues and defect prevention

✔ Capital spending avoidance

✔ Inventory and cash-flow issues

Regardless of the reasons why a manufacturer begins a Lean journey, after committing to Lean, they see improvement on all these fronts.

From batch to flow

Traditional methods of production work with batches, usually large in size and organized by function. This method of production is wrought with the seven wastes. Lean is not traditional. Lean is based on flow — single-piece flow, ideally. To achieve single-piece flow, you must change how you do business and remove all obstacles to flow.

Creating work modules

Organize manufacturing according to product groups or families. Lay out work in modules so that material flows counterclockwise. Have all equipment and fixtures required to manufacture a part or family of parts inside each work cell. Keep equipment as small and flexible as possible. (See Chapter 11.)

Base the operating pace on takt time. In the best module designs, support personnel never need to enter the main production area to replenish material or repair equipment — this is performed from the backside of the equipment. This approach improves both safety and productivity, because no one but the trained production team is in the direct production area.

Quality at the source

No large inspection stations are at the end of a process; quality is everyone's job along the way. In each operation, people perform standardized work, including steps to verify their own work as well as the work of the previous operation. Error-proofing "gadgets" (*poke-yoke*) prevent operators from performing incorrectly and advancing poor quality to the next operation.

An error-proofing gadget, or *poka-yoke,* can come in many forms: a physical guide that helps material positioning; software that monitors key characteristics and stops equipment if specifications are violated; or high-tech solutions like infrared cameras — or whatever you can dream up! If it prevents errors, it's *poka-yoke.*

Working as teams

Lean operators work as a team, performing standardized work. The team is responsible for customer satisfaction and quality. They're responsible for production and routine maintenance of their equipment and tools. The team runs the show!

Changing from batch to flow affects not only the physical layout of a facility, but also the organizational support structure. Lean organizations tend to use fewer layers of management, fewer managers, and fewer support people. With the hands-on team responsible for some of the tasks traditionally associated with first-line supervision or maintenance department, the roles of the individuals in those areas change. Supervisors act as coaches, mentors, and roadblock removers. The ratio of supervisors to team members is established so that supervisors have sufficient time to truly mentor and build capability in the team. Maintenance workers focus on preventive maintenance, equipment improvements to support kaizen, and error-proofing mechanisms.

Reducing inventory

Flow manufacturing changes how you treat inventory because inventory is waste. It ties up cash and it's at risk for obsolescence. Every time inventory is touched, it can be damaged or destroyed. Inventory consumes energy and space and it stops the flow of production.

When you transition from traditional department-oriented manufacturing to cells, you no longer need the work-in-process (WIP) inventory that waited until it could be transported to the next step, sometimes located in another building. Equipment is close; pull systems reduce inventories required in a process. "Point of use" becomes the design philosophy for in-process material storage. What is the absolute minimum amount — based on takt usage — that can be stored where you use it?

Sometimes process constraints or risk mitigation prevent perfect module designs, and you need in-process inventory stores (type-1 *muda* — see Chapter 6). In this case, you install controlled inventory stores, or "supermarkets." Your goal is to always reduce inventory, but unless you can figure out a different way to remove the constraint or risk, implement a well-managed and controlled solution with planned, standardized, minimized in-process stores, located as close to the point of use as possible.

To handle inventory, you need material handling equipment. But instead of fork trucks to move large gondolas weighing tons or conveyor systems connecting buildings housing different functional areas, go smaller: Consider using bins, hand trucks, and push carts. This improves safety — no more speeding lift trucks ready to run you over or take out a building column! Costs go down — no building repairs and fewer high-tech pieces of equipment to maintain. And quality improves — less risk of transit damage.

Proclaiming that you'll reduce inventory isn't effective. You must use all the elements and practices of Lean, working together. If you cherry-pick one technique of Lean, such as inventory reduction, you're more likely to use it out of context — and make the situation worse.

Kanban, just-in-time, and the pull system

The Lean system of consumption-driven replenishment has long-proven itself in manufacturing, across tiers of supplier and distribution networks. It is now a compelling alternative to traditional push systems like material requirements planning (MRP) for a few reasons.

- ✔ **Push-style systems rely on forecasts to determine what and how much to replenish.** Forecasts can be useful indicators of general demand, but they're poor predictors of precisely which products will be needed and when. In multi-tiered supply chains, push-systems distance manufacturers farther from their customers and push forecasts farther from reality. Information is diluted in each layer of the system. As a result, excessive inventory builds and costly last-minute change orders create ripples and bullwhips through the supply chain.

- ✔ **Push systems cause manufacturers to incur large inventory-carrying costs.** Over-buying creates excess inventory, which must be carried and managed. And push systems still run out of parts! Stock-outs, of course, wreak havoc in production systems, delaying customer shipments, increasing premium freight charges, and disrupting plant operations by forcing unnecessary and expensive changeovers. Errors in MRP also cause people to work outside the system to expedite materials and to conduct repeated physical inventories. It becomes a vicious cycle.

Lean pull-type systems are not like forecast-driven replenishment systems. Pull-based manufacturing synchronizes production with consumption in real time, increasing on-time delivery performance, and reducing stock-outs and costly last-minute changes. A *kanban* system (see Chapter 11) reorders parts and components based on actual consumption at the point of use. As orders arrive, material is pulled from the end of final assembly, which instantly sends an order to the final assembly production module to produce more.

- ✔ **The "two-bin" method:** An operator has two bins of material: One is being consumed and the other is full. When the first bin empties, the operator keeps working, using the second bin. The empty bin, which acts as a *kanban* or signal, is sent out for replenishment. A full one returns before the operator runs out.

✔ **The kanban-card method:** A *kanban* card travels with the inventory, containing information such as the description of the item or part number, and its location. When inventory is consumed the card triggers replenishment.

Volume and variety

Lean applies in manufacturing whether you make one a month, a hundred a day, or thousands every hour. A custom cabinet facility may look different from a commercial wood bookcase manufacturer, but both use wood, cut to a specific dimension, sand, and finish — and they both do it over and over again. The starting place for implementation is the same: Understand the customer, map the flow, 5S, identify value, and standardize work. Beyond the basics, the manufacturers may choose a different tool to apply first, but it all applies.

High volume, low customization

Numerous books and case studies describe high-volume Lean production; after all, it's where Lean started. When you make the same thing, the same way, every day, you have a great foundation for implementing any of the Lean techniques, like standardized work, work modules, error-proofing or pull systems. Lean is perfect for high-volume, consistent environments.

Low volume, high customization

In contrast to the high-volume production environments of a Toyota, Motorola, or Dell are thousands of companies who specialize in low-volume, highly customized manufacturing. Whether your company is a machine shop, sign maker, cabinetmaker, or salad maker, the concepts of Lean apply to your business. It's not a question of how few you make, or the differences from one item of design or production to the next. The details may include different ingredients or different dimensions, but you're still performing similar processing steps each time.

Look for elements of commonality and repetition in what you do — there are more than you may think. Standardize all that is common, and compartmentalize what is unique. If you focus only on how different you are, and how new everything is, you'll make it difficult to see how standardized work can help your situation. The more you can define standardized work, the more benefits you can begin to accrue from Lean practices.

Applying Lean to the office is also important, because your customer interacts mostly with sales, service and accounting. Your product may be unique, but your office functions are the same, regardless of what your customer orders. How will you eliminate waste from business processes?

The getting-started tools are the same, regardless of what you do. After you have the basics, examine your processes with an eye toward eliminating waste. A Formula-1 pit crew changes tires very differently from your local service station, but they're both doing the same job. The Formula-1 crew eliminated waste from the real-time process and creatively developed different techniques. Wouldn't you, the consumer, like to have your tires changed that fast?

When you're producing in a high-mix, low-volume environment, Lean can actually be *more* valuable. Customers get their orders faster and margins are improved. Think about this: If a low-volume producer builds a bad product, they don't have the volume over which to amortize mistakes. So if you're building one satellite that doesn't work or you're a gourmet food provider that has to throw out spoiled ingredients, your margins are reduced. Lean can help you.

Lean in Services

Nearly 80 percent of the U.S. economy and increasing percentages of the global economy are now services, rather than manufacturing. Lean provides some of the greatest opportunities and most powerful results in service businesses. Although service organizations have different processes, different key metrics, and different root causes of problems and challenges, Lean methods are just as effective.

Lean practices improve service business performance, by

- Reducing the time spent performing business activities
- Reducing the total cost of doing business by eliminating wasted time and effort
- Increasing customer satisfaction by improving the timeliness and quality of deliverables
- Improving employee morale and increasing enthusiasm by engaging staff in the development and implementation of improvements

By applying concepts that until recently had been alien to most service businesses — attacking speed and quality, simplifying complexity, scaling differentiation, and empowering employees — service organizations can share in some of the productivity gains already enjoyed by the makers of autos, planes, trains, appliances, and other products. Savings will vary significantly by company and industry, but it is realistic to expect reductions of 25 percent in costs and 50 percent or more in response times and in-process errors by implementing Lean practices in service businesses. In addition, revenue gains of 5 percent annually are not uncommon.

Commercial services vs. internal services

Commercial services are those businesses that offer their services to other businesses and the general public. The services they offer represent their core competence and form the basis for their profit and loss (P&L). By contrast, internal service providers are company overhead departments and functions that provide support to other profit-generating departments. (We address the internal group in Chapter 14.)

Examples of commercial service businesses include everything from airlines, communications (voice, cellular, data) companies, cable and satellite TV providers, computer services, and mail and shipping services, finance and mortgage companies, education and training services, repair and maintenance services, and much more. Some of these services are labor and equipment based, while others are transaction based. In addition, most government agencies are in the service business, but they're a special case and we address them later in this chapter, in the "Lean Government" section.

In all service businesses, Lean is an attitude and approach anyone can understand, and it's a set of practices and tools everyone can apply. The Lean techniques don't require extensive employee training or complex technical support. In a service context, going Lean means getting back to the reason why everyone got into the service business in the first place: to serve people!

Embedding Lean practices within a service organization is not a quick fix or rapid overhaul. It requires the same diligent and holistic approach to transformation as in manufacturing or any other industry. Lean in services means:

- Improving service processes to focus on the customer and deliver more customer value
- Empowering your people to deliver outstanding customer service
- Decreasing waste in the service value stream
- Reducing batch processes and moving increasingly toward a flow of activities to deliver the service
- Striving for the perfect service

Because service businesses are often even more labor intensive and dependent than manufacturing businesses, the respect for people in the service value chain is of utmost importance.

A service is a product!

Services are like products in many ways. Services begin with a customer need or want, and they end when it's delivered to them in a satisfactory manner — at the right time, in the right way, and at the right price. The service is the result of a process or series of processes acting in a coordinated fashion to produce the desired results. There's a value stream of activities and support information. The service is a result of design, development, and delivery. And the service is prone to defects and rework — just like products.

You must think of a service as a product, because

✔ Services are architected and designed to meet customer requirements and to fit the "manufacturability" of a production and delivery system.

✔ Services have specifications — for quality, performance, timeliness, and price.

✔ Services have a value chain comprised of components on both the supply side and delivery end.

The seven forms of service waste

Service process waste is waste, just like product or material process waste is waste. Service-business waste may look a little different, but it happens the same way:

✔ **Transportation:** Transportation waste in a service environment is the unnecessary and non-value-added movement of people, goods, and information in order to fulfill the service obligation to a customer.

✔ **Waiting:** If people, systems, materials, or information are waiting, that's waste.

✔ **Overproduction:** Are your services producing sooner, faster, or in greater quantities than the customer is demanding or requiring?

✔ **Defects:** Defective services are those that do not deliver the correct requirements to the customer, the first time.

✔ **Inventory:** Do you have service products no one wants? Do you have an excess to capacity to deliver services?

✔ **Movement:** Are activities, paperwork, and other efforts unnecessarily juggled?

✔ **Extra processing:** How much extra paperwork or effort do people go to in order to deliver the service? Could any of these steps be eliminated?

Improving services the Lean way

Services naturally benefit from one of Lean's fundamental tools: the pull system. In most cases, the delivery of a service to a customer is based on the action of the customer requesting the service, which stimulates the value chain to assemble and deliver it. The key to Lean service is in common services — the building blocks that permit flexible assembly in real time as the customer requests it. All other Lean fundamentals also apply.

5S in services

The 5S of the workplace applies to service businesses:

- ✔ **Sort:** Workplace organization is universal. Sorting office materials, maintenance materials, or other tools is fundamental to the delivery of quality and timely services.

  These days, many service businesses are computer-based or computer-facilitated. Sorting your computer environment — your e-mails, your files — is a Lean activity. Keep your computer desktop and file system Lean and clean.

- ✔ **Straighten:** The tools of services should be arranged in standard locations for consistent and easy access. This includes desk items, databases, repositories, references, operating procedures, or process definitions. Information, including file and system names, should be consistent.

- ✔ **Scrub:** Maintain service tools in a neat and clean condition. This includes any work areas, whether in the office or in the field.

- ✔ **Systematize:** As always, don't wait for things to build up. As part of your regular routine, go through your work environment and maintain it. Define a certain time or regular event as the basis. This includes both private and common areas.

- ✔ **Standardize:** Exercise discipline in maintaining your workplace, and institute processes that ensure that this regular maintenance occurs, in a standard manner to standardized levels. Don't overdo it — just do it.

Speed and quality

As a Lean service organization, always be moving to deliver customer value ever more quickly with consistent quality. By consistently increasing the speed of operations, service businesses are more flexible and can respond with greater agility to changing customer demands and market conditions. Faster services are delivered by fewer hands, and by streamlining and eliminating unnecessary steps. In processing more quickly, the organization reduces opportunity costs. And, of course, the customers are more satisfied to receive services faster. Ensure that the customer has the same quality experience regardless of where they receive your services or from whom.

Focus equally on quality. Lean service businesses significantly reduce the time spent on reworking deliverables. Be sure to establish specification limits and collect metrics on quality, applying tools to reduce variance, prevent failures, and attack root cause.

Checking variety and reducing complexity

Service complexity arises from providing a well-meaning effort to become an intimate, highly-tailored or engineered service. But any increase in complexity directly increases the risk of both slower and defective services, and indirectly increases support and maintenance costs — in the form of overtaxed back-office processing procedures, too many customer-service systems, and too much staff training.

Analyze service processes for variety and complexity. Sort the routine, commodity services from the specialized services and treat them differently. Standardize the routine services, and manage the lower-volume, higher-complexity services as specialty items. Where necessary, assemble these services in a value chain.

Frontline power

To enable services to deliver on the promise of both quality and speed, shift decision-making closer to the customer. The segmentation and production of highly structured service components enable frontline staff to engage customers more independently — with less management oversight.

Lean service operations enable people to make more of their own customer-facing decisions. Frontline employees are empowered to operate, instead of having to seek approval for decisions. This setup also frees them from focusing solely on basic transactions and allows them to give more, personal attention to customers, which ultimately increases revenue.

Nothing better exemplifies frontline empowerment than the Ritz-Carlton Hotel Company chain, where every member of the staff has a discretionary budget for settling disputes. Each staff member has the personal authority to provide such perks as room upgrades, complementary food, and other amenities on a case-by-case basis. When a guest has an issue, staff is both enabled and required to break away from regular duties and immediately address the customer concern.

Transactional Lean

Transaction businesses are a specific form of service businesses, where the product is purely data and information, and it's processed according to specific procedures. Examples include reservations and online order businesses, select banking businesses, payroll processing, and insurance claims. Success in transaction processing businesses is based on speed and accuracy. How can Lean help?

Once again, the fundamentals of Lean apply: focusing on the customer, improving the value stream, focusing on flow, striving for perfection, and maintaining a high respect for people. Transaction businesses are typically professional office environments, with a highly educated workforce, using computers and data processing capabilities to perform the tasks. Lean transaction businesses do the following:

✔ **Explicitly map the value stream to understand precisely what is required to complete the process task for the customer.** Use this map as the basis for continually eliminating wasteful practices.

✔ **Understand that information transactions are products.** Design, develop, source, assemble, and deliver transactions.

✔ **Regularly employ kaizen to examine and optimize your transaction processing processes.** Keep the changes small, local, continuous, and practical. Ensure that management responds and implements changes quickly, and rewards the employees quickly.

Lean in Healthcare

The healthcare field is one of the most exciting frontiers of Lean. In an environment where patient care needs are climbing, and the availability of skilled resources and reimbursement for services are shrinking, Lean is helping. Lean Healthcare focuses on the needs of the patient (the customer) and strives to improve turnaround time, contain costs, reduce space, increase speed of delivery, and eliminate mistakes — in short, improve the quality of care. Although no definitive data exists on the global impact of errors and preventable diseases, consider these two statements from the World Health Organization (WHO), "Errors in medical care affect up to 10 percent of patients worldwide," and "At any one time, some 1.4 million people worldwide suffer from hospital-acquired infections."

Improving healthcare through Lean

Lean healthcare is not about eliminating people or eliminating assets. Lean healthcare is improving activities and processes within the system. This is accomplished by identifying and removing wasteful activities and focusing on patient value-based activities. Health industries applying Lean principles across their organization are experiencing increases in benefits and performance:

- ✔ Reduced incidents of mistakes
- ✔ Improved patient education
- ✔ Reduced wait times for patients
- ✔ Improved clinical outcomes
- ✔ Increased staff productivity
- ✔ Reduced clinic and management costs
- ✔ Improved employee satisfaction for nurses and staff

Defining waste in healthcare

Open any paper in just about any country and you'll find an article about healthcare. Public or private, they all have issues. If you've ever encountered a healthcare establishment, you know some of these issues firsthand. Consider some of the ways that the classic seven forms of waste translate into a healthcare environment:

- ✔ **Transportation:** Patients are moved excessively for testing and treatment. Samples and specimens needing analysis travel excessively to reach the labs and within the labs.
- ✔ **Waiting:** Patients wait for diagnosis, treatment, discharge, beds, or testing. Physicians wait for patient lab results. Teams wait for specialists.
- ✔ **Overproduction:** Excess testing is performed for the convenience (and liability protection) of the organization, not to meet customer demand.
- ✔ **Inventories:** Equipment, materials, medicines, testing regimes, beds, appointment times, lab samples and specimens for analysis, lab results awaiting distribution, dictation ready for transcription . . . the system is replete with inventory!
- ✔ **Movement:** Unnecessary and excess movement of equipment, materials, charts, and medicines is common in healthcare. Doctors and staff have excess motion while performing procedures. Even patients themselves are moved unnecessarily!

✔ **Defects:** Mistakes are widespread: wrong patient, wrong procedure or medicine, misdiagnosis, unsuccessful treatments, re-sticks, redraws.

✔ **Excess processing:** Staff makes multiple bed moves, retests, data entry, excessive paperwork, and so on.

In healthcare when evaluating the value stream, you look at seven specific areas of flow: patient flow, family flow, provider flow, medicine flow, equipment flow, and information flow.

According to WHO, "there are 234 million operations performed globally each year. At least half a million deaths per year would be preventable with effective implementation of the WHO Surgical Safety Checklist worldwide. This Surgical Safety Checklist has gone from a good idea recognized in a 2008 pilot study to a global standard of care, which already has saved many thousands of lives." In addition to the Checklist improving outcomes, it also improves communication among the surgical team, and ultimately the quality of care.

Lean in Government

Of all industrial sectors outside of manufacturing, Lean practices are taking hold in government as strongly as any other. At first, this might seem a paradox. After all, most governmental entities seem to be the opposite of Lean! Like any institution, governmental agencies face constant budget restrictions. At the same time, they're being asked to fulfill greater needs on the part of their constituents. Sounds a lot like doing more with less, doesn't it?

The choices are limited. Delivering less isn't received well by voters. And it's not a matter of simply working harder. The challenges are not solved by any singular approach like defect reduction, constraint management, or measurement and reporting, although those are all useful tools that have a role. And any viable solutions must be a workable cultural fit into the nature of the government environment.

Lean is ideal for implementation in the public sector, especially when you consider that governments at all levels need to plan for the long term, whether planning services, infrastructure or defense. With many factions competing for the same limited resources, Lean enables governments to deliver more effectively to more people. *Kaizen* has been used globally to standardize processes, create regular policy reviews, improve natural resource utilization, repair military vehicles damaged by war, just to name a few examples.

In the public sector, Lean practices help organizations:

✔ Shorten cycle times to completing and delivering services

✔ Improve service quality

✔ Increase productivity and resource utilization

✔ Dramatically increase customer (constituency) satisfaction

✔ Reduce waste in all forms, including bureaucracy

The largest barrier to implementing Lean in government exists only in terms of providing the appropriate skills, capabilities, and experiences to those responsible for carrying out the processes.

Lean in Retail

The retail environment is where the value stream meets that last customer — the consumer. Retailers experience customer needs and wants firsthand: exactly what the customer wants, where they want it, when they want it, and in the desired quantity and quality. In today's world, consumers have become more demanding than ever: innovation has set high expectations, access is global, brands and SKU's have proliferated.

It's been difficult for retailers to keep up with delivering value from the standpoint of the consumer. Retailers are challenged with layouts and store flow, product categorization, packaging, backroom storage, backroom push, corporate marketing initiatives, leftover seasonal stock, and of course pricing. Consumers experience product proliferation, duplication, and complexity, confusing promotions, ineffective signage, clutter and hard-to-find merchandise, poor service, and long checkout lines. No wonder consumers feel stress, procrastinate about making purchases, and shop less often or on-line!

Lean practices improve customer service, by decreasing wait times and ensuring that the right products are on the right shelves at the right time. Point-of-sale data directly stimulate supply and delivery based on real-time purchases. Lean helps them with flow to the store shelves and in minimizing inventory levels.

The next time you go to a retail store, look for evidence of Lean practices, and you'll be likely to find it. Figure 15-1 shows an example of visual standard work instruction for something as simple as cleaning the restroom. See what other Lean techniques you notice, from customer service to products on the shelves.

Diagram of area to be cleaned
with Process Step

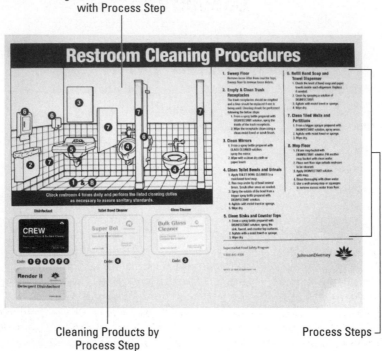

Figure 15-1:
A visual
aid for
standard-
ized work
instructions
in a retail
environment.

Cleaning Products by
Process Step

Process Steps

Graphic provided by Diversity, Inc., now part of Sealed Air

Lean Everywhere

The future of Lean across all industries is limitless. The principles, methods, tools, and techniques apply in any situation. Looking at a business, organization, or industry through Lean eyes will open up new pathways for improvement opportunities. In the following Chapter 16 are several case studies.

Chapter 16

Real-Life Lean

*I*n this chapter you learn about real-life examples of Lean in practice. You see Lean across several organizations in three industries — healthcare, manufacturing, and financial services. These stories include increasing laboratory throughput, maximizing consumer appointment capacity, operating room changeover, a high-tech assembly area's first *kaizen* after a merger and on-boarding employees. In each case, a variety of Lean practices resulted in dramatic improvements in performance and customer satisfaction. Lean can be applied in many ways to any type of process in any industry — use these case studies as inspiration to improving all areas of your organization.

As you read these, you may have to adjust how you think about applying Lean concepts to your own processes. In this chapter, you see that "inventory" can be defined as available appointment times, and single minute exchange of die (SMED), a quick changeover technique (see Chapter 11), applies to the changeover of operating rooms. Both are direct applications of Lean techniques.

Improving Healthcare

This section looks at three distinct applications of Lean in healthcare settings. The first, from Master Black Belt Erica Gibbons, focuses on workflow improvements in a hospital laboratory. The second, from Linda LaGanga, shows how one organization, the Mental Health Center of Denver (MHCD), improved their performance rate for consumer intake processes. Finally, the Healthcare Performance Partners show the use of SMED to improve the safe changeover time of operating rooms at a medical center.

Laboratory queuing and workflow

The laboratory in a Midwest hospital needed help keeping up with their growing blood work demand. Blood work requests arrived from all over the 260-bed short-term acute-care hospital areas, especially during two periods: between 5:30 AM to 8:00 AM, and from 2:30 PM to 4:00 PM, Monday through Friday. Hospital leaders prescribed Lean to assist business leaders in eliminating issues in the facility. The laboratory had yet to participate in a Lean activity. Initially, both the laboratory leaders and staff doubted Lean would help their situation.

Initial conditions

The laboratory staff worked three 8-hour shifts with 30-minute lunches and two 15-minute breaks. No swing shifts were available. Several day-shift staff members had quit in the prior few months due to high-pressure and time-sensitive working conditions.

To process blood specimens, the staff received specimens through two sample elevators in various-sized packages. They'd separate urgent and routine requests and immediately spin specimens in one of their four centrifuge machines. After spinning the tubes, the staff distributed specimens to the appropriate machines for loading and processing. Once the lab work was completed, the staff recorded the results and phoned nursing personnel with any abnormal results. They were required to complete urgent requests within 30 minutes from the recorded lab draw time on the tube and routine requests within 120 minutes.

Urgent requests started increasing at a faster pace than hourly lab volumes could handle. Spoilage rates averaged 7% per hour with higher rates during their peak hours of 5:30 to 8:00 AM and 2:30 PM to 4:00 PM. During these peak periods, results often took considerably longer than the standard specified timeframes to process, resulting in irate calls and visits from hospital staff and managers.

In response, the lab brought in new equipment, which caused space constraints. Managers also placed an entry computer between sample elevators and beside each processing unit. Typically, managers assigned one processor per unit and had one to two receivers per shift. Figure 16-1 shows the layout of the lab.

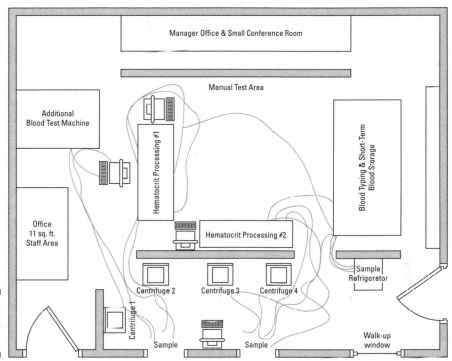

Figure 16-1:
Initial lab
layout.

Lab kaizen

To begin the *kaizen* improvement effort, Lean practitioners, in conjunction with the lab personnel, characterized the current state by collecting data on the lab specimen types and arrivals per hour for the prior three months. The hematocrit and other blood samples represented 78 percent of lab specimen volumes. Figure 16-2 shows the data.

Figure 16-2:
Initial lab
specimen
volume and
staffing
by hour.

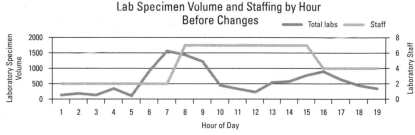

Each blood sample was separated in one of four available centrifuges. A centrifuge could separate up to 24 samples in a 7 minute timeframe. With a 24 sample load, it took an additional 3 minutes to load and 2 minutes to unload. The total time to centrifuge 24 samples was, therefore, the 3 minute load-time, plus 7 minutes centrifuge, and 2 minutes to unload, for a total of 12 minutes — or 0.5 minutes/sample.

The hematocrit machines then processed the 24 centrifuged samples in a rack that took 6 minutes with 1 minute to load. Additional blood tests were performed in a larger blood test machine, which processed up to 48 centrifuged samples per rack in 9 minutes, on average, with a 2 minute load-time.

Both machines automatically uploaded their results into hospital information systems. Urgent requests acted as interrupters in the system. The staff processed urgent requests immediately, no matter the order received. Although both machines required daily maintenance, practitioners ignored downtime in the analysis.

> Hematocrit processing = 24 samples/7 min. → 0.29 min./sample
>
> Additional blood processing = 48 samples/11 min. → 0.23 min./sample
>
> Distributing samples = 0.1 min./sample (may be done in groups)

The team used Little's Law, which is the fundamental mathematical principle for queuing theory applied to a steady-state process, to analyze the sample arrival process. For a given arrival rate, the time in the system is proportional to packet occupancy.

N = λ * T, where:

> N: Average number of packets (specimens) in the system
>
> λ: packet arrival rate per unit of time
>
> T: average time in system per packet (including distribution, waiting and processing time)

The packets' time in the system is determined by subtracting lab result time (departure time) from lab receipt time (arrival time). Generally, staff processed lab requests in a first-in first-out (FIFO) order. They required additional time to notify nursing and shift handoffs.

The team used the hourly takt time for specimens to determine the required staffing, especially during peak hours.

After they collected the initial data, the Lean practitioners formalized the project improvement team, which included a blend of lab workers and Lean. As the lab personnel became more involved in the project, they began to see how Lean could help their situation.

Involve staff as early as possible in your projects. When they help to identify and solve their workflow issues, they begin to own the project and in the long term will sustain the results. You will save time and improve buy-in with early involvement.

The improved lab

The team worked together to identify improvements to lab processes that would result in more effective sample processing and better customer service. The next future state included several highly effective process improvements:

- ✔ **Lean the laboratory layout:** By adding one centrifuge and moving all of the centrifuges in line with hematocrit and alternative blood machines, the specimens flowed through lab in a more linear fashion, reducing distribution time by 0.1 minutes/sample. Figure 16-3 shows the post improvement layout.

- ✔ **Flexing staff hours:** Two day-shift technicians modified their hours to accommodate high morning volumes. This shifted capacity enabled the lab to meet the workload demands with no increase to the head count. As an added bonus, the new schedule allowed these two technicians to be with their school-aged children after school.

- ✔ **Error-proofing labels:** Errors due to misaligned labels were the primary reason that they required an additional blood test machine. To reduce errors and associated rework, the laboratory staff worked with test tube vendors to include a guideline for hospital personnel to better position the label on the tubes.

- ✔ **Educating the customers – redefining *urgent*:** Like the boy who cried wolf, lab customers realized their lab work moved to the front of the line when they labeled it urgent, so everything became *urgent*. To overcome the everything-is-urgent syndrome, lab technicians met with the laboratory users around the hospital, who sent the most "urgent" requests. They listened to them to understand what drove "urgent" sample needs. With this understanding, the technicians created a standard definition for "urgent" and began to educate hospital staff about urgent requests using face-to-face meetings; they also create a communication campaign to spread the word about the new definition of *urgent*. The team effort made the difference. By improving overall sample turnaround and standardizing the *urgent* definition, fewer urgent requests came into the lab.

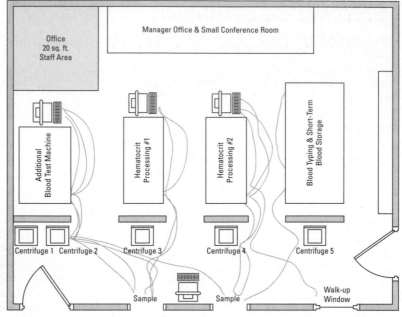

Figure 16-3:
Improved
lab speci-
men volume
and staffing
by hour.

Results: We love it!

The new layout and staffing changes dampened the peak hour effect. Peak routine samples were completed within 45 minutes. Staff completed urgent requests on average within 25 minutes. Inappropriate urgent requests decreased by 80 percent as turnaround times improved. Figure 16-4 shows the lab specimen volume changes after the improvements.

Figure 16-4:
Improved
lab speci-
men volume
and staffing
by hour.

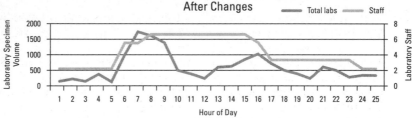

Laboratory technicians liked the new, less-stressful staffing. With faster test turnarounds, technicians worked on testing rather than fielding complaint calls from hospital staff. Most importantly, the empowered technicians were proud of their accomplishments, every step of the way, and owned their results.

Getting new consumers to show-up to scheduled appointments

The Mental Health Center of Denver (MHCD) is a private, nonprofit organization and the community mental health provider for the city and county of Denver (http://www.mhcd.org). MHCD believes that people can — and do — recover from mental illness; that treatment works to improve the lives of people of all ages; that MHCD's work and mission are vital to the community; and that the quality and effectiveness of MHCD programs save the community money. It is important to them that people have services available to them, and that people show-up when scheduled to receive services. MHCD refers to people who use services as *consumers*.

Getting started

MHCD had a persistent problem of high no-show rates for initial intake appointments. With the support of the chief executive officer (CEO) and other executive-level staff, they decided to use Lean to tackle it. The first Rapid Improvement Capacity Expansion (RICE) project (*kaizen* project) aimed to increase the number of consumers admitted. The project focused on the elimination of waste caused by appointment no-shows and the increased utilization of intake resources.

Top management support and careful team selection are essential to the long-term success of the Lean team. Management support helps to guarantee project participation and resources over time. The right people on the team — those who value operational improvement and are impacted by the issue — can help to build support throughout the organization, especially when Lean efforts are just beginning.

Select initial Lean projects that people care about and that address a significant operational problem, preferably ones closely tied to the organization's mission and values. Success with these types of projects builds momentum and acceptance of Lean in the organization.

MHCD selected the initial Lean team members based on the Lean Respect for People principle, as well as their roles in the organization and their contributions with designing and operating effective, customer-centered processes. The team consisted of clinicians, administrative staff, managers, quality systems staff, and consumers, who had experienced the access process. They met over a period of four days to study and analyze all of the individual processes and activities that made up the scheduling of consumers for their initial intake appointment at the various adult and child sites within the organization.

The team used several Lean tools, such as value-stream mapping, fishbone diagramming, identification of current and target state conditions, and gap analysis (see Parts III and IV). Through their analysis, the team identified several processes to improve. Improvements to these processes would result in more consumers scheduled into appointments and improved consumer show-up performance. It is vital that the consumers actually show up to the initial appointment because it is the only way that they will be admitted to receive services.

The team decided to define *inventory* as "available appointment slots." They viewed the process of scheduling consumers who call for appointments as an inventory consumption and distribution system.

Clinicians performed new consumer intakes. These clinicians were on separate teams located away from the access center. The clinical intake teams gave the access center lists of times and days for appointment slots with clinicians. The access center then filled these slots with consumers, who called to request admission. When all of the allocated slots had been filled, the consumers, who called for appointments, were turned away and told to call back in a later week. Figure 16-5 shows the high-level value-stream for the consumer access and intake-to-services process.

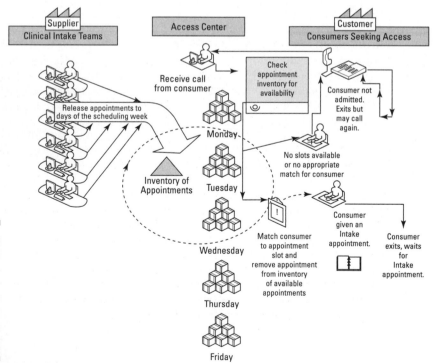

Figure 16-5: High-level value-stream for consumer access and intake process.

Understanding the issue and generating improvements

The consumer participants on the RICE team provided insight into the factors that influenced their decision to attend an intake appointment after they had missed the first several appointments that were scheduled — in other words, the team heard the voice of the customer (VOC). This sparked ideas from the clinicians on what they could do to welcome new consumers, alleviate their anxiety, ensure that they had reliable transportation to the appointments, and knew how to get to the clinic.

The VOC provides crucial insights that drive effective process improvement. In this case, including consumers on the team helped the staff to understand how their actions affected consumer behavior and to generate new ideas for process improvement.

The team characterized the current state by measuring and analyzing information on appointments and no-show rates by day of week. Figure 16-6 shows the measurements before and after the Lean improvement project. The team utilized clinicians' experience and the data to identify additional improvement opportunities. For example, they determined that Tuesdays were good days for intakes because no-show rates were relatively low and reminder calls could be made a day in advance, unlike Mondays. The team also noticed that Thursdays had relatively low no-show rates, but few appointments scheduled.

Turning "no-shows" into admissions

These insights led the team to redesign appointment schedules to add more Thursday appointments. This change increased the calling consumers' chances of obtaining an appointment the same week without having to wait until the next week when clinical intake teams released new schedules. The newly developed process engaged consumers to understand the importance of their appointments and the need to cancel ahead of time, if they could not attend. This provided an opportunity to recycle appointment slots so that consumers, who called later in the week, could use them.

They combined separate steps in the workflow (such as an orientation appointment and the actual intake assessment), which originally occurred on separate days, into a single step to eliminate the possibility of a no-show after orientation. Moderate overbooking was also used for group orientations to mitigate lost capacity from no-shows. If more consumers showed up than expected, flexible capacity was put in place by calling upon program managers and interns to conduct the individual intake assessment following the orientation. By having the right participants on the Lean team, the new practices were implemented quickly and effectively.

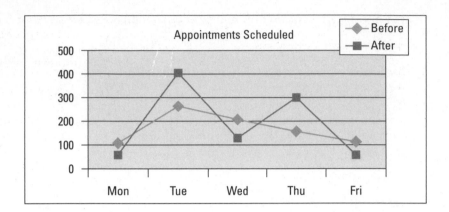

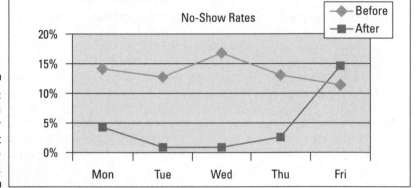

Figure 16-6:
Data before
and after for
appointment
and no-
shows.

Results

In just the first month of operation, the number of scheduled intake appointments increased by 22 percent over the same month in the prior year. The increase in scheduled appointments, combined with an immediate 5.67 percent decrease in no-show rate, resulted in a 30.26 percent increase in the number of completed intake appointments.

A one-year follow-up analysis of the results showed that this initial Lean project resulted in a sustained increased intake service capacity of 27 percent, decreased no-shows 12 percent, and gave 187 additional people access to services, all without increasing staff or other expenses.

MCHD recognized how important measurement and validation are to the improvement process. An analysis of the process after one-month confirmed that the system was working and provided feedback and motivation for the organization to continue its Lean initiative. The ultimate test of success was the large analysis that compared a full year of data one year after the implementation to a full year of data from the year before the improvements.

By focusing on what adds value for customers and eliminating waste, the Lean process at MHCD resulted in expanded access to services for consumers, who need them, and a more cost-effective use of resources. The program fostered innovative approaches and a commitment to improving quality throughout the organization, in both clinical and business areas. Through sustained leadership and organizational commitment and demonstrated results, Lean at MHCD thrives. Employees love the process, and consumers appreciate the results!

SMED operating room turnaround

Smooth transitions and hand-offs of operating rooms (OR) between procedures are critical to overall hospital performance. Healthcare Performance Partners (HPP) used Lean practices when working with a 260-bed for-profit medical center in Georgia, to maximize OR turnaround time performance. Efficient and safe turnarounds are important because they govern whether the next case will begin on time, with all necessary conditions and tools at the ready. Like a Formula 1 pit stop, a smooth OR transition means taking only the time required with well-choreographed team using standardized work (see Chapter 11) to make sure nothing is overlooked. The OR *kaizen* developed and implemented improved procedures for general surgery room turnarounds at this facility.

The current condition

The OR team was meeting the 20-minute corporate goal for turnaround time only 66 percent of the time. The *kaizen* team observed that, if everything went perfectly, the nurse alone had nearly 20 minutes of work to do. The number of team members involved in the turnover, including technicians and orderlies, varied between cases, as did the number and types of tasks. Looking at the process with new eyes, the team wondered:

- ✔ Which tasks truly had to be done during the critical turnaround time?

- ✔ Which could be performed before or after, or as part of other work?

- ✔ What efficiencies could be gained for the remaining tasks performed during turnaround?

Internal versus external tasks

When you think of turnaround time like a pit stop, it is easier to see that only the most critical tasks should be performed during the *internal* or live time — the time when the cars pull into the pits. For example, the pit crew only tightens the lug nuts during the pit stop. Other tasks, like filling the tires, are done during *external* time — the time before or after the turnaround.

In one example of the *OR pit stop*, the team saw that the OR technician would use critical internal time to go to another area of the hospital to pick up instruments for the next case. The team found a way to free up the technician's time during the prior case to gather the instruments needed for the next case — in other words, they moved the activity to the noncritical path. Pushing this task into external time made the technician more available during the critical turnaround minutes.

In another instance, the nurse often used turnaround time to deliver a specimen to the laboratory. The *kaizen* team found a way to create a drop-off area for specimens, freeing that nurse's time to focus on the turnaround.

Mastering the quick-change

The team continued to evaluate all of the OR changeover activities and find more ways to move activities to external time. The *kaizen* team also looked at ways to reduce wasted steps, confusion, and extra motion during the critical turnaround period.

For example, the team watched the nurse transport the patient to the post-anesthesia care unit (PACU), then return to the OR where the computer was located, complete the charting there, and then go to the pre-op holding area to retrieve the next patient. To reduce wasted time and effort, they located a computer right in the PACU, where the nurse could complete charting closer to the patient and eliminate an extra trip back to the OR. This change saved a crucial 2 minutes (10 percent) of key RN time during turnaround, and made their job easier.

The team also found variation in the number of people working during a turnaround — between three and eight staff members. They created a way to level and standardize the workload, making the number of people involved more predictable and sensible.

Above all, the OR must be clean. The cleaning solution they'd been using required 10 minutes for soaking surfaces. The team decided that this amount of wait time was too long and looked for another cleaning solution that would meet the cleanliness standards in less time. After they found a product that required only 1 minute of soak time to achieve the same level of cleanliness, the switch was on. Finally they updated the standardize work instructions for OR turnaround to reflect the new cleaner requirements.

The results

The hospital staff made several successful trial runs using their new procedures. Figure 16-7 shows the before and after data for the process. These results indicate:

- ✔ A reduction of 8 minutes (40 percent) in turnaround time, translating to 160 hours of OR time annually
- ✔ Improved quality of the turnaround
- ✔ Improved staff and physician satisfaction

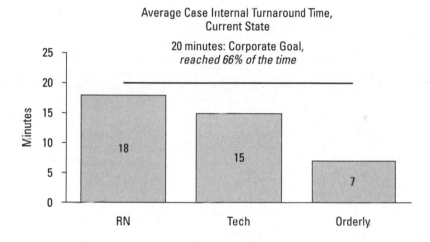

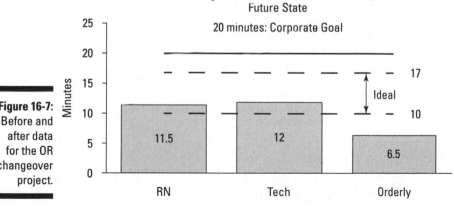

Figure 16-7: Before and after data for the OR changeover project.

First Kaizen Experience with a Post-Merger Team

Todd McCann, a *kaizen* leader and *sensei,* worked with a large-scale legacy telecommunications manufacturer that had diverse product offerings and a large plant. The company had just been sold to a new owner. Todd's team supported this new organization by conducting *kaizen* activities throughout manufacturing and assembly operations.

The first area targeted for improvement was the final assembly for 24/36-port routers. The team evaluated several process areas for improvement: external customer relationships, order entry, internally manufactured materials, purchased materials and procurement planning/logistics, internal manufacturing and assembly production planning, and the router final assembly work area.

Todd and his team also focused on the people and culture of the organization by respectfully instructing, challenging, coaching and mentoring plant personnel; building teams; and growing and nurturing the *kaizen* spirit in the hearts and minds of the workforce to create breakthrough thinking attitudes and behaviors. As a *sensei*, he knew that these activities would result in greater value for the customer, team members with greater skill and capability, and profit for the business.

Conducting *kaizen* activities early in a merger transition is critical to a successful transition and incorporation of a new team into an existing Lean organization. Through these activities, you can create faster cultural alignment among the organizations, rapid operational improvement, and smooth out the overall transition.

Initial conditions — before kaizen

The physical space for the router assembly challenge involved a three million square foot plant consisting of three interconnected buildings. One building contained wire manufacturing. Another building had component part manufacturing, final assembly, and material receiving. The final building housed finished goods storage and shipping.

Leadership approach

The new owners knew the existing work practices were not going to get the results they needed. They knew they had to change but weren't sure how. A

Lean approach, including *kaizen* activities, provided the way to achieve radical change and improved results.

Using hands-on instruction and learning-by-doing based in Lean, the workforce received new knowledge about how to approach and perform their job; they also learned how to identify and solve problems which were hidden in the current work practices. They learned new ways of thinking, which guided them in how they would continuously apply this new foundational knowledge. The use of Lean principles, practices, tools, techniques — in combination with new leadership behaviors and activities — enabled the team to achieve the results the new owners desired: increased value for the customer and improved profits for the business.

Perform instruction and training in short intervals. Create a high-touch — no-tech or low-tech instruction environment. Avoid committing students to death by PowerPoint. Spend less time in classroom and more time in *gemba* — learning by doing.

Current-state measurement system

The team, under the guidance of their *sensei*, conducted a collaborative two-week *waste walk* using a current-state value-stream map (created by the final assembly team). This walk provided them with empirical evidence of immediate areas of opportunity. The team found an abundance of all seven forms of waste (see Chapter 2), areas of constrained and no flow, no pull, lack of known standards, and standardized work. There were inadequate measures of safety, cost, quality, and delivery, and the majority of workers were unclear about what value they were delivering to internal and external customers and about how to create profit for the business. They also found evidence that the use of their Enterprise Resource Planning (ERP) system was causing product to be pushed through the production system, rather than pulled through it (see Chapter 11).

When they examined how the plant measured and tracked production progress, the team found many improvement opportunities. They discovered that current-state measurement disciplines were out of date and ineffective. Also, defect rates in final assembly weren't measured, and controls for detection and prevention of production defects were ineffective. Defects were regularly reaching the final assembly area. Far too often, supervisors and managers were receiving erroneous signals that work was proceeding defect free and according to plan.

Constantly and consistently evaluate and question your measurement system and related standards. Be concerned if you constantly observe *Good & Green*; it usually signals opportunity for improvement. By challenging the status quo, you will create breakthrough thinking.

Kaizen: People, process, and attitude

The *kaizen* team was a diverse mix of personnel consisting of final assembly *gemba* workers, zone production manager, zone production planner, a Six Sigma Black Belt/Industrial Engineer dedicated to the target area, plus ad hoc members including a zone forklift driver, external suppliers, receiving warehouse, and finished goods warehouse personnel. The team challenged themselves to identify and eliminate waste, and produce pull and flow.

Team diversity creates perspective and enables shared vision (*hoshin*). Be mindful of team mix, knowledge, position, and skill diversity.

Constantly reflect (*hansei*) to guide the growth of new thinking. Apply the Socratic Method and constant reflection as core disciplines — before, during, and after *kaizen* activities. Ask questions like:

1. What should be happening versus what is happening?

2. What will be the measurable benefits of our improvement?

3. Is the improvement real or apparent?

Using the current-state VSM to guide improvement

The team built and validated the value-stream map (VSM) by applying the discipline of 3 Gen (see Chapter 13), walking both material and information VSM activities through the value stream. They began with the customer, continued through finished goods in the warehouse, proceeded to final assembly and moved through the rest of the operations until they arrived at the beginning of their value stream — the order entry process.

The team used simple inquiry, standardized worksheets, direct observation, and fact collection through measurement. The team also learned to identify and measure waste and to build alternatives to eliminate waste and prepare for *kaizen* activities to trial and test. The team began to see how the end-to-end value-stream was operating. The efforts exposed many problems throughout the value-stream between internal suppliers, internal customers, and ultimately the final customer. When problems were identified, they shared them with the teams across the value-stream, and addressed them through the *hoshin kanri* (see Chapter 13). At this stage, the team was enlightened, yet they were still pessimistic.

Facing the fears

A Lean *sensei* is mindful of pessimism caused when people feel afraid or uncertain, and how this can be especially true when they've been part of a merger. Todd McCann knew that the only way to move beyond fear was to understand and address it — fear of the unknown, fear of failure, internal struggles, lack or trust, or conflict. Without addressing it, people would not move forward because when people are afraid, they often cannot see how to change or may refuse to believe change is even possible. In this condition, it's much more difficult to achieve the results you desire. In fact, without addressing the fears you may harm the organization and produce *muri* — waste due to overburdening or stressing the people or system.

Todd and his team created a safe environment where people could openly discuss and expose fears without ridicule or retribution. He recognized that the team was reluctant to make any improvements — not only were they unclear on the outcomes and benefits of the future state; they had a fear of the unknown. He began by instilling the discipline of 3 Gen — to go where the action happens, observe, and gain facts. This discipline enabled everyone to gain perspective, understand the overall process, reflect and freely contribute ideas. He was then able to inspire people, build positive and creative conflict, and increase confidence in others for the benefit of others — not for the benefit of the *sensei*.

When reflecting on his work with the team, Todd recalled one of the final assembly *gemba* workers, who said, "Todd, 24 minutes is impossible. We will be running around like chickens with our heads cut off." He simply replied, "I have more respect for you and others than to make you headless chickens." She smiled and her trust and confidence grew, even though fear of the unknown remained within her. The *sensei* was humbled by her comment and continued to hold high his standard of respect for others. He had built trust through respect, providing a reason for others follow him.

The value-stream mapping walk

The team found waste — *muda, mura, muri* — in all activities in the VSM and identified areas for improvement by going to *gemba*. They:

- Saw an increasing order backlog for 24/36 port router

- Measured the final assembly, test and pack out cycle time at 2.5 days

- Witnessed the absence of continuous flow and takt time — batch thinking prevailed (200 units per cart)

- Discovered ineffective point-of-use stocking and replenishment system in final assembly

- Characterized an inattention to work station ergonomics, poor lighting, numerous industrial safety hazards — no 5S (see Chapter 11) present in final assembly area

✔ Noted the absence of standardized work

✔ Identified reactive, unclear scheduling throughout VSM causing inconsistent, unpredictable and uneven material delivery from internal suppliers to final assembly

✔ Witnessed an ineffective layout of final assembly area, where the proximity of final assembly work stations were between 5 to 20 feet away from each other

✔ Discovered reactive scheduling of light duty automated assembly process located in final assembly area

✔ Observed no pull production planning and/or scheduling and no visual management or controls in final assembly area

In short, the team saw that the final assembly process and its personnel were suffering from years of inattention and neglect. Reasons for defects and defect rates were unknown, problem escalation and resolution was unclear — and it all resulted in compromised assembly schedules.

True north thinking: The ideal state

After reflecting on what they observed in the current-state VSM, the team established new thinking that was radically different from the past. They created new passion for their ideal state and began the change. *Kaizen* thinking and the spirit of challenge began to take root. Even the nonbelievers slowly changed their thinking after they experienced the benefits of the improvements.

When considering process change, remember that 90 percent involves people and 10 percent is purely mechanics. Look past the mechanics. Be mindful of past conditions that are present, humble yourself, and look respectfully within the minds and spirits of the people in the area being improved; they have much to offer.

Future state — after kaizen

The team produced their *hoshin kanri* for final assembly, creating the plan through thoughtful reflection, intense detailed review and selection of alternatives to implement and test. The team's mantra was two fold: "no wishful thinking or problem admiration allowed" coupled with "daily *kaizen* and challenge of current standards to eliminate waste."

Outstanding results

The team redesigned the work area to produce an assembly work module, radically modifying the layout from batch to one-piece flow. The results were significant:

- Final assembly lead-time dropped from 2.5 days to 24 minutes.
- Final assembly work-in-process (WIP) was reduced by 98 percent.
- Floor space required for final assembly was reduced by 65 percent.
- Material shortages dropped from 25 percent to 2 percent.
- A *kanban* system was installed with internal suppliers to create smooth and balanced material flow.
- Customer order backlog was eliminated in two weeks with no overtime.
- Assembly work station proximities shrunk from feet to inches.

Working the Lean way

The team achieved outstanding results through the direct involvement of *gemba* workers, production managers and all supporting suppliers. Key factors included the passion, skills, and knowledge of the workforce, their past struggles, and the team embracing new struggles created through learning-by-doing. New Lean behaviors took root:

- Takt time was calculated and daily production targets were developed and visually managed in the final assembly cell.
- Standardized work was created by the final assembly workers for use by themselves and production managers.
- 5S was incorporated during work module design efforts.
- Daily *kaizen* activities became a behavioral norm.
- External suppliers of purchased fasteners supported the implementation of a two-bin system for point of use replenishment and delivery.
- Daily shift stand-up meetings were held in the assembly area, with production managers present, and used new visual management display boards.
- A command center for problem escalation was formalized and began to remove problems from the *gemba*.
- Production managers were constantly visible in the work area, looking to lend a helping hand and to manage countermeasure creation, root cause analysis, and problem resolution and prevention.

✔ Internal manufacturing suppliers were switched off in ERP, and ERP was re-purposed to accommodate *kanban* system. Unionized production schedulers were more than happy to re-purpose their daily activities and improve the new pull scheduling system in *gemba*.

✔ Final assembly applied a *kanban* system to create just-in-time (JIT) schedule with internal suppliers:

- New custom carts were created and new right-sized containers were purchased, a Limbo bar system was installed for injected molded parts, resulting in 100 percent on time/complete delivery.

- Plating and high speed stamping operations adopted pull planning *kanban* system synchronized to final assembly schedule.

- Component part inventory reduced from 12 days on hand to 2 days on hand for all internal manufactured parts.

✔ Light-duty automated assembly machine internal to the work module was scheduled using *kanban*.

✔ Unnecessary inventory was reduced by 15 percent.

✔ Ergonomics and other associated burdens were addressed during work module design by the workers, with production management support.

Ensure that the results of a localized *kaizen* activity, like this one, do not produce unintended consequences, burdens and waste elsewhere in the value stream. Take time to 3 Gen, understand how your part contributes to and impacts the whole value stream, and share your improvement ideas with other areas. The goal is *real* improvement of the overall value stream.

Lean Reduction of Call Center Attrition

Financial services organizations, like many industries, rely on call centers for customer service and first call issue resolution. Consumers form opinions about a company based on their experiences with these call centers. Ultimately, many consumers make purchasing decisions because of these experiences. Companies know they need to ensure call center employees are well trained and are representing their companies in the best light.

One Fortune 100 financial services organization had 5,000 call center employees working globally. They had a retention issue: the average employee annual turnover rate was 55 percent. This sky-high turnover cost the company millions of dollars in recruiting, on boarding, and training new staff, plus they were putting the customer experience at risk with the constant influx of new employees.

Senior leaders recognized that they had to do something to change the revolving door on their call centers. They sponsored a Lean project — and they threw in an extra challenge: improve the situation in 4 weeks! Elissa Torres, a Master Black Belt and Lean practitioner, worked with a cross-functional team to understand and find ways to immediately reduce the on-boarding cycle time and increase value-added tasks. The team included members from the core business process, as well as human resources, information technology, and the training department.

Characterizing the problem

As the team began their investigations, they immediately found that the new hires with 4 to 7 weeks seniority had the highest rate of attrition. The team conducted exploratory discussions with employees, leaders, and trainers, using affinity diagrams (see Chapter 12). As the conversations progressed, a central theme emerged in these focus groups: the delay in obtaining required system access to complete the on-boarding processes. This included simple things such as signing up for benefits and obtaining the system access needed to perform job functions.

As part of the Plan phase (see Plan-Do-Check-Act or PDCA in Chapter 9), the team then narrowed the scope of their project. With management support, they narrowed their focus to reducing the time required to on-board an employee, particularly the time required to obtain all system accesses to enable them to perform their job. Next, the team met for 3 days and began mapping the processes that enabled system access for newly hire employees. The team found that an average new hire had to be set up and have access to in seven different systems in order to perform their job. Each of these processes could take as few as 5 days — but it could also take as long as 65 days!

Make sure you truly define the scope of a project, understand the process, and identify root cause in the Plan phase. Otherwise, you will waste time, effort, and resources solving the wrong problem. You will also not take advantage of the acceleration of improvement initiatives the Lean enables.

The team summarized the process maps into a graphic showing the high-level value-stream steps — making the larger barriers to cycle time more visible. Figure 16-8 displays the high-level value-stream format in Excel. This graphic captures the value-stream process steps and related information such as data from reports, timing, important notes, types of waste identified at each step, pain points, and opportunities.

TIP

Creating a high-level value stream in Excel can be a simple and quick first step to characterize the process and identify the linkages to waste, pain points, and opportunities.

VSM Step	Offer and Background Check	Leader Onboard and Employee Start	System Access Requested	System Access Processed	Leader and Employee Obtain System Access notification
Process Map Steps	Recruitment 10	Leader New Hire 20	System Access Request Process 8	Provision Access Network, Mainframe, System A, System B, Email, IntraNet, Internet 142	Communication Process from Systems Access Administrators 21
Average Time	7.2	1.5	4	15	5
Min	3	1	1	5	2
Max	15	2	8	65	10
Time Type	days	days	days	days	days
Source	HR system This step out of Scope	HR system	Sample from 6 month sample	Request Reporting	Request Reporting
Notes	Delay to acceptance. Delay of 4 days due to vendor for background check	Leader does not request system access until after employee starts day one	Leader delay in submitting request. 4 Different access request forms. Forms confusing which causes returns and further delays.	Multiple handoffs Manual processing of access in mainframe	Too many communications received.
Waste Type	Waiting		Over-processing Defects	Waiting Motion Defects Inventory	Over-processing
Pain Points	Vendor		There are four different processes for submitting requests for system access. New Leaders not aware of their responsibility for requesting access.	Group-lack of automated workflow. System Administrators limited on provisioning capabilities for first stop resolution. Manual set up of system access.	Multiple communications received. Most access is dependent on other types, notification on type B irrelevant without type A.
Opportunities	New SLA with existing vendor. New Vendor	Request system access prior to employee start date	Centralized new hire access requests from departments. Consolidate request form and process.	Automated request workflow. Train system administrator on provisioning of more systems.	Streamline communications and send dependent access communications at the same time.

Figure 16-8: High-level VSM in Excel.

After the team created and categorized their VSM, they found the biggest non-value-added culprit was one of the seven forms of waste: waiting. Then they had to understand *why* there was so much "waiting" happening. What they uncovered was that the inventory of system access requests was in a backlogged work queue because a required manual process was understaffed.

The Lean team's solution

As the team moved through PDCA, they brainstormed short-, medium-, and long-term solutions to reduce the time required to on-board an employee in the call center. Each team member was accountable for expanding on their assigned solution for review with the stakeholders and executive sponsor within one week.

They established reporting baselines for each of the systems and created a weekly scorecard for tracking progress and changes. The team began implementing the first short-term solutions by the end of second week, and the final automated solution was implemented within 60 days. In addition to focusing on the system access processes, the training department reconfigured their curriculum to be more hands-on before the employee had to work in a full production environment.

To ensure that they implemented solutions in a timely manner, over the life of the project, the team established a weekly scorecard for all of the system access types and monitored them throughout the deployment of solutions. The team also knew the importance of measurement to ensure that the project gains were sustained over the long haul. They implemented controls in the business processes and systems to monitor performance over time.

Always measure your progress, both during the project implementation and as part of the standardized work. It keeps your implementation on track and ensures your project solutions are sustainable over time.

Here are some of the results the team achieved:

- System access process went from a range of 5 to 65 days to a range of 1 to 4 days.

- The new target for average cycle-time was set at maximum of 3 days and was tracked on a weekly scorecard for new hires.

- The attrition rate for new hires for the call center immediately fell from 65 percent to 40 percent.

- Training time decreased from 6 weeks to 4 weeks and reduced the learning curve by 15 percent, after they implemented the new hands-on curriculum.

Because the solution worked so well for the call center, the company decided to implement them across all other new hire platforms. This resulted in a savings and cost avoidance of over $10 million dollars. The improved processes also increased organizational effectiveness and addressed employees' concerns that they did not have to tools to do their job.

Part VI
The Part of Tens

The 5th Wave   By Rich Tennant

"We're using just-in-time inventory and just-in-time material flows, which have saved us from implementing our just-in-time bankruptcy plan."

In this part . . .

1n this part, we steer you toward some excellent resources for more information on Lean. We also fill you in on the best processes to adopt and pitfalls to avoid. If you're pressed for time and you want to get some key information quickly, this part is for you.

Chapter 17

Ten Best Practices of Lean

. . . .

In This Chapter

▶ Satisfying customers and delivering value is at the heart of successful Lean practice

▶ Looking at Lean as a journey, not a destination

▶ Keeping things people-focused, simple and visual

. . . .

This book chronicles the principles, methods, tools, and techniques that comprise Lean. As you embark on your own Lean journey, recognize the following ten best practices. They'll help you keep your bearings.

But first, a key note: Leadership — not just the unwavering guidance and support from top managers, but also everyone's everyday personal leadership — is so fundamental to the success of any initiative that it precedes a place on a best-practices list. Leadership is the "zeroth" law of success. Enable it. Encourage it. Reward it.

Feel the Force (of the Customer), Luke

The Lean *sensei* is calling out to you: *feel the force.* Do you hear him? Can you feel it? That force is the will of the customer — calling out to you, pulling you, stimulating you, guiding your every action. Your mission is to align all your brainpower, your energy, your resources and your might to answer this call.

Keep the customer at the core; the customer is the center of your universe — the customer's wants, needs, and definition of value. Feel the customer's force like the force of gravity. It is constant, undeniable, and unrelenting, but it keeps you grounded.

People First — and Foremost

Customers, organizations, enterprises, suppliers — they're all about people. They're led by people, they're staffed by people, and they serve people.

And so Lean is all about people, too. People come first. They *always* come first. No matter where you are on your journey, you'll sustain a Lean practice only because people are engaged and supported.

Your people are motivated and rewarded by success, not tools. People are constantly tempted by the leverage and economies offered by technology and tools. But tools don't "win"; people do. Remember that tools exist to aid and assist people. Help people change their thinking and behaviors so they use tools subordinately. You need tools, but the people are what make or break a Lean initiative.

Genchi Genbutsu

This poetic expression says it perfectly: Go and see. Or, more bluntly, get up off your butt, get out there in the world, and see it for yourself! E-mails, reports, spreadsheets, conference calls, presentations, hearsay — they cannot and do not tell the whole story. You must see it with your own eyes. And not just your eyes — you must experience it with all of your senses.

The world is subtle and full of nuance. Nothing's black and white. Often these subtleties are not just important, but are the critical difference. Reports and data only tell one part of the overall picture. There's nothing like being there to get the whole picture — the actual place, actual products, and actual facts (3Gen; *gemba, genbutsu, genjitsu*).

Some people may label these efforts as boondoggles — or worse, outright *muda*. But you're adding value when your firsthand observations and experience enable faster and more effective processes and procedures.

The Art of Simplicity

It's the famous cliché: "Keep it simple, stupid" — but simplicity is one of the best practices of Lean. The world is complicated, and complications cause trouble — and waste. A best practice of Lean is to simplify and eliminate, before you automate and integrate. Always ask yourself "Which option is simpler?" Choose the simplest option before moving forward.

Note that *kaizen* is itself the art of simplicity. To make continuous improvement continuous, you don't implement complex and convoluted solutions. Ideally you change one thing at a time. Increased complexity increases the risk of failure and lowers reliability. *Kaizen* is the simpler alternative.

At a Glance

A Lean environment is a high-sensory environment. Design yours to convey critical information with a glimpse of an eye or a turn of an ear. Use simple techniques like *andon boards* (see Chapter 12) to show where trouble is brewing or has boiled over; have horns honk or bells ring to signal takt time (see Chapter 7), or tool boards to illustrate when something is out of place or missing. Use customer information centers, cross-training boards, and performance trend charts for key metrics to present information about the business in a way that you can respond to nonstandard situations.

A Lean environment should enable everyone — even an outsider — to understand the status and state of affairs. Are you running to standard? Is there an issue? How are you doing? All at a glance.

Step by Step, Inch by Inch

Success is not a big bang. You can have big wins along the way, but no single breakthrough event or project victory will sustain achievements over the long term.

Lean is a journey, not a destination. You live Lean every day, through successes and setbacks alike. Lean is the force of a million little things, all the time. Lean is trying, doing, learning, and trying again — and again.

Lean is the tortoise and *The Little Engine That Could.* Lean is "small ball" — scoring again and again by hitting singles, bunting, and stealing bases. Lean is the Lexus tagline: *The Relentless Pursuit of Perfection.*

The (Standard) Way

Standardize your work. Make routines routine. Be consistent. Find and follow a standardized way of working.

Standardized work provides the basis for the most effective operations — and for innovation. When you have standardized work in place, you can count on it, train to it, delegate it, or even outsource it. And then, you can build on it! That's because you don't have to reinvent the basics, or suffer performance variances because your work is, well, nonstandard. Standardized work is a building block that enables you to improve, move forward, and accomplish more.

Of course, certain practices are custom by definition — they don't fit a standard. But even then, you can standardize the parts that can be standardized. It's fine for the custom parts to be "custom" — make them custom officially. Over time, you can look for ways to standardize even them.

Turn Over a Rock

Turn over any rock, in any part of the organization, and you'll find opportunity. You might be tempted to confine Lean just to the manufacturing or line areas, but don't do it!

Most organizations find greater waste when they start flipping over those rocks in places that they've ignored or thought that Lean might not really apply — like new product development, customer service, or back-office functions.

You will find opportunities to apply Lean everywhere you turn. Your job is to apply Lean to them, in all areas of the organization.

Follow the Value Stream

Value "flows" toward the customer. Use all your tools of communication, leadership, and visual management to help people see alignment and stay in the flow towards customer value. Design your environments, your tools, your practices, and your habits to keep the value stream flowing and to recognize when it's not. Support people and processes in centering themselves, using tools like tugboats to nudge them back into place.

Sometimes, you can easily find yourself in an eddy current or a side pool, swirling 'round and 'round, spending energy but going nowhere. All the Lean techniques — for reducing waste, organizing into cells and teams, performing standardized work, and applying quality and control tools — are there to help you align your efforts to the center of the value stream.

The Balanced Diet

The wide array of Lean tools and techniques may look like a smorgasbord, enticing you to pick and choose whatever looks inviting and tastes yummy. You could be tempted to select a few tricky tools (too many sweets!) and neglect other elements (fruits and vegetables). But Lean requires you maintain a balanced diet and complete nutrition. You're healthy only when you're whole. Don't neglect any of the parts.

You must not just follow lofty principles of Lean — you must also use the tools. But you can't just apply technical tools — you must apply the people tools as well. Short-term projects are effective, but only within the context of the long-term view. Lean applies to the whole body of the organization — and not just your organization, but all of the organizations in the value stream.

Chapter 18

Ten Pitfalls to Avoid

*L*ean is different from traditional western-style thinking, organizational structures, and management styles, so keeping your bearings can be difficult. Traditional ways of working have force and momentum. Many people — some well-meaning, and some not so well-meaning — can quietly conspire, either accidentally or purposefully, to knock you off course and derail your initiative. Many large and well-meaning companies have fallen prey to one or more of these traps, and suffered mightily for it.

In this chapter, we fill you in on the most common causes of problems with Lean initiatives, and tell you how to avoid them. These issues are real — and they can be real trouble if you're not careful. Pay attention to these pitfalls, and stay alert for signs of disaffection or discontent. Doing so can save your initiative and, ultimately, your organization.

Shiny Objects

There are multiple approaches to improvement. And new improvement ideas and tools constantly emerge on the landscape. What's so special about Lean? What's wrong with these other paths? It's simple: Like fad diet and exercise programs, these other paths can distract you from your improvement journey. Although innovation is good — and many initiatives have something to offer — understand how best to include these approaches in a way that is consistent with your Lean principles and methods.

Take Six Sigma, for example. The statistical tools most commonly associated with Six Sigma can be very useful in the reduction of variation *(mura)* and the elimination of defects, but the approach and infrastructure of a Six Sigma initiative differs greatly from Lean. You can easily include Six Sigma tools within Lean, but because Lean is a fundamental methodology, it cannot be wholly subjugated into other methodologies or frameworks. Lean is a holistic and complete system. If you're practicing Lean, be careful and thoughtful in how you adopt other methods and tools.

Why Do This? It's Just Not For Us

You may find people in your organization have a preconceived notion or belief that Lean isn't for them — or even for you. These people may have other ideas, or are used to thinking another way and don't want to change. Or perhaps they think that Lean is strictly for manufacturing companies, like Toyota, and you are not a product manufacturer. Or, if you are a manufacturing company, they might think Lean is applicable only on the manufacturing floor and not in other processes like order management, invoice processing, or customer on-boarding.

It's now proven that Lean applies everywhere — for enterprises in any industry and for all functions and processes. Remember that *how* you apply it is unique to circumstances: Lean isn't formulaic, so everyone tailors it to how it best works for them. But don't let anyone tell you "Lean? That's not for us." Because it is! You'll need to help people understand why it's the right thing to do and how each individual will benefit.

Complacency

Complacency is the number one killer of initiatives like Lean. It's tough for people to really change their behaviors and stay the course. Even if things aren't going well, it's often difficult for people to change, take on a new initiative, and carry it forward; if there's not a crisis, people often can't see the compelling reason to change.

And even if you have a Lean initiative underway, people will naturally tend to think the problems aren't theirs. After all, if it's somebody else's problem, why should they change?

In addition, because Lean is a continuous, incremental-change process, it's sometimes difficult for some people or organizations to perceive the significance or the value of the small, continuous *kaizen* changes. And if they can't see it, and if it doesn't appear significant enough, they're going to wonder why they should do it.

Resistance to change is natural to any change initiative, and it's no different in Lean. But Lean almost intensifies this resistance through its incremental, baby-steps approach.

How do you get people to adopt Lean practices if they can't readily see the results? You fight complacency with several weapons:

- ✔ **Customer awareness:** People need to know what the customers want, how they are changing and what they say about your organization.

- ✔ **Communications:** Have strong communicators who are unrelenting and convincing in the purpose and goals of the Lean initiative, as well as its proven, time-tested methods and tools.

- ✔ **Information updates:** Be sure to communicate the results and benefits from Lean improvement activities as they occur — both in your company and elsewhere.

- ✔ **Competition:** People need to know what your competitors are doing, what industry practices are, and what it takes to keep pace.

- ✔ **Lean measurements:** Create performance measures that reinforce Lean behaviors.

- ✔ **Punitive measures:** Sometimes, you have to use the stick. In every group, there are some who will not board the train.

Same-Old Same-Old Senior Managers

Like with any program or initiative, if the senior managers aren't fully embracing Lean, you have a very, *very* difficult road ahead. Many in the industry would tell you that your chances of a successful Lean implementation are nil without senior management's full commitment and action. Why? Because the initiative is so all-encompassing and life-changing, that without management's active participation, it simply won't happen.

Senior managers can't go on living the old ways and expect a change in the way the organization functions. Senior managers must change how they lead the organization every day, if Lean is to become the way the organization does business. The management functions can't be delegated or handed off; they must be practiced and performed by the managers themselves. All managers have to participate in *kaizen* events; they must take the *gemba* walks. They must focus on how results are achieved as much as the results themselves. They question and guide versus order and demand.

Furthermore, senior managers must regularly communicate the nature of the change to the business culture and practices, and reinforce why they have chosen to change to Lean. The senior managers must be visible and available to talk to people at all levels inside and outside the organization.

The revolving door of senior managers, particularly through merger and acquisition, has also been the source of Lean initiative failures. Replacing enlightened Lean leaders with traditionally minded ones has caused the demise of some very noteworthy companies in record time. You cannot have a successful Lean journey unless all the leaders understand and are committed to its success.

Stuck in the Middle Again

Traditional middle managers really are in the middle: They get it from both ends. The senior managers are forever beating on them to increase productivity and performance, and to "lower overhead" (that is, reduce headcount). Meanwhile, their subordinates are often like a herd of cats, who won't always do what they're asked to do and, furthermore, don't necessarily like being "railroaded" into yet another new initiative that they didn't ask for. They think of their immediate managers more as roadblocks than enablers.

Welcome to classic middle management — a lot of pressure, often in a thankless position, struggling to satisfy two disparate constituencies, and trying to make do with inadequate tools and insufficient support.

The roles of middle managers and supervisors are very different in Lean from traditional hierarchical, order-giving organizations and systems. In Lean enterprises, the supervisors become coaches and mentors. They relinquish considerable authority and decision-making to the employee teams, who find their own solutions to problems and challenges. The middle managers guide, question, listen, and enable their people. Their job is to break down walls that inhibit team success.

These roles of middle management and supervisors are different from traditional western-style systems. Managers and supervisors must be properly trained, equipped, and supported in order to perform within a Lean system. It's not an easy transition for people. Some of them just don't make it.

It's a Quick Fix!

Do not sell yourself or your organization on Lean as a quick fix. You can realize short-term benefits and gain momentum through a special Lean project or a *kaizen* blitz event; however, the true success of Lean does not come through short-term special events. The true power of Lean is through continuous, incremental improvements over the long term.

If your organization is so severely damaged that you must take immediate action and slamma-jamma a miracle overhaul in order to dramatically improve results in the upcoming quarter, Lean is not a silver bullet. If that's your situation, best of luck to you, but shop elsewhere.

 Use Lean as a long-term solution. Use Lean to more patiently, orderly, and consistently change people's thinking and behaviors, change the culture, and improve continuously and incrementally forever. You don't create that kind of change overnight. You can make progress in the short term, but to truly change you need time.

Cherry-Picking

One of the most common faux pas of Lean implementations is the piecemeal application of individual tools. Companies who believe that a couple of tools will solve their world-hunger problems are grossly mistaken.

The piecemeal efforts always backfire. Because Lean is a complete system, picking up a few tools and hacking away is a recipe for disaster. Without the holistic understanding, adoption, and support of the principles and methods of Lean, the tools are out of context. Of course, you never implement all the elements of Lean at the same time, but keeping in sight the interrelationships of the all the elements in the overall system is critical.

The most flagrant abuses have lacked the Respect-for-People aspect of Lean, attempting to implement Lean tools within traditional management, accounting, and operations frameworks. It just doesn't work.

With Lean, do it, or don't do it. But don't think you can do it halfway and sustain your gains.

Playing the Shell Game

Let's say that a nugget of waste is sitting there on the table, under the shell of your organization. Your operations manager — fully trained in Lean practices — deftly pulls out two additional shells: one for a supplier, and one for a distributor. He starts moving shells around and, suddenly — presto! — the nugget of *muda* is no longer under your shell. It's now under one of the others. He's eliminated waste from your organization, and aren't you the better for it?

You've just committee a Lean infraction: You've moved the *muda*. Moving the *muda* doesn't count in Lean, because improving yourself at the expense of someone else isn't really improvement. You're all interconnected through the value stream. Ultimately, the aim of Lean is to improve the *entire* stream. You have to eliminate the waste — period.

The Grease Monkeys

Many people around you will happily pick up a tool and use it — Lean tools included. A new technique, a new form of analysis, a new software program — they're all good. People love tools. They seem like toys. When you get a new toy, you get to play with something different that you haven't had before. You look for opportunities to show off your new toy, er, tool. But you need to remember to pick the right tool for the job.

A carpenter cannot build a bookcase with just a hammer, and you cannot build a Lean organization with just a *kanban* card. One tool does not a transformation make. You need to figure out how to use the full compliment of tools in your toolbox and pick the right tool for the job.

Beans Are Beans

Do not expect traditional accounting methods and systems to reflect the improvements accomplished through Lean. Eventually, results will hit the bottom line, but even these results don't properly account for the whole picture. Of all the nemeses to befall Lean initiatives, this is perhaps the most insidious: Believing that the old ways of accounting for the business are the only ways to account for it.

A Lean implementation will redefine boundaries, breaking down traditional functional walls and changing the nature of how you define cost and value in the organization. They will further change how people's contributions are measured, incentivized, and rewarded. Floor space will be reduced, flow will be improved, and cycle time will be faster. You cannot make all those changes operationally and continue to perform accounting the old way — all the numbers don't overtly show up with traditional cost accounting.

The accounting managers may tell you how difficult it is for them to change, or even wave the risk flags (think Sarbanes-Oxley). Help them understand how they can be part of the solution instead of the problem. Show them the results, and challenge them how best to account for the improvements you make. Bring them onboard, and they can make a key difference!

Busy Bees

Activity ≠ Progress. Everyone knows that people can be busy — very busy — without being at all productive. Bureaucracies are replete with useless activity, wasting people, time, and effort without producing anything of value. Make sure that the Lean improvement activities you undertake really add value.

When you have *kaizen* events, make sure that they're well organized, with defined objective and teams creating lasting results aligned with your long-term vision. Be certain that managers are participating in them, to ensure people with authority and accountability understand and support the results. For example, if the objective is to free up floor space, then make sure it is freed up in usable, collective areas, rather than isolated pockets that don't create value for anything.

Busy bees should be busy making honey. Make sure your bees are making honey, too.

Chapter 19

Ten Places to Go for Help

This book is a great introduction to Lean. We provide you with a broad understanding and working knowledge, showing you the principles and practices, the methods and tools, the language and jargon. But as complete as this book is, there's so much more to Lean than could ever fit in 408 pages.

Fortunately, Lean is so well-known and widely practiced that many, many sources of help — on every aspect and element of Lean — are available to you. Researchers and practitioners, businesses and organizations, blogs and websites, societies and associations, authors and historians — they're all out there, accessible, and available to help. Whether you want more knowledge, education and training, consulting and project assistance, tools and technologies, or reference publications, you've got it. In this final chapter, we introduce you to the greater world of Lean support that can pick up where we leave off.

Books and Publications

Believe it or not, *Lean For Dummies* is not the only book about Lean! (It may be the best one, but it's not the only one!) There are hundreds of books on Lean, written from every angle. Whether you want to know about a particular tool or technique, or about implementing Lean in a certain business or industry, chances are there's a book for you. You can search for these at any of the major online bookstores.

Check out Productivity Press (www.productivitypress.com), which offers the broadest selection of books and learning tools about Lean and the methodologies based on the Toyota Production System (TPS). Many of their books are translated directly from the Japanese versions.

Several interesting books exist about building a culture to support Lean. Three that offer unique perspectives are *Toyota Culture* by Jeffrey Liker, *Toyota Kata* by Mike Rother, and *Stomp the Elephant in the Office* by Steven Vannoy and Craig Ross.

 Lean Hospitals: Improving Quality, Patient Safety, and Employee Engagement (second edition), by Mark Graban is the award-winning go-to book on implementing Lean in hospitals. He is also the co-author of another important Lean in Healthcare book, *Healthcare Kaizen: Engaging Front-Line Staff in Sustainable Improvements,* (2012). Both books are from Productivity Press.

Online Information

In this age of the Internet, you can find an almost limitless amount of reference material online. Use your favorite search engine to find information on nearly any topic. If you want more direction, check out the following sites:

- ✔ **Wikipedia (**www.wikipedia.com**):** This site has general information on a wealth of topics, including Lean, its history, and the people behind it.

- ✔ **The Improvement Encyclopedia at Syque.com (**www.syque.com/quality_tools/index.htm**):** UK quality consultant Dave Straker has implemented an extensive online reference library that includes useful information on Lean and other quality tools.

- ✔ **The Lean Library (**www.theleanlibrary.com**):** Founded by Jamie Flinchbaugh of the Lean Learning Center, the Lean Library is a clearinghouse for book reviews, papers, links, and industry news.

- ✔ **The Lean Enterprise Institute (**LEI; www.lean.org**):** Founded by James Womack, the Lean researcher, this site provides Lean resources, products, and event information. LEI's network extends globally.

Blog Sites

Want to stay apprised of ongoing trends? Have a specific issue you'd like to address? Want to participate in discussions with the real experts in the Lean community? Check out the following blog sites:

- ✔ **The Lean Blog (**http://leanblog.org**):** Senior Lean practitioner Mark Graban maintains one of the most active Lean blogs on the Internet.

- ✔ **The Lean Insider (**http://leaninsider.productivitypress.com**):** This is the blog site of Productivity Press, the company that translated most of the Japanese books about quality and continuous improvement into English.

- ✓ **Evolving Excellence (**http://superfactory.typepad.com/blog**):** Bill Wadell and Kevin Meyer, founders of the Superfactory knowledge products company, host a lively blog.

- ✓ **Lean Healthcare Exchange (**http://www.leanhealthcareexchange. com**):** Charles Haygood, founder of Healthcare Performance Partners, and associates share case studies and cutting-edge information about Lean in Healthcare.

- ✓ **Gemba Panta Rei (**www.gembapantarei.com**):** Kaizen Institute Executive Director Jon Miller hosts this informative blog on many aspects of Lean. This blog is now affiliated with the Kaizen Institute (www.kaizen.com).

In addition to blog sites, you can find many virtual groups to connect with peers. Look on LinkedIn, Facebook, and Yahoo!

Professional Societies and Associations

Several professional societies and associations have dedicated Lean efforts, and you can contact them for additional information:

- ✓ **Shingo:** The Shingo Prize was established in 1988 to promote awareness of Lean concepts, and recognizes companies across North America that achieve world-class status. The Shingo Prize is administered by the College of Business of Utah State University. (www.shingoprize.org)

- ✓ **The Society of Manufacturing Engineers (SME):** SME is the world's leading professional society supporting manufacturing education. SME promotes an increased awareness of manufacturing engineering and helps keep manufacturing professionals up to date on leading trends and technologies. The society has members in 70 countries and is supported by a network of hundreds of chapters worldwide. Lean certification information is found on their website. (www.sme.org)

- ✓ **The Association for Manufacturing Excellence (AME):** AME is a not-for-profit organization dedicated to cultivating understanding, analysis, and exchange of productivity methods and their successful application in the pursuit of excellence. AME is practitioner-based, and events and workshops focus on hands-on learning. AME publishes the award-winning *Target* magazine and puts on several regional and national events each year. (www.ame.org)

- ✓ **Manufacturing Extension Partnership (MEP):** Sponsored by the U.S. National Institute for Standards and Technology (NIST), MEP is a nationwide network of over 350 centers, funded by a combination of federal, state, and private monies, providing resources, expertise, and services to manufacturers. It helps companies to compete globally, improve supply chain integration, and gain access to technology for improved productivity. (www.mep.nist.gov)

Conferences and Symposia

Numerous organizations regularly sponsor conferences and symposia around the United States and the world on Lean, quality, and business process improvement. These conferences are outstanding forums for meeting with peers, surveying product and service providers, and attending seminars on current topics of interest. Major Lean conferences and organizations include the following:

- The Society of Manufacturing Engineers (SME) hosts a variety of technical events and expositions. Check the events section on its website. (www.sme.org)

- A number of Lean Summits are sponsored by the Lean Enterprise Institute. (www.lean.org/Summits/Index.cfm)

- ASQ is a source of global quality excellence. It offers several conferences per year that are focused on quality, and presents an annual conference that combines Lean, Lean Six Sigma, and Six Sigma to explore trends in continuous improvement. (http://asq.org/conferences)

- Productivity, Inc. holds a variety of conferences and workshops throughout the year. (www.productivityinc.com)

- Topical conferences are held regularly throughout the year. Examples include the Lean HR summit (www.leanhrsummit.com), the Lean Accounting summit (www.leanaccountingsummit.com), Lean in Healthcare (www.leanhealthcareexchange.com and www.lean healthcarewest.com), and the Lean Educators Conference (www.leaneducatorconference.org)

- Lean Enterprise China is a Lean Enterprise Institute-sponsored event for Asia-Pacific. (www.leanchina.org)

- Lean Central Europe presents a lot of good information. (www.lean-kanban-conference.de)

- Lean Summit UK is a Lean Enterprise Institute-sponsored event for Europe. (www.leanuk.org/#summit)

Consultants, Facilitators, and Trainers

If you're embarking on a Lean initiative, or you have an initiative underway, you may need assistance in the form of expert advice, training, and experienced facilitation of *kaizen*, *kaikaku*, or other events. Worry not! The Lean community has experts available to help you in all of these areas.

You can find and apply expertise in several forms:

- **Methods and tools:** Most training and consulting organizations special-ize in the methods and tools of Lean — everything from value-stream mapping and Kano modeling to performing statistical analysis and con-ducting *kaizen* events.

- **Change management:** Leading an organization through the change process to understand and practice the philosophy of *kaizen* is very dif-ferent from learning and applying the tools. Look for a different kind of expertise to help you through the change process.

- **Rent-A-Sensei:** Sometimes, you just need an expert who can facilitate your team through a project or phase of an initiative. Certain consultan-cies have such experts, in the form of experienced leaders, or *senseis*, who can assist you.

To find people to help you, just enter "Lean consultants" into your favorite search engine.

Interview consulting organizations carefully to ensure that they have applied experience in the areas of your greatest needs and interests.

In addition to private consultancies, an increasing number of academic insti-tutions are teaching and training Lean practices. An organization known as the Lean Education Academic Network (LEAN) is group of university educa-tors who are pursuing Lean education in U.S. higher academia, as well as con-tinuous improvement of Lean education in the classroom through sharing of knowledge and teaching materials, collaboration, and networking among col-leagues. You can find out more at www.teachinglean.org. Toyota and the University of Kentucky created one of the first partnerships. You can find out more at http://www.lean.uky.edu/. The Center for Competitive Change at the University of Dayton has been helping companies become more com-petitive for over 20 years. You can find more at http://www.competitive change.com. The University of Michigan, home of Jeffrey Liker (author of several books about Toyota), offers several continuing education courses on Lean. More at http://interpro.engin.umich.edu/proedhome.htm.

Lean Periodicals

Subscribing to Lean periodicals will bring you regular joy and knowledge, via your mailbox! The following established periodicals are manufacturing-oriented:

- *Assembly Magazine* (`www.assemblymag.com`; subscription: free; 12 issues/year)

- *The Manufacturer Magazine* (`www.themanufacturer.com`; subscription: free; 12 issues/year)

- *Industry Week* (`www.industryweek.com`; subscription: free; 12 issues/year and yes, it's called *Industry Week,* but it comes out monthly)

- *Lean Directions,* an SME e-publication (`www.sme.org/leandirections`; subscription: free; 12 issues/year)

- *Target,* an online AME publication (`www.ame.org`; free access; 4 issues/year)

- *The Superfactory* online newsletter (`www.superfactory.com`; subscription: free; 12 issues/year)

Software Providers

Technology vendors are building increasing knowledge in the methods and tools of Lean. In addition to their products — which have considerable online help and tutorials — they provide education and support services.

- Software AG (`www.softwareag.com`) is an enterprise-class provider of tools for integrating information and processes across extended value-chains. Software AG's ARIS includes a value-stream mapping capability, along with SIPOC, Fishbones, and process analytics.

- iGraphx (`www.igrafx.com`) provides business process analysis tools, including value-stream mapping.

- Systems 2 Win (`www.systems2win.com`) provides Microsoft© Excel templates for a variety of Lean tools, including standard work, *gemba* interviews, spaghetti maps, and more.

- eVSM (`www.evsm.com`) provides simple value-stream mapping tools as extensions to Microsoft© Visio and Excel.

- A variety of software companies offer information display and visualization tools and provide toolkits that help you build your own add-ons and displays. You can search the Internet or ask your Lean *sensei* for more information.

Practitioners

Chances are you know someone who has been involved in Lean, perhaps even a specialist of some type. If you're working in a Lean company, you're surrounded by experienced professionals. They have the expertise and reference material available for you.

Even if you don't know of anyone personally, you may be surprised by just how few degrees of separation lie between your interest and a Lean expert. Ask colleagues in professional organizations, go to your local university, search for connections via social media like LinkedIn or search the web.

Before engaging in a relationship with a Lean practitioner, be sure they are the right fit for your organization.

Related Genres

Lean is so broad and all-encompassing that it touches and affects many related disciplines and genres. Conversely, Lean in and of itself does not have all the answers. You must maintain a broad perspective to and a complete picture. Look into these related disciplines for important supporting information:

- **Ergonomics and industrial engineering:** How consumers use products and services, and how workers use machinery and tools

  - Usernomics: www.usernomics.com/ergonomics-standards.html

  - The Institute of Industrial Engineering: www.iienet2.org

- **Supply chain and logistics:** Optimizing supply, delivery, inventory, and readiness

  - The Council of Supply Chain Management Professionals: www.cscmp.org

  - The Association for Operations Management: www.apics.org

- **Project and program management:** Controlling project scope, schedule, and resources; configuration management; getting the most out of project teams

  - The Project Management Institute: www.pmi.org

  - The Project Manager's Homepage: www.allpm.com

- **Statistical analysis:** In-depth understanding of the behaviors that influence outcomes

  - The American Society of Quality: www.asq.org

  - The Online Statistics Textbook: www.statsoft.com/textbook/stathome.html

✔ **Six Sigma community:** Because defects are a form of waste

- The Online Six Sigma Forum: www.isixsigma.com

- The International Society of Six Sigma Professionals: www.isssp.com

✔ **Business Process Management:** A rapidly growing field that is becoming a clearinghouse of all things process

- The Business Process Management Initiative: www.bpmi.org

- Business Process Trends: www.bptrends.com

✔ **One Page Business Plan:** Concise descriptions of goals, mission, and strategies; not just for small, startup businesses anymore — it's applicable as the one-page description of any project or program plan.

- The One Page Business Plan: www.onepagebusinessplan.com

✔ **Organizational Development (OD) and Training:** Training, facilitation and Organizational Development resources and professionals

- Organizational Development Network: www.odnetwork.org

- American Society of Training & Development: www.astd.org

- International Association of Facilitators: www.iaf-methods.org

- Free Management Library — OD Information: www.managementhelp.org/org_chng/org_chng.htm

Glossary

3Gen: Derived from three Japanese words — *genchi (like gemba), genbutsu, genjitsu* — it is the practice of going to where the action is, observe what is happening and get real data/facts to solve problems and improve processes. Sometimes the words are written with *"gem"* rather than *"gen"* because of the transliteration from Japanese characters.

3P: Production Preparation Process is the act of applying Lean concepts in the design phase, usually involving a cross-functional team to bring all perspectives and eliminate waste before a process implementation.

5S: The principle of waste elimination through workplace organization. Derived from the Japanese words *seiri, seiton, seiso, seiketsu,* and *shitsuke,* which have been translated into English as *sort, straighten, scrub, systematize,* and *standardize.* Safety is often included as a sixth S.

5 Whys: A method of root-cause analysis that entails the progressive asking of "Why?" at least five times or until the root cause is established.

andon: A signal to alert people of problems at a specific place in a process; a form of visual management.

A3: A one-page reporting format, named for the international paper size (11" x 17" in US sizes). It contains, on one page, critical information about an issue, such as description, cost, timing, data, planned solution, and planned resolution.

consumer: The person or entity who obtains goods and services for his or its own use. *See also* customer.

continuous flow: The ideal state where products move through a manufacturing process — or people move through a service process — one at a time, without stopping or waiting.

current-state value-stream map: A value-stream map that depicts things as they currently exist within the value stream. *See also* value-stream map.

customer: The person or entity who is the recipient of what you produce, either within your organization or outside your organization. *See also* consumer.

cycle time: The total amount of elapsed time from the time a task, process, or service is started until it is completed.

future-state value-stream map: A value-stream map that depicts an improved view of the value stream, which advances toward the ideal-state.

gemba: Where the action occurs. *See also* 3Gen.

genchi genbutsu: Go and see. *See also* 3Gen.

heijunka: The technique of smoothing or leveling schedules.

heijunka **box:** A tool used to control the volume and mix of production through the controlled distribution of *kanban* at standard, fixed intervals of time.

hoshin: A system of planning, forms, and rules that engages everyone in addressing business at both the strategic and tactical levels. It is also known as *policy deployment* or *hoshin kanri*.

hoshin kanri: See hoshin.

ideal-state value-stream map: a value-stream map that depicts a value stream composed of only value-added activities.

information flow: The uninterrupted progression of supporting data and instructions along the value stream.

jidoka: Transference of human intelligence to machines via automation. The automation enables the equipment to detect defects and stop until someone comes to fix the problem. This supports quality at the source and the prevention of defects from progressing along the value stream. Additionally, the person in charge of the step in the value stream is responsible to resolve the issue or stop the flow to get outside assistance.

just-in-time (JIT): Providing what is needed, when it is needed, in the quantity needed, and the quality level needed.

kaikaku: Radical improvement activity to reduce waste.

kaizen: Incremental continuous improvement that increases the effectiveness of an activity to produce more value with less waste.

kanban: A signal that triggers replenishment or withdrawal in a pull system. *Kanban* is often in the form of a card on a container in production environments. The signal regulates the production flow in the value stream.

Lean: An improvement methodology based on a customer-centric definition of value, and providing that value in the most effective way possible, through a combination of the elimination of waste and a motivated and engaged workforce.

muda: Any activity that consumes resources, but creates no value. *Muda* is categorized in two forms: Type-1 *muda* is necessary for the process, but non-value-added; type-2 *muda* is both unnecessary and non-value-added.

mura: Waste due to unevenness or variation.

muri: Waste or stress on the system due to overburdening or unreasonableness.

non-value-added: Any activity, product, or process that does not meet the value-added criteria. *See also* value-added.

Plan-Do-Check-Act (PDCA) or Plan-Do-Study-Act (PDSA): An iterative improvement scheme at the core of the *kaizen* process. This four-step process includes (1) defining the objectives, issues, and potential solution; (2) carrying out the plan in a trial mode; (3) verifying and studying trial results; (4) fully implementing and standardizing the solution. It is also called the *Shewhart cycle* or *Deming cycle.*

poka-yoke: A device to prevent the production or occurrence of defects.

Respect for People: The engagement of and investment in people, including training, empowerment, safety, job security, contribution and respect of ideas, and morale. It is foundational to Lean and essential for the creation of a culture where *kaizen* thrives.

sensei: Master or teacher, in this context, of Lean.

seven forms of waste: Transportation, waiting, overproduction, defects, inventory, motion, and excess processing are the seven forms of waste identified by Taiichi Ohno, one of the pioneers of the Toyota Production System, as waste normally found in mass production. Also known as the seven wastes or the seven *mudas.* Sometimes includes an eighth form — an unengaged workforce.

single minute exchange of die (SMED): Term used to describe the compilation of tools and techniques used to dramatically reduce the time required to complete the changeover of production and support of one "product" to another. Think Indy pit-crew tire changes.

SIPOC: An acronym for Suppliers, Inputs, Process, Outputs and Customers. It is a form of defining a process that includes the relationship between these entities; often depicted graphically.

standardized work: The definition of a process step characterized by takt time, a set work sequence, and established in-process inventory. Deviations to standardized work constitute an abnormality, which is then an opportunity for improvement.

takt time: *Takt* is the German word for "beat." In Lean, takt time is the pace of production based on the rate of customer consumption. It is calculated by taking the available minutes of work divided by the units required by the customer in that period of time.

value: The worth placed upon goods or services, as defined by the customer. *See also* customer.

value-added: Defined by the customer and must meet all of the following criteria:

- The customer must be willing to "pay" for it. Payment is generally thought of in monetary terms, but could also include time or other resources.
- The product or service must be done correctly the first time.
- The product or service must be transformed.

value stream: The flow of materials and information through a process to deliver a product or service to a customer.

value-stream map: A graphical representation of how all the steps in any process line up to produce a product or service, and of the flow of information that triggers the process into action.

voice of the customer (VOC): The collective needs, wants, and desires of the recipient of a process output, a product, or a service, whether expressed or not. The VOC is usually expressed as specifications, requirements, or expectations.

waste: Any activity that uses resources, but creates no value for the customer. Usually expressed as *muda*, *mura*, or *muri*.

Index

ple & Mac

ad 2 For Dummies,
d Edition
8-1-118-17679-5

hone 4S For Dummies,
h Edition
8-1-118-03671-6

od touch For Dummies,
d Edition
8-1-118-12960-9

ac OS X Lion
r Dummies
8-1-118-02205-4

ogging & Social Media

tyVille For Dummies
8-1-118-08337-6

cebook For Dummies,
h Edition
8-1-118-09562-1

om Blogging
r Dummies
8-1-118-03843-7

itter For Dummies,
d Edition
8-0-470-76879-2

ordPress For Dummies,
h Edition
8-1-118-07342-1

siness

sh Flow For Dummies
8-1-118-01850-7

vesting For Dummies,
h Edition
8-0-470-90545-6

Job Searching with Social Media For Dummies
978-0-470-93072-4

QuickBooks 2012
For Dummies
978-1-118-09120-3

Resumes For Dummies,
6th Edition
978-0-470-87361-8

Starting an Etsy Business
For Dummies
978-0-470-93067-0

Cooking & Entertaining

Cooking Basics
For Dummies, 4th Edition
978-0-470-91388-8

Wine For Dummies,
4th Edition
978-0-470-04579-4

Diet & Nutrition

Kettlebells For Dummies
978-0-470-59929-7

Nutrition For Dummies,
5th Edition
978-0-470-93231-5

Restaurant Calorie Counter
For Dummies,
2nd Edition
978-0-470-64405-8

Digital Photography

Digital SLR Cameras &
Photography For Dummies,
4th Edition
978-1-118-14489-3

Digital SLR Settings & Shortcuts
For Dummies
978-0-470-91763-3

Photoshop Elements 10
For Dummies
978-1-118-10742-3

Gardening

Gardening Basics
For Dummies
978-0-470-03749-2

Vegetable Gardening
For Dummies,
2nd Edition
978-0-470-49870-5

Green/Sustainable

Raising Chickens
For Dummies
978-0-470-46544-8

Green Cleaning
For Dummies
978-0-470-39106-8

Health

Diabetes For Dummies,
3rd Edition
978-0-470-27086-8

Food Allergies
For Dummies
978-0-470-09584-3

Living Gluten-Free
For Dummies,
2nd Edition
978-0-470-58589-4

Hobbies

Beekeeping
For Dummies,
2nd Edition
978-0-470-43065-1

Chess For Dummies,
3rd Edition
978-1-118-01695-4

Drawing For Dummies,
2nd Edition
978-0-470-61842-4

eBay For Dummies,
7th Edition
978-1-118-09806-6

Knitting For Dummies,
2nd Edition
978-0-470-28747-7

Language & Foreign Language

English Grammar
For Dummies,
2nd Edition
978-0-470-54664-2

French For Dummies,
2nd Edition
978-1-118-00464-7

German For Dummies,
2nd Edition
978-0-470-90101-4

Spanish Essentials
For Dummies
978-0-470-63751-7

Spanish For Dummies,
2nd Edition
978-0-470-87855-2

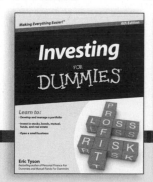

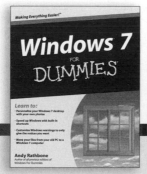

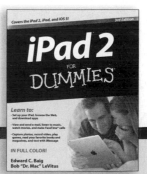

ailable wherever books are sold. For more information or to order direct: U.S. customers visit www.dummies.com or call 1-877-762-2974.
U.K. customers visit www.wileyeurope.com or call (0) 1243 843291. Canadian customers visit www.wiley.ca or call 1-800-567-4797.

Connect with us online at www.facebook.com/fordummies or @fordummies

Math & Science

Algebra I For Dummies,
2nd Edition
978-0-470-55964-2

Biology For Dummies,
2nd Edition
978-0-470-59875-7

Chemistry For Dummies,
2nd Edition
978-1-1180-0730-3

Geometry For Dummies,
2nd Edition
978-0-470-08946-0

Pre-Algebra Essentials
For Dummies
978-0-470-61838-7

Microsoft Office

Excel 2010 For Dummies
978-0-470-48953-6

Office 2010 All-in-One
For Dummies
978-0-470-49748-7

Office 2011 for Mac
For Dummies
978-0-470-87869-9

Word 2010
For Dummies
978-0-470-48772-3

Music

Guitar For Dummies,
2nd Edition
978-0-7645-9904-0

Clarinet For Dummies
978-0-470-58477-4

iPod & iTunes
For Dummies,
9th Edition
978-1-118-13060-5

Pets

Cats For Dummies,
2nd Edition
978-0-7645-5275-5

Dogs All-in One
For Dummies
978-0470-52978-2

Saltwater Aquariums
For Dummies
978-0-470-06805-2

Religion & Inspiration

The Bible For Dummies
978-0-7645-5296-0

Catholicism For Dummies,
2nd Edition
978-1-118-07778-8

Spirituality For Dummies,
2nd Edition
978-0-470-19142-2

Self-Help & Relationships

Happiness For Dummies
978-0-470-28171-0

Overcoming Anxiety
For Dummies,
2nd Edition
978-0-470-57441-6

Seniors

Crosswords For Seniors
For Dummies
978-0-470-49157-7

iPad 2 For Seniors
For Dummies, 3rd Edition
978-1-118-17678-8

Laptops & Tablets
For Seniors For Dummies,
2nd Edition
978-1-118-09596-6

Smartphones & Tablets

BlackBerry For Dummies,
5th Edition
978-1-118-10035-6

Droid X2 For Dummies
978-1-118-14864-8

HTC ThunderBolt
For Dummies
978-1-118-07601-9

MOTOROLA XOOM
For Dummies
978-1-118-08835-7

Sports

Basketball For Dummies,
3rd Edition
978-1-118-07374-2

Football For Dummies,
2nd Edition
978-1-118-01261-1

Golf For Dummies,
4th Edition
978-0-470-88279-5

Test Prep

ACT For Dummies,
5th Edition
978-1-118-01259-8

ASVAB For Dummies,
3rd Edition
978-0-470-63760-9

The GRE Test For
Dummies, 7th Edition
978-0-470-00919-2

Police Officer Exam
For Dummies
978-0-470-88724-0

Series 7 Exam
For Dummies
978-0-470-09932-2

Web Development

HTML, CSS, & XHTML
For Dummies, 7th Edition
978-0-470-91659-9

Drupal For Dummies,
2nd Edition
978-1-118-08348-2

Windows 7

Windows 7
For Dummies
978-0-470-49743-2

Windows 7
For Dummies,
Book + DVD Bundle
978-0-470-52398-8

Windows 7 All-in-One
For Dummies
978-0-470-48763-1

Available wherever books are sold. For more information or to order direct: U.S. customers visit www.dummies.com or call 1-877-762-297
U.K. customers visit www.wileyeurope.com or call (0) 1243 843291. Canadian customers visit www.wiley.ca or call 1-800-567-4797.

Connect with us online at www.facebook.com/fordummies or @fordummies